COURTLY LOVE

COURTLY LOVE

The Path of Sexual Initiation

JEAN MARKALE

TRANSLATED BY JON GRAHAM

Inner Traditions
Rochester, Vermont

Inner Traditions International
One Park Street
Rochester, Vermont 05767
www.InnerTraditions.com

First U.S. edition published by Inner Traditions in 2000

Originally published in French under the title *L'amour courtois* by Éditions Imago 1987

Library of Congress Cataloging-in-Publication Data

Markale, Jean.
   [Amour courtois, ou, Le couple infernal. English]
   Courtly love : the path of sexual initiation / Jean Markale.— 1st U.S. ed.
         p. cm.
   Includes bibliographical references and index.
   ISBN 0-89281-771-2 (alk. paper)
    1. Courtly love in literature. 2. Goddesses in literature. 3. Adultery in literature.
   4. Women in literature. 5. Goddess religion. 6. Troubadours. I. Title.

PN682.C6 M2813 2000
809′.933543′0902—dc21

                              00-059780

Printed and bound in Canada

10 9 8 7 6 5 4 3 2 1

This book was typeset in Minion with Mason and Mason Alternate as display fonts

Inner Traditions wishes to express its appreciation for assistance given by the government of France through the ministère de la Culture in the preparation of this translation.

Nous tenons à exprimer nos plus vifs remerciements au government de la France et le ministère de la Culture pour leur aide dans le préparation de cette traduction.

Contents

The Game of Love and Knightly Prowess

A massive reevaluation of all the tenets of Western Christian society was prompted by the widespread turmoil that shook the period customarily known as the Year 1000. The extensive self-questioning did not, however, mount any serious challenge to society's fundamental animating principle: the well-known law of three classes, really none other than the reappearance of an ancient trifunctional partitioning of Indo-European civilization.* This particular Christian society was seeking to discern—in events, in the intellectual speculations of a few individual thinkers, in the disorder that accompanies any new mode of inquiry—what meaning could be given to a world that people believed was suffering the throes of its last stages of existence and that (in spite of the doomsayers, the ravings of the poets of eschatology) was now showing signs of enduring—at least until the next crisis. While awaiting that crisis, it seemed necessary to organize the world in a manner that complied with God's divine plan. It was in the interpretation of this divine plan, revealed symbolically in the Scriptures, that disagreements began to appear. The era awkwardly termed the "age of heresies"

* *Translator's note:* The three classes consisted of the clergy, the nobility, and the commoners.

was just beginning. Fortunately, at this time, pyres for sinners were a rare phenomenon; it took the creation of the Inquisition to push the situation past the tragic point of no return.

In the early years of the eleventh century, a new and unrecognizable Europe awoke from the nightmares of the Year 1000. This Europe had only just begun to integrate the various aspects of its long gestation period into an increasingly harmonious synthesis when it was rendered sterile, at the end of the Middle Ages, by the Roman Catholic Church's taking over the realms of spirituality and knowledge. But from the eleventh century through the thirteenth century, a fantastic revolution was under way—a revolution in the true sense of the word, not a change of direction, as is assumed in the modern acceptance of the word, but a process that ends with a return to its departure point. This time was the era of courtly love. Actually, *fin'amor* ("refined love") would be a better choice of words, at least when referring to the specific period during which courtly love was apparent in the spiritual, intellectual, speculative, as well as literary life of an era.

The literary world is the only one in which courtly love has left meaningful and enduring traces, but it is not enough to consider courtly love only through its literary aspect, which is just the visible tip of the iceberg. The submerged portion is much larger. The problem with this submerged portion is that its revelation includes a great risk: the risk of overturning the established view of this era and of calling into question the entire system on which medieval society was based.

We should stop and reflect momentarily on the terms *medieval* and *Middle Ages*. They are convenient designations for the period extending from the theoretical fall of the Roman Empire to the Reformation. As such they simply describe a chronological benchmark. But this stretch of time is formed from many diverse, even conflicting eras, and it is vain to try and make of it an organized and coherently structured totality. There are as many "Middle Ages" as there are attempts to explain the world and human beings, following the many interpretations given them by earlier civilizations—including both those that could be called indigenous (hence "barbarous") and those that were established, willingly or by force, in all the countries making up western Europe.

If the importance of Latinity (this term being preferable to *Romanity*) is absolutely undeniable, we must still recognize that Latinity was not the only component of what was in the process of construction at that time. Far from it. Western Europe certainly defined itself as Latin with respect to eastern Europe, which was Greek. The Latin language—either directly or indirectly, and especially in the religious sphere—was undoubtedly in a dominant position, if not an outright hegemony. But this is to forget that the Latin language as introduced into Gaul by its Roman conquerors was what linguists call "dog Latin," that is, a form of classical Latin that had definitely evolved and been *perverted* under a wide array of influences. This is also to forget that the term *Latin* covers a vast area that would be very different indeed without its Hellenistic component. It is well known that the civilization of the Roman Empire had nothing in common with that of the original Latinium—it would be more accurate to speak of a Greco-Latin civilization. And then, also, we should not forget the contributions of the Near Eastern civilizations to Imperial Rome. There are many arguments that seriously contradict the prevailing simplistic notion of a western Europe emerging fully armed from the brain of Rome: mistress of the world, mistress of the arts, philosophy, and civilization in general. To tell the truth, the only people claiming direct descent from Imperial Rome were the popes and the emperors, thus anyone holding any kind of rank in the structures established by imperial and pontifical authorities. This was an abuse of power as well as an abuse of confidence.

To add to the confusion, Christianity is usually ranked in with Latinity. This judgment is a bit hasty. Christianity is certainly responsible in large part, and especially in France, for the victory of Latin over the indigenous tongues, but Christianity is not just another Latin ideology. It is something else entirely. Calling it the Roman Catholic Church—justified by the important role that has been played and still is played by Roman authorities—camouflages realities that are much more complex and clearly heterogeneous. It should not be overlooked, for example, that Christianity was born, under Roman control, in a

Jewish milieu strongly influenced by Hellenistic culture and indelibly colored by Neoplatonic doctrines, all of which had traveled through Hellenic Greece before terminating in a Rome already undermined by triumphant atheism and the mystery cults, particularly the Eastern cults. Under these circumstances, it is difficult to ascertain the exact role played by any single element in the delicate operation of sociocultural alchemy.

This Latinity is not the only element, even if it may be considered the dominant one. The Middle Ages would have been quite different, for example, without the German contribution. This contribution was twofold: one aspect was continental in origin, brought by the Franks and the different peoples called "barbarian," of whom the Visigoths were the most remarkable; one aspect was insular and Scandinavian in origin, brought by the later waves of men from the North. By profoundly modifying the original structures of the Roman Empire, or by occupying those structures, the Germans prompted an evolution of a depth that is still often unrecognized but whose traces are still visible today in every country of western Europe.

To this is added the Arab influence. Depicted as conquerors and destroyers of the Christian faith, the people then commonly considered Saracens were nevertheless just as much a civilizing force as all the others. And even though Muslim civilization was a synthesis of various elements picked up by Mohammed's disciples during their travels, it offered for all this an opening into a previously unknown world, making just as considerable a contribution in the realms of philosophical thought, art, and the esoteric or hermetic traditions. From the eleventh century onward the Muslim influence upon the Mediterranean regions is particularly clear. The Iberian peninsula is a crossroads where Muslims, Jews, and Christians came together, mingled, and eventually fraternized. Their convergence is partially responsible for the birth of the brilliant Occitan civilization. For this reason it is a good idea not to overlook possible Mediterranean archetypes in the formation of courtly love and the literature for which it is famous.

There is one element that historians tend to neglect, since it is the oldest, the most subtly discreet, if not to say secret, and this is the Celtic influence. The greater part of western Europe was invaded and actually colonized, over the course of the two Iron Ages, by Celtic-speaking people. In certain regions such as eastern Gaul (though it is considered Germanic), the Armorican peninsula (Brittany), the Massif Central, and Great Britain especially, signs of the Celts' presence are far from having disappeared. On the contrary, everything seems to show that Celtic substructures were not at all in ruins during the eleventh century. They actually formed the foundation for all that was in the process of being built.

These are all the different facets that must be borne in mind while seeking to understand how and why, during the eleventh century, there arose a new way of posing the question of relations between male and female—relations closely linked to intellectual and spiritual speculations. These questions concerned only a tiny minority of people, always high in society, a circle centered on a rich lord and especially a great lady, a court striving toward new heights of elegance and refinement, including what could be called the great minds of the time. And great minds there were. But the bulk of the populace, all classes included, were barely touched by this new "fashion." It is not without good reason that the term *courtly love* prevailed over *fin'amor* (refined or pure love). And even though this fashion subsequently became the rage throughout European aristocratic society thanks primarily to the songs of the troubadours and the "courtly" romances, its birth remains thoroughly obscure—like the causes that prompted it, for that matter.

During the eleventh century people had just emerged from the "terrors" inspired by the Year 1000. Without exaggerating these terrors, it should be recognized that they made an effective contribution to the reevaluation of society during the high Middle Ages. The commotion affected all levels of society. The empire, which Charlemagne had restored in a Christian context, was in complete decline. The empire was still "holy," but despite the best efforts of Otho III and Pope Sylvester II (the monk Gerbert d'Aurillac), it had become merely Germanic. Although provoked by Gerbert, the dynastic change within the Frankish kingdom overturned all political assumptions. The Capetians would never become the emperor's suffragans, and they became increasingly marginalized, conferring upon their sovereignty an increasingly obvious sacred character. But whether in the territories of the emperor or in those of the Frankish king, the process of disaggregation accelerated: Charlemagne's great dream of a Christian—actually a somewhat Germano-Roman—universality was succeeded by the day-to-day reality of particularism and the investiture of numerous principalities, all independent of one another and sharing no common union apart from the Christian faith.

Historians have sought to analyze this phenomenon and have come up with various interpretations, but no one has discerned the resurgence of the old Celtic mentality, which had been repressed for centuries and yet which deeply imbued the territories of this changing Europe. The social structure of the ancient Celts is, in fact, quite distinctive.[1] It is different in every possible way from the Latin idea of civilization, which is centralized, constructed around a city *(Urbs)*, and confounded with the community of citizens *(Civitas)*. The Celts' society, on the other hand, is characterized by a refusal of any central authority and by the formation of autonomous social groups, functioning almost as self-sufficient units whose sole tie is their community of origin and culture. In the feudal Europe that is about to emerge, one can see many Celtic tendencies toward a horizontal-type society.

The subdividing that was taking place within the old Roman empire reveals the resurgence of ancestral themes, themes that had in fact never really been forgotten but that—with the help of large-scale invasions and the synthesis of Latinity and Germany—had found an entirely new form of expression. Feudalism is a system resulting from the realization of the day-to-day nature of reality, a realization of the actual material difficulty of ensuring a good equilibrium among all the different forces of an immense entity, understood on a world level, if not on the level of the universe. Feudalism was established at that moment in time when people began to understand that *they had to make do with what they had*. And what did they have, if not the mental—and thus social—structures rooted in the ancestral fields?

This understanding is important because the new phenomenon of courtly love could do no other than reflect these profound tendencies. It was not a matter of *satellization,* a term that implies an ideal or, rather, ideological center with forces revolving around it endowed with a certain autonomy. The matter actually goes much further than this. To risk an astronomical metaphor, the new phenomenon resembled a succession of solar systems, independent of one another yet all bound to a universal system of gravity. The lady of courtly love was like a resplendent sun, around whom played out the deeds of the amorous knights (and lovers)—to the greater benefit of the community thus illuminated and to the greater benefit of the individuals themselves, who emerge from their trials by necessity much better than before.

The turbulence and disturbances made themselves felt also in the Roman Catholic Church and involved the intellectual culture as well as spiritual and cultural life. Until the Year 1000, intellectual culture had been confined to the episcopal seats. The famous "Palace Schools" (attributed a little too lightly to Charlemagne) were the most consistent models of intellectual life in this time. The culture was episcopal, aristocratic, and royal. The general character type was Gerbert d'Aurillac, the future Pope Sylvester II. Reared and educated under the auspices of the cathedrals, a zealous servant of the princes of the Church and the princes of this world, this doctor of divinity was the official curator of a culture drawing from both biblical texts and the great Latin tradition. A student of the times owed it to himself to write and speak like Cicero or like Titus Livy.

After the Year 1000, however, it would no longer be under the auspices of the cathedrals that cultural artisans would prepare for war but under those of the monasteries. This shift is important. And here again we see a phenomenon of subdivision, a process of disaggregation. In fact, even though the Roman Catholic Church—after the fluctuations of the first centuries of Christianity, after the first so-called heretical protests, after successive repressions of the "national" churches—had succeeded in imposing a monolithic structure and a dominant ideology over society, it remained no less vulnerable and exposed to internal con-vulsions.[2] For it was from within that the Church had evolved, starting in the eleventh century, and in particular from the increasingly active role played by the monasteries.

There is nothing new about monachism. It made its first appearance on French territory with the missions of Saint Martin de Tours, but its greatest era must have been the seventh century. It was of dual origin: one source was the Benedictine monachism of Italian (perhaps even Roman) inspiration, which had a solid foothold in French territory; the other was a monachism that would best be described as Celtic, that of the Irish Saint Colomban and his disciples, especially noticeable in the north and east of what is today France. The difficulties that Colomban and his companions experienced with the Merovingian princes led the new monasteries to seek protection from temporal authorities, as well as from the local ecclesiastical authorities (who were all too often depen-dent upon those very same temporal authorities). The consequence was that a direct connection was established between the monasteries and the papacy, which in practice led to great autonomy for these establish-ments and for the groups of monasteries that followed. Monachism became a kind of state within a state, a church within the church, espe-cially when the Colombanian monasteries (heirs to the Celtic tradition stifled by the papacy) combined with the Benedictine monasteries, infusing in the latter the desire for an increasingly real independence from all other powers. During the Year 1000 the divide between the sec-ular and the regular clergy intensified. The low clergy of the rural areas—kept in ignorance, or springing up out of popular spontaneous sentiment—played no role except to echo the will of the high clergy at the very top of the pyramid. The high clergy, in fact, could make or unmake kings; witness the transfer of power from the Carolingian dynasty to the Capetian dynasty.* In France there were six bishops or archbishops to be found among the twelve peers of the realm. The high clergy became increasingly political, sharing in the life of the states (as

* *Translator's note:* The transfer of power from Carolingian to Capetian took place in A.D. 987.

much as we can speak of states in the modern sense of the word) and showing very little concern with spirituality or culture. Politics were a good enough occupation for the monks. After all, what else did they have to do?

In fact, monks from all orders profited from the windfall they were given. They actually did concern themselves with spiritual and cultural matters, and it is thanks to them that the general ethos of the time began to change. As keepers of knowledge—the sciences and arts as well as religious tradition—monks of the eleventh century not only preserved the cultural patrimony of the West but also gave it life. They extended it and allowed it to ripen. It is an incontestable historical reality that what is customarily referred to as the Middle Ages is their doing.

It goes without saying that, from the perspective of this era, intellectual disciplines were not subject to specialization. To become a philosopher one needed an encyclopedic as well as a synthesized understanding of all existing knowledge. To become a philosopher, one did not learn only to deliberate on cause and effect, as Pangloss* would have said; one learned to integrate culture into spiritual life, for neither culture nor spiritual life could function without the other. This point is essential for anyone wishing to understand even a little about the medieval mind.

During the eleventh century, however, there appeared for the first time a new and dazzling reality, a reality so dazzling that no one had ever seen anything like it before. This was the sudden realization of the woman standing at the side of man. One could well say that this was nothing new, nothing that human beings had not been aware of since the dawn of time. Of course. But what is new is that this awareness took root in a Christian society, which was built essentially for men by men, a society that accepted women only as some form of inferior being. Saint Paul's message, distorted by the Church Fathers, had been well received and put into practice. At the beginning of the eleventh century, and more so than ever before, woman was the servant of man, in the

---

* *Translator's note:* Pangloss was the name of Candide's tutor in Voltaire's satire of the same name, which lampooned the positive philosophy exemplified by Pangloss's repeated assertion that "Everything happens for the best in the best of all possible worlds."

sense that her role was to aid him to achieve his own fullness.

The new awareness manifesting at this moment, at least in certain milieus where there was time enough to question things, has a dual nature. On one hand, in the everyday world, women were often heirs to domains or fortunes, thus they were *interesting*[3] because they represented an economic force without which men could not accomplish the divine mission they had abrogated exclusively to themselves. On the other hand, theologians and mystics (who refused to credit the mysterious Mary Magdalene with any influence over Jesus Christ) were beginning to perceive that this same Jesus Christ had found physical incarnation in the very belly of a woman—to whom he owed his humanity and thus his embodiment as the Son of God among men.

These theologians and mystics were intelligent enough to see the contradictory character of these contentions, which inspired a good deal of confusion around the concept of the *Theotokos.* Did Mary Magdalene copulate with Joseph? or was she inseminated by the Holy Ghost without any physical contact? We know how the Roman Catholic Church answered this question: Mary, Mother of God, remains a virgin. The crux of the matter lies in the exact meaning of the word *virgin,* but since no one has ever been able to really explain the term, we can still lose ourselves in a meandering maze of etymology and speculation. And although the great Christian minds of the era had not yet arrived at the idea of the Immaculate Conception (and there was still a considerable way to go before they could justify a physical virginity and predestination), they are in fact still at the most elementary level when it comes to admitting Mary's role of mother while refusing her any sexual role at all. Poor Joseph! The Savior's genealogy was so arranged, however, as to make Jesus also a descendant of Joseph. It is hard to understand.

This is to show the extreme complexity of the problem raised, essentially by ninth-century monks, and the ensuing fallout for both the ethics of the time and the theological conception of a *Theotokos* rendered so sterile she became an image emptied of all meaning and all humanity. By presenting Mary as the model for all women—the universal mother, the Virgin of virgins—the new thinking reawakened impulses hidden deep

in the unconscious. What was reawakened, it should be added, was the
ancient image of the mother goddess, an image of the female from times
long before the Christian era, that particularly in its Celtic form has
been authenticated by archaeological discoveries as well as by the great
myths from the British and Irish traditions. Here again it is necessary to
remember the primordial contribution made by the Celts toward the
elaboration of the double face (in reality a single being with two faces)
of the woman of the courtly era—simultaneously Universal Virgin,
mother of all mankind as well as of God, and Royal Whore, the Sacred
Prostitute stepping right out of the temples of Babylon or some fairy
mound of pre-Christian Ireland.[4]

The people who mattered, the ones making human law and preaching divine law in the eleventh century, were men. But where, then, was
the love that Jesus, if we are to believe the Gospels, extolled so much? To
be fair, this love did exist, but it was within the shadow of the monasteries. And here is the great revolution of this century, which will see its
triumph in the writings of Bernard de Clairvaux, as formidable a politi-
cian as he was mystic. Love is in the monasteries—love of God, of
course, but the time is not far off when the troubadour Uc de Saint-Circ
would declare that one can reach God only through the intermediary of
woman. From now on we find ourselves far from the *ancilla domini*. It
is striking that the triumph of the cult of the Virgin Mary actually coin-
cides with the triumph of the lady of courtly love. Everything happens
as if the same conception of woman—that is to say, of a human being in
all her fullness and endowed with all her means and all her functions—
had appeared under two contradictory but in reality complementary
forms. One, purified of its carnal context, exists on a higher, transcendental plane; the other is also transcendent but is devoted to the profane
sphere, that is, etymologically speaking she remains *before the temple*.
On first analysis we find here the classic distinction between the sacred
and the profane.

The dichotomy is artificial, although it may have been deliberately presented as natural and been adroitly exaggerated for the needs of the cause.
We are so caught in the undenominational character of the secular

(which is treated by all beliefs with indifference, if not hostility, on principle, toward all things sacred) that we no longer see that the two separate faces are actually of one single reality. The secular lady of courtly love is none other than the sacred Virgin Mary, to whom pious invocations abound in Christian liturgy.

Indeed, starting from the moment when society posits the fundamental principle that woman is the necessary and essential hub of its functioning, there could be no other recourse than to render the feminine image more socially acceptable, and this by all available means. Thus woman now appears as a marvelous fairy, looming out of the mists on the Isle of the Apple Trees; as a horrible witch, endowed with negative, castrational powers; as a Virgin with magnified, purified features, who miraculously gave birth to a Child-God, himself the phantasmagorical projection of human beings in search of their own transcendence.

This revolution does not take place without hesitation, confusion, and an overflowing of boundaries throughout the value system, as if demarcation lines dividing biology, psychology, sociology, and religion have become a veritable strainer in which osmosis takes place in all directions and no longer in conformance to natural law.[5] The theoreticians of *fin'amor* tried to pull proposals out of this confusion in an attempt to dam up a wave no longer under control. The problem was serious and concerned the very foundation of the social structure.

The new mentality that was evolving can best be described as the valorization of woman—and through her what is called femininity—as the motor force of life and the foundation of a spirituality based on nature. But this is a profane and erotic mysticism that has scarcely any Christian roots. The woman takes on the look of a savior goddess: "But this deification is not without danger to a patriarchal civilization that is not taken in by the image. Very quickly the official ethics, represented by a self-affirming Christianity, will enclose femininity within the image of Mary."[6]

> The society of men was well aware of the danger and retreated
> before it. They preferred the Law and the prohibition that comes

with it, which ensured their power, to the woman's transgression, which called this power into question in its entirety. . . . The experience of the Mother to many seems a terrifying mystery, bordering on madness—so much so that they have not yet understood the process whereby it is from the Mother that spring forth both soul and woman: the soul I recognize in the woman before me and the woman I see thanks to the soul she gives me in discovering it within me, in a perpetual exchange between archetype and reality.[7]

The danger represented by the intrusion of the sacred into daily life was felt by patriarchal societies as an attack on the privileges certain members of these societies had reserved for themselves. Thus it was necessary to "break" any link that created a symbiosis between carnal impulses and metaphysical aspirations. Out of this emerged the image of the Virgin Mary treading the serpent underfoot, even crushing its head, for she was not to be bitten in the heel. In doing this, no one realized that the serpent was actually, originally, an integral part of the Virgin Mary.

Secular societies were mistaken in closing their eyes to the mysteries of the irrational. Clerical societies abused their power in denying all rational connotations in their affirmations, not realizing that in so doing they were using the most simplistic and narrow-minded vocabulary of rational language. This is why the "Virgin" Mary can only be, in the most basic sense, cloaked in a physical virginity excluding any interpretation that might bring symbol and metaphor into play. However, Bernard de Clairvaux said unambiguously: "We are carnal, and born from the concupiscence of the flesh; thus also it is necessary that our love begins in flesh," which still did not prevent this incomparable individual from becoming a devotee of Our Lady and from dedicating to her a form of worship that no longer had any specific relationship to the flesh. Saint Bernard was a contemporary of the great troubadours and of the first authors of the courtly narratives. The people of the Middle Ages were in fact far from prudish. Long before Boileau, they knew how to call a spade a spade.

Here we are at the very heart of the problem of courtly love. It concerns a new art of loving, but also a new art of living, for to live is to love and vice versa. Is this not the essential meaning of Jesus Christ's message, at least to judge from what words of his others have thought worthy to pass down to us? Have we paid enough attention to the fact that the Latin name of Rome, *Roma*, is the exact reverse of the Latin word *amor*, meaning love? Is this really mere coincidence, or random chance? Perhaps, but it still offers food for thought.

For love to exist, and for there to be *fin'amor*, requires a bare minimum of two people. Although it is possible to imagine autoeroticism, it is impossible to imagine the existence of an auto-love, the myth of Narcissus notwithstanding (he came to a bad end, anyway). An auto-love becomes egoism, egocentrism, or egotism, according to the deviance under consideration (even including autism), each of them a negative attitude based on pure impulse and contrary to the definition of humanity. Hegel repeated often enough that God, in the absolute state—that is, with no creature, with no other, before him—is the equivalent of nothing and therefore does not exist. Without the other, there is only nothingness, unaware of its own existence.

This is to say that courtly love—encompassing the art of loving, the art of living, the symbolic code for learning to love, and whatever its social, economic, literary, or simply sentimental components—poses a problem of metaphysical ontology. To speak of courtly love forces an opening onto horizons that no longer have anything in common with the individual himself, opening wide the gates of awareness onto realms both subtle and invisible.

Starting in the eleventh century, the intellectual elite of Europe, freed from its millenarianist terrors, began to ask if love was, in fact, merely a game, a simple copulation intended to perpetuate the species, or if it might not be a means to achieve transcendence, a means to surpass the human sphere and move toward the divine. It was then that woman, until that time the object of scorn and suspicion (partly because of the Church Fathers), came out of the shadows where she had been kept—sometimes against her will, sometimes with her own well-meaning complicity, always entailing a certain masochism condoned by the clergy, who themselves profited from such a state of affairs. Of course this upsurge of femininity took place with extreme discretion and surrounded with numerous precautions. The Christian populace had not forgotten that our remote ancestors worshiped a mother goddess, most often wearing three faces—a Trinity, as if by chance, but this was not at all by chance. The Virgin Mary was a recovery of this sulfurous figure, presenting an image of her that had been purified, if not expurgated. Sanctuaries would be built for *Our Lady,* the Mother of all Christians, our "Good Mother," the one through whom we are obliged to pass in order to attain God.

But Our Lady is universal: everyone must share her with his brothers. If we take away the amorous aspect, and the sexual aspect, she is no longer anything but the Mother. What becomes of the lover in all this? She is repressed from the cult, and from devotion, but she lurks on in the unconscious. In the countryside, people continue bizarre ceremonies in honor of a goddess who lives in the woods, who could be encountered near fountains. Is she Artemis or the triple Brigitte of the Celts? It does not matter. Sorcery has a hard life, even when its cults are practiced in the greatest secrecy. The folktales from oral tradition preserve the memory of this goddess under the guise of the fairy, who can be good or evil, young or old, beautiful or ugly, according to circumstance or to the storyteller's fancy.

This spills over into intellectual life. Poets recover the old myths and get to know the old legends. Morgana is still much alive in folk memory; she reigns over the marvelous isle of Avalon where there is no illness, no weakness, no death, where fruits are ripe all the year round. Now, Morgana is a "Lady," that is to say, a *Domina* or "mistress," the feminine form of *Dominus,* "lord." We can see the parallel between the couple made up of God and Mary and the couple made up of the lord and lady. But when the lady of the legends, most often embodied in the person of the lord's wife, actually becomes visible, as she lives within the framework of a socially determined but restrictive group, she individualizes or, rather, serves as a prism to crystallize each person's desires: she is no longer *Our Lady* but *Milady.*

This is where the *lover* comes in. For Milady to exist, she must have a subject who contemplates her. From the perspective of the court, this subject must be the knight, the model of the masculine for that era. But it could also be the troubadour, singing the praises of she who is inaccessible (at least theoretically). Thus the notion of the couple appears, since there can be no lady without the suitor. Attracted by the lady's beauty, either real or symbolic, the wooing knight or poet would try to approach her. The best way to get close, to catch her eye, is to accomplish great feats of martial or literary prowess. Thus a subtle game is established between the lady and the lover, a refined game not very different from the liturgies celebrated in church in honor of the *Theotokos*. The lover becomes the priest of a new religion—a religion that dares not give itself a name but which develops in parallel with the one that sees the Virgin Mary enthroned upon the altar of the Church. The profane reunites with the sacred, for the very good reason that they actually form one single reality, considered under two different but complementary aspects.

Courtly love concerns the lady and the lover not as individuals, therefore, but as the real or imaginary couple they form when all necessary ritual conditions have been fulfilled. Out of this is born the "service of love." It is the basis of the renunciation, sacrifice, loyalty, enchantment, prayers, and especially that meaningful behavior that seeks always to outdo itself in what is seen as the exploit. For one must deserve Milady in the same way one must make every possible effort to attract the compassion of Our Lady.

The game risks becoming dangerous. Freed of her reassuring maternal aspect that is not only tolerated but also magnified by the Church, there is a strong risk Milady might find herself reclassified as erotic. And then the diabolical element reappears, emerging directly from the ancient feminine cults of antiquity, either Greco-Roman or barbarian. One text, though courtly, says that "woman is more artful than the Devil," and in the *Quest for the Holy Grail* the Devil appears to Percival in the form of a lascivious, thoroughly seductive woman, and the hero scarcely manages to avoid succumbing to her. The old antifeminist terrors are still in evidence, intensified by the disabused considerations of certain Church Fathers. Tertullian was both married and a father, but did he not say "we are born between shit and urine"? There is no doubt that woman is an impure being against whom one must be on one's guard, because impurity is the mark of Satan.

This explains the somewhat sulfurous connotation that will be applied to the lady-lover couple, whatever form their relationship takes, be it purely sentimental (or platonic, as it was once called) or unabashedly sexual. For the idea of marriage is totally excluded from such a couple. To the contrary, it would even seem that for a courtly couple to be perfect, the lady must be married, so there must be either actual or symbolic adultery. After all, the perfect model of this couple is Lancelot and Guinivere, or Tristan and Iseult. But this couple is far from representing the moral and religious ideals of Christianity. Or could there by chance be nothing at all subversive in this courtly love, which numerous authors have described as a simple social game of no consequence serving primarily the needs of that era's privileged class?

Contrary to what one might think, subversion of any kind is never born among society's most disadvantaged classes. It is significant that during those troubled times when the common people are agitated, there is talk of leaders or even of a "clandestine band leader." It is well known that mobs are easily manipulated. It was the people who made the Revolution of 1789, but it was not originally their idea. That came from an intellectual elite, which took advantage of the people's unconscious impulses and legitimate social demands. The same holds true for all historical upheavals: it is the alliance between power and knowledge that transforms the world, a fact that clarifies the full and total responsibility of those who are keepers of knowledge, or who claim to be. In the case of the period spanning the eleventh through the thirteenth centuries, the keepers of knowledge, clerics as well as certain so-called enlightened aristocrats, acted as manipulators of opinion. They infused some very strange elements, gleaned from what is called the Tradition, into the social and moral rules of a society that to all appearances was Christian.* But this Tradition is far from being innocent.

---

* *Translator's note:* "The Tradition" refers to spiritual paths outside the church—magic, the occult, shamanic practices, mysticism, alchemy, and so forth.

If we actually analyze the events leading up to the formulation of courtly love, we cannot help but encounter currents whose orthodoxy is more than suspect. First, there is the great tradition of the Occitan troubadours (as a term, *Occitan* is far preferable to *Provençal*, since the so-called troubadours were for the most part natives of Toulouse, Auvergne, and Limousin), a tradition colored by Catharism* and by cultural memories dating back to Visigoth times. Next, there is the persistence of Celtic elements—in the Occitan mountains and the Valley of Lot, in particular, where these elements are maintained under a fragile veneer of Roman influence and a more or less marginalized version of Christianity. This "Celticity" appears all too clearly in the architecture and the ornamentation of the Roman churches, in the oral folktales, and in the very foundations of the Occitan vocabulary—which was, in the last resort, much closer to the Gallic spoken in the times of independence than to the *langue d'oïl*† perverted by numerous influences and more directly exposed to a certain Latin radicalism. And there is another, most essential factor: the roles played by Eleanor of Aquitaine and by Chrétien de Troyes in the twelfth century. Eleanor, twice queen (of France and of England), crystallized around her not only the fantasies of the troubadours but also the legends of Celtic origin, to which her stunning personality gave new shape. Chrétien de Troyes, the true creator of the courtly romance, was a converted Jew and heir to a long kabbalistic tradition. This is not insignificant. We must also not forget that it was in Champagne, around the area of Troyes, that the so-called Cathar heresy first appeared before spreading (as is well documented) throughout the Toulousian area of Occitan.

This makes for many fairy godmothers around the cradle of courtly love. And these godmothers all share a nature that the Middle Ages labeled diabolical or infernal. To the line of conduit dictated by pontifical authorities

---

* *Translator's note:* The Cathars (from the Greek *Katharos,* meaning "pure") were a twelfth- to thirteenth-century Manichaean sect that viewed the established church as the antichrist. They became quite powerful in the Occitan and were eventually destroyed as heretics by a crusade mounted by the church and the king of France.
† *Translator's note:* the language spoken north of the Loire at that time.

and echoed to their hearts' content (even if there was temporal conflict) by the various European monarchies, the new intellectual elite born in the shadows of the monasteries responded with proposals that threatened to endanger the whole dogmatic edifice of Christianity. The Roman Catholic Church actually conceals its own share of mysteries also, and if the so-called Gothic architectural reform was actually the resumption of control over the flock of faithful by an alarmed clergy, it nevertheless allowed the infiltration of some unusual epiphenomena—due to the secret rules of the guild of builders, who easily found ways to cloak in orthodoxy what was pure heterodoxy. The charm of the Middle Ages lies in the fact that it pulled off a brilliant synthesis of the most contradictory lines of thought.

Therefore, we must be prudent and examine with care everything concerning this agreeable game called courtly love. If we keep to the amusement theory, it becomes the sign of an intellectual aristocratic elite seeking to call attention to itself and to distinguish itself from the lower classes. If we venture beneath the surface, however, we find ourselves in the presence of otherwise formidable realities that challenge the very foundations of the society that courtly love was claiming to express and codify.

Woman is not the only problem raised by the elegant casuistry of the courts of love: there is also the problem of *the couple*. This is of primary importance because, until this time, men and women had been considered separate beings, each with particular qualities and flaws (the flaws of women being obviously more numerous). Before the eleventh century it had been established once and for all that man worked, prayed, and waged war whereas woman, while maintaining her necessary reproductive role, was the warrior's rest, the worker's diversion, the cleric's object of fantasy. In fact clerics had no trouble at all in gratifying their fantasies concerning women. The chastity of the clergy was always the source of an impassioned debate at the heart of the Church, even if the celibacy of the priests and the chastity of the monks had become official rules (which were rarely heeded). Now, suddenly, the mentality changed: it was clear that male activity, especially warfare, could be linked to sexual activity and thus could be linked to woman.

We could almost say that eleventh-century thinkers gave themselves over to a psychoanalysis of sexuality, bringing to light each sex's respective contribution to everyday life. The old androcratic notion—summed up so well in the Jewish prayer "Lord, I thank you that I was not born a woman"—suddenly loses its value, at least on a primary level, for it overlooks the fact that biblical women, especially in the beginning, did not hesitate to establish a wide dominion over society and to intervene in its actual functioning. To be more specific, for as little as we might care to view courtly heroines such as Guinivere, Enide, and Iseult from any angle other than through the romantic mirror (all too often our sole frame of reference), we see that these heroines are actually far from passive figures, merely putting up with men's adoring gaze and thereby reducing love's field of play to its sentimental dimension. These heroines have nothing in common with those heroines popularized by nineteenth-century literature in the image of the romantic woman wasting away and dying of love. Iseult's dying from love has causes that are not all from the world of the emotions, even if this world seems the most emphasized in the story that has come down to us.

Denis de Rougemont, in his long meditation on love and the West called *L'Amour et l'Occident*, insists that courtly love played an essential role in fashioning the modern conception of love. By demonstrating that sentimental love was incompatible with marriage, and by codifying sexuality and integrating it into the sentiment of love, eleventh-, twelfth-, and thirteenth-century theoreticians prompted the birth of an authentic Christian marriage built on feelings of love, and its corollary adultery, the crystallization of passionate love. All of this was completely new. Earlier eras had known only the *economic* marriage, intended to perpetuate the species or the lineage, a marriage in which sexuality was merely a means to an end and feelings of love were futile. In this respect, we could say that our own era seems a regression, to the extent that sexual liberation through its aberrant forms has led to the abandonment of sentimental and even passionate love, to the benefit of pure sexuality and the marriage of convenience. Thus the problem of courtly love, put back in proper context, should inspire us to reflect on our own behavior.

For it is a matter not so much of an intermittent, temporary questioning of the existence of the couple in a context determined by social and historical circumstances as it is a matter of the fundamental, ongoing debate concerning the relations in which a man and a woman could engage, as well as concerning the necessity of defining their relations within their social group.

Early Christianity offered a model that was not very different from the Greek model, as revised and corrected by Rome: the domination of woman by man, whereby she is all the while coddled and protected, but relegated to the role of procreator and dispenser of pleasures to the male. Christianity merely added a notion of sacred duty, in order to ensure the success of God's plans. It was also the beginning of a long period of making woman culpable: she was suspected of perverting the divine mission embodied by masculine activity.

In the eleventh, twelfth, and thirteenth centuries, instead of diverting man from his divine mission, woman to the contrary began to assist him (as shown in *Erec et Enide,* by Chrétien de Troyes), and, even more revolutionary, she began to actually motivate that activity. Woman now abruptly becomes the most perfect image of the divine incarnated in all forms, the initiator of human activity, which without her intervention would risk remaining empty of all meaning and significance.

The change does not take place without hesitations, and especially not without transgressing prohibitions that until that time had been considered definitive and unbending. The fact that courtly love condoned extramarital love is enough to make it suspect—a thoroughly logical reaction considering that marriage is the keystone of society, be it Christian or otherwise, and any venture knocking a breach in this sacrosanct institution must necessarily be subversive and thus (to use medieval terminology) tinged with diabolism. The problem becomes more complex, in that courtly love—as it appears in its theoretical codification and as it is lived in the fictional narratives of the era (see Lancelot and Tristan)—claims to substitute new rules for behavior, at the very core of society, to the detriment of the old laws hitherto considered definitive and endorsed by Christian morality. By associating love with what was most absolute and most exalted about masculine activity, theoreticians of courtly love managed to formulate a profoundly different, even contradictory, authentic philosophy of behavior.

This association of love, previously considered an easy, soothing pleasure and truly the warrior's well-deserved rest, with the war-making activity itself, which allowed a man to attain prowess through exceeding his own limitations, this is the new idea that was making its way from the eleventh century, timidly at first, to arrive at a mad and sometimes exaggerated exaltation of the new relationship between man and woman. It did not concern just any kind of relationship, as it did not concern just any kind of man or woman. Woman is idealized, transcended, deified. She is a woman of high rank, the wife of a lord no less. As for the man, the wooing lover is never the husband, for the husband is his wife's equal, which makes the game of courtly love an exercise in futility. The man must be of lower social standing than his lady. Most often this knight in fact owned no domains nor had a personal fortune. But he possessed an *existential potentiality*. Thanks to the woman he would adore and serve to the best of his abilities, this potentiality would be set in motion, letting him achieve exploits that would cause his adored to return his love and (if all necessary conditions were met) give him his just reward. By doing this he would accomplish the different steps of an evolutionary process and undergo in some way a rigorous initiation, which would lead him to a higher rank that he would never have been able to attain without the motivation caused by his lady. His "service of love," even immorally directed toward the wife of his lord, would engender a beneficial effect upon the society in which he lives. In the final analysis the entire society benefits from this strange adulterous love. It seems the crowning achievement of ambiguity.

This is why it is impossible to consider courtly love, a very productive social and literary game of the Middle Ages, without making serious reference back to the couple it forms and animates. The lady of courtly love is certainly very important in that she forms a hub around which turn her possible lovers. But this lady is also nothing without these lovers who, blinded by her luminous beauty, are caught in the trap and gather in a pack around her. This lady, when all is said and done, would also be nothing without the one whom she chooses from among her suitors, the one with whom she will undertake a veritable ritual of "possession," a magical ceremony, leading the man to transgress social, moral, even sexual prohibitions in order to attain a state of grace where anything is possible. The notion of the individual disappears at this point, giving way to that of the couple. The lover-knight has no more validity on his own than does his lady in her haughty silence. To understand courtly love we must first understand the couple, which formed under the force of circumstances and in view of the then current codes of conduct.

This cannot happen without revealing some strange patterns of behavior. Was the couple thus formed as innocent as we are led to believe? Is it a matter of a couple linked solely by vows of a love so pure, spiritual in the extreme, worthy of the devotion Saint Bernard de Clairvaux felt for the Virgin Mary? Was it simply a convenient and extremely refined means of binding a valiant knight to his lord through the intermediary of the lord's lady? After all, the prose narrative *Lancelot* is very clear: King Arthur asks Guinivere *to do all in her power* to keep the brilliant Lancelot of the Lake at court. The essential thing is to know when one should not go too far, but then, what would be too far is never very clear.

This is the outline of the couple as it emerged from an intellectual speculation overturning the entire order of things. Because of its ambiguous and imprecise nature, this couple can never be more than marginal, and quite often, as a result of the religious and moral assumptions of the time, it was given a diabolical cast, as much for the lady's as for her lover's attitude and as much for the curious nature of the couple as for its acceptance by society. Later, in the seventeenth century, because of the precious nature of its style, courtly love would become integrated into the map of Passionate Feelings, but this would be no more than a cerebral game whereby ladies of high estate in that era would be courted all their lives without ever having to respond to their suitors. And the suitors entertained no hopes of any kind. What had been a game of love and knightly exploit became simply a drawing-room diversion, challenging society in no way whatsoever. In fact, society became more puritanical. During the eleventh, twelfth, and thirteenth centuries, it is an entirely different thing. The spiritual, intellectual, and carnal aspects of life are so closely interwoven it is difficult at times to see them separately. It seems, moreover, that no one would have dreamed of separating what was by necessity to remain as one. Courtly love is a whole: it should be no cause for surprise if Guinivere and Lancelot's relationship goes as far as actual adultery; it could scarcely be otherwise.

It makes no difference if we analyze the processes of courtly love from a strictly literary point of view or if we subject them to psychological, sociological, or even political readings. The end result will be the same and will reach one fundamental observation: the couple formed by the lady and her lover, whatever their admitted or ulterior motives, is a kind of infernal couple that throws itself in the way of medieval Christian society and troubles its good conscience.

Is it not the devil's role to *throw himself in the way?* Let us not forget that it is *in hell* that Dante meets Francesca di Rimini, guilty of having read too many adventures of Guinivere and Iseult, of succumbing to the infernal charm of the passions they represent. There was considerable work to be done to tap into the energies awoken by courtly love and to direct them toward the quest of the "holy" grail or toward the reassuring worship of the Virgin Mary, mother of God and all humanity. It must be acknowledged that the energies awoken this way were sexual in origin and did not always find their culmination in mystical ecstasy. Would the infernal couple be a necessary stage in the development of the individual seeking fulfillment?

ONE

THE LAWS OF LOVE

Any behavior that is recognized in public and that claims to be equally applicable and valuable to everyone must one day or other be codified by a theoretician. It is quite clear that moral regulations are the consequence of innate principles being applied within any specific society, principles that are generally codified when they are actually no longer useful. The problem then becomes that the matter is not taken any further and said rules are not changed, a task that never receives universal support and is never undertaken without pain. We know that Boileau's *Art poétique* marks the end of the so-called classical era; all the works that could fit the definition provided by this *Art poétique* had already been written well before he felt obliged to write his treatise, which in one fell swoop prompted the poetic sterility of the century to follow, and the eternal disgust for literature experienced by generations of students ever since, no matter how well disposed toward it they may have been before beginning their education. Courtly love did not escape a similar fate; it was codified with marvelous precision at the exact moment that it ceased to be in practice, at the beginning of the fourteenth century. The sole purpose of an otherwise quite lackluster and unreadable codification was to memorialize the essential features of what had been the greatest intellectual adventure of the Middle Ages.

This codification took the form of a text written in Latin, *De Arte amandi,* part of a manuscript dating from the early years of the four-teenth century and presented as the work of a certain André le Chapelain.[1] This mysterious author (of whom we know nothing save that he was a member of the clergy, specifically a "chaplain") was sup-posedly a contemporary of Philippe-Auguste, but it is more than obvi-ous that this is just a convenient assumed name, as was common prac-tice during that time. The text is written in a style closer to that of the reign of Philippe le Bel. It serves as a kind of final period at the end of a theoretical exploration of courtly love.

Whatever the truth concerning the author and the circumstances of its composition, this text is unimpeachable testimony to the doctrine of courtly love. Furthermore, the purpose of the text is pedagogical: Capellanus* addresses his work to a certain Walter, "who wants to serve in the knighthood of love." Scholars have lost their way in endless discus-sions trying to find historical traces of this Walter, but to no avail. The subject of the dedication, whether real or imaginary, is nothing more than the model of a young knight who must serve his apprenticeship before he can gain entry into the bizarre kind of sect formed by the "servants" of love, as the fanatics of Milady were sometimes called. *De Arte amandi* thus presents itself as a mandatory code to be known and practiced by any knight wishing to become a priest in the religion of love.

This code, however, is buried in a heap of considerations, which might be helpful to a sociologist trying to understand the society of that era but which primarily record an intellectual mannerism that is hard to tolerate. The essence can be found in two chapters where the theory is presented in its pure state, one concerning "precepts of love," the other concerning "rules of love."

The Precepts of Love

This is certainly not the first edition of an "Art of Love." The famous Indian *Kama Sutra,* with its roots going back to time immemorial, is the

---

* *Translator's note:* In English his name would be Andrew the Chaplain. He is more com-monly known by the Latin version of his name, Andreas Capellanus.

most characteristic example, and it has numerous implications for the level of metaphysics as well as for the level of sexual technique. As for classical antiquity, the best example must be Ovid's *The Art of Love*, an ambiguous work that is more a mirror held up to a corrupt society than a code of amorous behavior. This in no way prevented the people of the Middle Ages from taking an impassioned interest in Ovid, and from translating and adapting his *Art of Love* on several occasions. We know, for example, that Chrétien de Troyes, a man tormented by love's casuistry and making large use of it in his romances, did a translation of Ovid's work for which the manuscript has been lost. But Andreas Capellanus's text has nothing in common with Ovid's and does not concern itself at all with techniques described so well in the *Kama Sutra*. We are here in the presence of pure theory, and by virtue of this, love appears as a transcendental state of Being, which one can attain only by carefully following the different stages of an initiation that is at the same time social, psychological, and moral. Thus what are referred to as love's precepts are justified at the very outset. There are thirteen of them—a fatidic number that doubtless has not been chosen accidentally.

The first precept reveals the social range claimed for the "service of love": *"Flee avarice as if it were a dangerous plague and, in contrast, be generous."* So altruism is emphasized immediately. Any given society is based on the solidarity of the individuals forming it, and he who forgets this not only places himself outside that society but also abandons any hope of becoming integrated within it. Within the "brotherhood" forming the "knighthood of love," the law of exchange is absolute. It is certain that avarice, which seals off the individual and isolates him completely, obstructs the easy functioning of the social group. Furthermore, we must consider greed in the larger sense of the word. It is not a question of not hoarding material wealth, but, rather, of remaining *open* to others, remaining constantly available to respond to any request. Generosity here is more an attitude of heart and mind than a habit of giving away money and goods. The first precept is an inherently moral one: it is futile for the neophyte to seek acceptance into the knighthood of love if he remains ignorant of his responsibilities toward the group, as well as toward the lady of his dreams. The other members of the community, like the lady, have a right to share in the exchange.

The second precept is equally moral in character: *"Never lie."* In other words, he must always be who he really is and not project a false appearance. The lie thus avoided concerns the beloved woman, from whom he should never hide the truth, as much as it concerns the community, which should never be deceived as to the true feelings and intentions of the lover-knight. Certainly there may be contradictions in his doings: the love that binds the knight to his lady must be kept a secret, and this, practically speaking, may amount at times to not saying things, which comes close to lying by omission. The rationale behind this is subtle; it eliminates the lie in favor of discretion, which is not quite the same thing. The accent is placed on sincerity, without which love either cannot exist or else is reduced to caricature. Numerous texts from the era, romances or judgments handed down by the famous courts of love, attest to the repulsion inspired by false lovers, those who not only fool themselves but also deceive society—and especially the abstract god of love, who serves as a vigilant guardian and symbolic guarantor of the paradise courtly love was trying to establish on earth. "He who binds himself to a false love, traffics with the devil and has no need of another rod with which to beat himself," wrote the Gascon troubadour Marcabru with his customary intensity. And Bernart de Ventadour exhibits a certain amount of bitterness when he observes: "The ladies, in my view, are making a great mistake when they don't return the affection of their faithful lovers. Of course, I should pass over in silence everything but what they want, but I suffer when a knave enjoys as much or more love than the faithful lover."*

The third precept stems from the second: *"Speak no ill."* Speaking ill, rumormongering or spreading evil rumors, is necessarily lying, for it is inventing falsehoods about others and entertaining negative thoughts about them. It causes therefore a serious breach in the mandatory soli-

---

* *Translator's note:* Markale did not provide specific references for quotes from the troubadour literature but it is quite possible that he used Pierre Bec's *Anthologie des troubadours* (Paris: 10/18, 1979) for many of them.

darity uniting the membership of love's knighthood. The poems of the troubadours are filled with warnings about slanderers, *lausengiers* who spy on lovers, try to invade their privacy, and are always ready to spread a nasty rumor—whether from jealousy or envy or simply from the thrill of wrecking someone else's game and disturbing a dearly purchased peace of mind. The warning that the neophyte should never speak ill of anyone is imperative because it concerns not only the other couples, the other members of the community, but also the very object of adoration, the lady. If the lady becomes the subject of evil rumor she will lose all her symbolic value, all the purity she embodies. A man speaking ill of his lady will find his perfidious attack turned back on himself, since it would be dishonorable and improper to love a woman deemed unworthy.

The fourth precept evokes the specific atmosphere in which the ritual of love should unfold: *"Never divulge lovers' secrets."* We are touching here the depths of the ambiguity in courtly love. On the one hand there should be no lies or falsehoods in amorous relationships, but on the other these relationships must be so secret, so wrapped in mystery, that they necessarily lend themselves to perilous speculations and fictional constructions. Under these conditions the well-kept secret may become a lie if only through the nondenunciation of something that could possibly be detrimental to the knighthood of love. The essential nature of courtly love is to be *furtive*. It so happens that the word *furtive*, whose etymological sense derives from a Latin word meaning "thief," is masked by a vague connotation of hypocrisy. However, in order for the love between the lady and her lover to be authentic, secrecy and mystery, hence hypocrisy, are indispensable elements. In all their poems the troubadours promise their most absolute discretion to the lady whose loving slave they wish to become. The Chaplain himself insists on this precept and revisits it when clarifying this idea: "All lovers are obliged to keep their love secret. If they submit their disputes to the judgment of ladies, the names of those involved should never be revealed to the judges, at least before the judgment is announced. If they use letters to communicate, they must refrain from writing their names. They should never affix their seals on these letters, unless they have one known only to them and their confidant."

The lover always has a confidant, who can perform the same role for the lady as well, and this precept is addressed to that individual. The confidant knows everything about the love binding the lady and her lover, and it would be a very serious shortcoming for him to divulge what he knows. We might ask why it is necessary to have a confidant. It is, however, part of the game. There must be at least one witness for the amorous relationship to be legalized in some way. Moreover, is it not more exciting, imaginatively, to know that someone else knows and could break the code of silence and at any moment place the couple's security and harmony in jeopardy? Love feeds on fear, and how can one ever be completely sure of the faithfulness of the friend taken on as confidant?

Furthermore, this confidant plays the ever-important role of messenger between the lady and her lover. He is in charge of organizing discreet rendezvous, where the lovers can find a haven from the *gelos* (the "jealous") and the *lausengiers* ("rumormongers"). If necessary, the confidant could send someone else off on a wrong scent. We are certainly given the impression that the confidant "held the candle."* This is close to the truth, and there must have been a fair amount of voyeurism attendant to this duty. The well-known but strangely dramatized twelfth-century poem *Aube* ("Dawn"), written in *langue d'oïl*, contains dialogues between two lovers, their confidant, and their lookout. The confidant is charged with protecting the lovers' peace of mind. He addresses the guard: "Watchman on the tower, watch well the surrounding lands, and may God protect you! For at this very moment, the lady and her lord are closeted within, and thieves are lurking about seeking their prey." We suspect that the lurking thieves in question are the jealous and the rumormongers. So the confidant's role is essential. He diverts all suspicion from the lovers, he lays out false trails, he serves as a guardian. In certain cases he even becomes the lover's duly appointed representative if his charge is forced to absent himself or is hampered by a wound or illness. He is authorized to make

* *Translator's note:* "Holding the candle" is a French expression denoting someone who helps a love affair.

remonstrations to the lady if she neglects her lover or commits an act of infidelity. He can even represent the lover before the courts of love (formed by ladies of high estate) when a matter of conscience is laid before them so they can judge it in complete composure. The confidant is actually the *secretary*, in the etymological sense of the word, the "keeper of secrets" for those who entrust him with their confidences. Of course it is expected that the favor will be returned when the "secretary" has his own amorous relationship with a lady.

This said, the nondisclosure of secrets lends to courtly love a dimension that escapes social control. The ambiguity that this supposes leads simultaneously to the retrenchment of the couple outside the group and to the functioning of this group through the transcendence required of the lover for him to merit his lady. It seems contradictory, but logically we must allow that private life, although respected and kept secret, does have repercussions on collective life. Even if "the lovers are always alone in the world," even if their relationship is more often than not based upon adultery (which under normal conditions would lead to the destruction of the social base represented by marriage and the legal family), every single action must sooner or later have an influence on collective behavior. It is as if the theoreticians of courtly love had measured the intensity of human progress within the social network against the reasoned and reasonable transgression of enforced prohibitions that serve as guardrails for that social network. In any case we must recognize that, even though society is made up of individuals, it is not individual mentalities we find at the collective level but another reality, different, heterogeneous, but linked just the same to individual mentality. The problem involves much more than just a game played by lovers.

So now we can speak of *connivance*. There have always been, in both ancient and modern societies, the transgressions of taboos, but these transgressions have always been performed *in secret* and have been reserved for individuals who are uncommon, either because of their birth or because of their behavior. The best example is that of ancient Egypt, where incest, as in most societies, was a serious sin, except for the pharaoh, who was required to marry his own sister in order to realize the *dyad,* the divine couple par excellence—a formidable duty that only exceptional individuals could take on and manage. It would be puerile to conclude that the matter entailed just abuse of power, or just toler-ance for the great people of this world. The famous "droit de seigneur," the subject of great condemnation, was in fact the degenerate form of an ancient ritual whereby a sacred figure, a priest or a king, would person-ally take on the curse entailed by the deflowering of a virgin, a magical act if ever there was one, considered dreadful in its consequences for the social group in question. Only a king or a priest was powerful enough to support the gravity of such an act. The transgression of a taboo is not within everyone's capability. This is the idea that appears in the amorous relations of a lady and her lover-knight, the active element thanks to which the society will endure. The main thing is to find a balance, a har-mony, between the law in general on one hand and the specific cases on the other. Hence the secrecy that is required of everything concerning the privileged—but naturally illegal—amorous relationship joining the lady to her knight, and hence also the obligation for those in the know to guard their silence under pain of committing a breach of duty.

This is the spirit of the fifth precept: *"Do not make several people con-fidants of your love-affair."* It goes without saying. If we multiply the obliging ears, we multiply also the mouths that may speak of it. The privileged relationship that is possible with one confidant risks being degraded if it is shared with several, with conflicts from jealousy or envy showing up in a context that grows less and less under control. There is a good illustration of this in the prose version of the Lancelot legend. During the early days of his liaison with Guinivere, Lancelot had only one confidant, the mysterious figure known only as Galehot, lord of the "faraway isles," the "son of the Giant," a person with whom he main-tained, furthermore, a relationship that to say the least revealed a some-what homosexual nature.[2] Everything was going quite smoothly and Galehot's discretion, amounting to active complicity, allowed Guinivere to preserve her "honor" and Lancelot his credibility at the court of King Arthur. But later—when, following the lovers' imprudence, the secret of their liaison is shared among a few more people, most notably Gawain's brothers and Morgana—the worst can no longer be avoided. Oddly enough, it then becomes apparent that Arthur's ideal kingdom is sinking into decrepitude and anarchy, which are the first signs of its future destruction in the battle between Arthur and his incestuous son, Mordred. In fact, the power and balance of Arthur's kingdom rest on the feats of Lancelot, who is bound to the king and the king's most reliable active element, also the most faithful, despite the consummated adultery between the queen and this most valiant knight in the world. Once the secret is out, nothing can hold together. The kingdom collapses. Arthur, deprived of his wife's lover, is no more than the king of a ludicrous chess game, waiting for checkmate. And all this is the fault not only of the *gelos* and the *lausengiers* swarming around the couple of lovers but also of their confidants who could not stop their tongues from wagging.

Courtly love as a factor of social cohesion is one of those secret, mysterious recipes without which nothing can run smoothly in this world. It depends on the necessary transgression of a taboo through the subterfuge of an infernal couple striving to create paradise. By the same token, and through a slight displacement of the facts of the matter, we can get a glimpse of the role played by hermetic thought in the evolution of medieval European society. Something subversive, capable of transforming the appearance of things, must be kept hidden from the great majority of people. On one hand, this large majority cannot comprehend the full scope of the action thus engaged in; on the other hand, this same majority is not capable of truly appreciating the power of transgression and would make use of it to satisfy mediocre ends, that is to say, ends emptied of their authentic potential. From this perspective it is not beyond the range of possibility to consider courtly love, in all its visible and invisible manifestations, as a hermetic doctrine that loses its effectiveness when divulged in an uncontrolled manner to those who have not received a preliminary initiation.

The sixth precept no longer concerns the lovers' relations with society but instead the knight's disposition toward his lady: *"Keep yourself chaste for your lady."* This is similar to the advice once deliberately given young girls to remain virgins until married. It is something of great satisfaction for the husband, who can take pride in being the first man to have *had his* woman. Such advice makes us smile today when it does not provoke outright hilarity, especially following on the heels of sexual liberation. However, this sixth precept must be considered an essential element of the logic of courtly love.

Certainly, its formulation is ambiguous. Is it purity before meeting the lover, or purity during their liaison? The text never says. Furthermore, just what is meant by the word *purity?* Should it be considered physical purity, such as actual chastity, or should it be understood as a state of mind, a concentration of energy directed toward the beloved individual, in which case would it be more appropriate to substitute the word *fidelity?* It is difficult to find answers for these questions. Perhaps, in terms of the fictional narratives of the courtly era, it would be appropriate to drop the concept of chastity and keep only fidelity. After all, we have the examples of Tristan and Lancelot to demonstrate that there is a crystallization of desire upon a single individual, Iseult or Guinivere, where there is no chastity and that purity defined in this light is a transcendence of human love in the direction of a divine domain, where woman represents—through a still perfectly erotic image—the terrifying God one does not yet dare to look straight in the face for fear of being burned by his insupportable light.

By all evidence woman was granted exclusive rights. She was unique in the way God is unique to a Christian. And in the same manner a Christian approaches the altar to receive communion after uttering words of purification,[3] the lover presents himself in all purity before his beloved's face. "When the entire world was covered in darkness, everything was shining where she was," sings the Gascon troubadour Cercamon, "and I will pray God that I may one day touch her again, or look upon her while she sleeps." With no exaggeration, we can draw this comparison: the lover's attitude differs not one whit from that of a believer receiving the Eucharist. And Bernart de Ventadour admits his complete communion with the divinity in these terms: "I no longer have any control over myself since the day she let me look into her eyes, the mirror I find most delightful." The point of fusion has been attained.

Bernart adds elsewhere: "I think of nothing else in the world half so much: and I cannot hear said a word of her without my heart turning in her direction and my face lighting up, whatever it is one is saying about her." And one should not claim that this communion is strictly the lover's accomplishment in the presence of his lady. It is also the behavior of the lady thinking about her lover: "Listen," says Raimbaut de Vaqueiras, in the voice of a woman character: "sweet breezes coming from over yonder where my beloved lies sleeping, bring me the libation of his sweet breath! My mouth opens from my great desire to have it."

The idea of purity, linked to that of exclusiveness, should be, if we have grasped it correctly, a permanent state of the lover ready to pursue his lady. In the same way that he must rid himself of all base and vile thoughts if he wishes to commune with God, he must present himself with a virgin heart—and a body no less stained—if he wishes to achieve the ultimate fusion with his beloved. This equivalence clearly shows that courtly love is a veritable religion, whose mysterious elements are highlighted and even exaggerated by the profane, if not erotic, aspect they cloak.

It is, pure and simple, a question of remaining unstained and available for the exclusive service of one's beloved lady. Under these conditions it is impossible to think about another woman, especially if that woman is already bound to another man by a contract of love. This is the meaning of the seventh precept: *"Do not knowingly seek to steal another's beloved."* This would be a double betrayal, both toward one's own lady and toward the *other,* the other who by law and deed belongs to the knighthood of love. This prohibition is easy enough to understand. But what are we to think about the word *knowingly?* Would stealing another's beloved be justifiable if one did not know she was already another knight's lady? This is what the formulation of the precept would seem to imply. But in this case there is the lover's own good faith. And then there was always the possibility of referring the matter to one of the famous courts of love presided over by great women such as Eleanor of Aquitaine and Marie de Champagne. They would have had numerous cases of this kind brought before them, if we are to believe the various testimonies from the time.

The eighth precept is of particular importance: *"Never seek the love of a woman you would be ashamed to wed."* This obviously contradicts the duly noted principle in the courtly system of logic concerning the incompatibility of love and marriage. But let us not forget that marriage is primarily a social act, a contract by which a man gives his name to a woman and makes her the generator of his offspring. Therefore, it is necessary for the generator to be equal or higher in rank than the man; otherwise it would be cause for disgrace. And even if there is no question of marriage between the lover and his lady, the concept of the woman's parity or superiority remains more valid than ever. In fact, it is the concept of superiority that predominates. The lover who sets his cap for a lady of higher station has a goal that, if not inaccessible, is at least capable of spurring on his own growth by encouraging his actions and exploits.

There is nothing in the least extraordinary about this in a feudal society. In the same way that a knight is bound to a more powerful lord by his oath, he must be his lady's vassal and obey a similar oath of fidelity. And in the same way that a vassal could have several different suzerains (given the many interlinked chains of feudal society) yet must declare himself the liege man of only the one to whom he owes his primary allegiance, this same vassal would be his lady's liege man, if accepted, by virtue of an oath of love that is the equivalent of the oath of vassalage he exchanged with his lord. Thus were woven together in a very subtle network interdependent individuals at the heart of a society that was definitively hierarchical and incapable of accepting the slightest flaw, at least theoretically.

The avowed goal of the lady is thus to *improve* her lover. Her duty is to do her utmost to better him, to aid him through the necessary steps required for him to blossom, at the cost of the harshest restraints, the most painful trials, the most glaring injustices. Lancelot in Chrétien de Troyes's *Le Chevalier à la charrette* ("The Knight of the Hangman's Cart") had personal experience of this, for he was at times obliged to submit pathetically to Queen Guinivere's slightest whim. But Guinivere's whims are something quite different from a mere manifestation of coquettish ways. By subjecting her lover to these vicissitudes Guinivere was measuring not the extent of Lancelot's obedience to her but his ability to handle any given situation. This is quite different, although at times one may have the impression that the queen was eaten up by sadistic cravings and although it is perfectly legitimate to ask whether Lancelot might not be drowning in sleazy delights of masochism.

Numerous poets have complained of being spurned or scorned by the lady who rules their thoughts, but this in no way has prevented them from receiving their due. Examples are not lacking. The odd figure of Eleanor's grandfather Guillaume IX of Aquitaine, a pugnacious and thoroughly lewd fellow when opportunity allowed but also a great poet, expressed himself thus on the matter: "My lady wishes to know what kind of love she feels and holds for me. No matter how hard the quarrel she seeks, never will our bond be loosened." Raimbaut d'Orange did not shy away from the excess that would be the standard fare of the seventeenth-century baroque poets when he wrote: "Your beautiful eyes are like rods to me that punish my heart with *elation*" (fairly revealing an authentic quest for pleasure through suffering). We are not far here from the "Venus in Furs" or even the leather-wearing woman always equipped with a whip. But Raimbaut d'Orange, it is true, added that these same eyes, though cruel, "cured me of baseness," and this changes profoundly the meaning behind this undeniable masochism. For as Bernart de Ventadour said, "One day of good adventure is worth one hundred of suffering." And Cercamon is even more explicit: "I am delighted that she drives me mad or leaves me gaping at air and moon-ing in futile waiting; I am delighted that she snubs me or mocks me to my face or behind my back, for good follows on ill will, if such be her own good pleasure."

At bottom courtly love is a trial during which, no matter what suffer-ings have been endured, the lover desires with all his being to reach the perfection embodied by his lady. The couple brought together this way is infernal, to the extent that it is immoral (with respect to traditional morality) and that it brings pain and suffering to someone who in com-plete awareness has surrendered to the divine—or diabolical (the nuance is hazy)—woman he has chosen. This is also the possible signification of the myth of Merlin the magician, prophet, and seer who of his own free will allowed himself to be immured within an invisible castle in the air. At this exact moment the infernal couple represented by the wizard and the fairy transform into the divine couple—beyond this world, invisible to human eyes, but who can sometimes be heard in the breath of the wind.

The chief thing is for the lover to accept the lady's superiority and to recognize the cogency of her requirements (actually her scorn and acts of cruelty), which are, in the final analysis, just so many divine commands that the individual must take into account if he wishes to reach this divine place. Under these conditions it should be easy to see how impossible it would be for a lover-knight to love a woman whom he would be ashamed to take as his legitimate wife.

This exclusiveness of love for a lady and the absolute obedience that is its consequence do not excuse us from broadening the discussion. If the lady is the model of all virtue and every perfection, it is because she is a woman. Without going as far as the mystical sublimation of the devotees of the Virgin Mary, courtly lovers recognize a certain superiority in every woman, hence the ninth precept: *"Be ever mindful of all the commands of the ladies."* The heroes of the fictional narratives were well aware of this— those who, searching for their lady who has been carried off by an evil lord or a monstrous giant, are always finding themselves diverted from their essential mission by the *service* they owe to the ladies and maidens in difficulties whom they meet along the way. This is no betrayal of their lady; it is the perfecting of this approach concerning the lady through the acts of prowess they are forced to accomplish in the service of others. This is the great lesson of solidarity and fraternity that is offered us by courtly theory. And it also explains the tenth precept: *"Strive to be ever worthy of belonging to the knighthood of love."* The eleventh is of the same nature: *"Show yourself polite and courteous in all things."*

The last two precepts, the twelfth and the thirteenth, are perhaps the most obscure of all, or at least the most likely to lend themselves to contradictory interpretations. This is because their vagueness is great, and it seems intentionally so, as if to allow more leeway to those wishing to enter love's knighthood. They are as follows: *"When devoting yourself to love's pleasures, do not allow your desire to exceed that of your lover"* and *"Whether you are giving or receiving the pleasures of love, always maintain a certain modesty."*

If I understand aright, in the relationship thus defined, the initiative is the exclusive prerogative of the woman. This is the heart of the revolution that took place in the eleventh century. The woman was no longer the object of man's pleasure, as she had been both in classical antiquity and in the early years of the Christian Middle Ages (along with the accepted reservations and the specific reference to the necessities of procreation). She has in some way become the leader of the game. The lady's desire surpasses all else, and desire is a command. The lover-knight must never take the initiative; he must be content to respond to his lady's desire. Without seeming to, this actually recalls the famous debate that comes down to us through Hebrew legend, concerning the mysterious Lilith. This individual, according to traditions that are most probably extremely ancient, was in fact the first Eve, the first woman *given* to Adam. But she would not stand for being *given*.[4] She quarreled violently with Adam on their respective positions in coitus: the woman underneath or the woman on top? If we look at the famous "missionary" position, androcratic society tries hard and by all means available to prove that man is superior to woman—at least in his active role, while the woman is relegated to a passivity that borders on resignation. Lilith's rebellion, claiming the right to be on top, is a symbolic element in the reversal of values, at the very least an attempt to establish sexual equality. We know that Lilith, unable to obtain satisfaction, left Adam, thus transgressing divine orders. Pursued by the angels of the Lord, she escaped annihilation because she knew the ineffable name of God, knowledge that gave her the right to live despite all. This is why God made her the wife—or the companion, who knows?—of Sammael, that is to say, the fallen Archangel Satan, or the Devil himself. No doubt the Evil One had the presence of mind to satisfy Lilith's just demands, even drawing some substantial benefits from doing so. Thus was established a new formulation for the couple, at least in fable.

The twelfth precept, even if it is vague and remains well within "courtly" limits, is no less explicit concerning this state of mind. It is incontestable that we can see here just one image (a reassuring one, it is true) of the infernal couple of Lilith and Sammael. There enters here not one implication of the moral order. Everything takes place on the level of the psyche, but this leads on to a social interpretation. The deciding element is no longer man, but woman. This is the radical transformation that first made its appearance in the amorous relationship.

Not only does this new kind of relationship completely eliminate rape and any form of verbal, moral, or social violence that might substitute for actual rape, but in his recognition of woman's superiority the lover-knight has considerably enriched the playing field as well. The woman has become the initiator, and by not exceeding his lover's desire, the man is not chastising his own desire but making it the very desire of the other in a perfect harmonious union where there is neither aggressor nor victim, vanquisher nor vanquished, but the birth of a single being, dual yet unique, multiple yet singular.

It remains to determine the exact nature of the pleasures of love that are thus codified in this precept. Finding support from the somewhat stereotypical formulations of the troubadours and referring to the era's so-called Christian morality, medievalists have unanimously insisted on the spiritual aspect of courtly love, denying its physical reality and invoking a certain platonism, revised and corrected by scholasticism. For these medievalists, love's pleasures can be nothing if not intellectual or spiritual, commingling with a great mystical leap toward the perfect and the absolute. This is a somewhat truncated view of medieval thought, which before submerging in the tragic asceticism of the fourteenth and fifteenth centuries was quite capable of expressing the spiritual in carnal terms and the carnal in spiritual terms. René Nelli, through a rigorous analysis owing much to Cathar principles (matter is necessarily evil, and all desire, even spiritualized desire, is related to matter, so there is no difference between sin of the flesh committed in thought only and sin of the flesh committed in real action), has opened the way toward a new interpretation, and since his work we must be a lot less peremptory.[5] Courtly love is one whole, in which mind and matter are indissolubly linked. It all becomes a matter of temperament: there are men and women who are chaste and others who are not. That is all there is to it. And everyone has free choice in how to live his or her life. Everyone has the choice of loving spiritually or physically, or loving in a way that even synthesizes the two, which are, after all, only two aspects of a single reality.

It is quite evident that the "faraway princess" whose praises are sung by Jaufré Rudel is an imaginary character. "When I shall see her I know not," he says, "as our lands are far apart." But he adds, "I shall never take pleasure in love if it is not to revel in that love far away, for I know of no woman, near or far, who could be prettier or better." Cercamon, on the other hand, asks God to give him physical contact with his beloved: "May the Lord allow me to touch her again." Arnaud Daniel takes pleasure in a very physical contemplation of his lover: "I look at her golden hair, her spirited body, delicate and young." And later he clearly expresses his desire: "May she receive me with her body, not her soul, secretly in her chamber!" It is true that other troubadours are more explicit and more direct, such as Raimon de Durfort: "There isn't a noble lady in all the world, who if she showed me her 'arse' and her cunt, just as nature made them—while saying to me, Sir Raimon, fuck me here in the behind—to whom I would not bow down my head and face as if I wanted to drink from a fountain!" But we would be mistaken to see in this frankness any kind of pornographic game. To the contrary, it seems that the majority of troubadours, although enjoying physical love with their ladies—or their substitutes—all sublimated this love. This is what Raimon Rigaut had to say on the subject: "Never for love of cunt have I demanded love from my lady, but rather for the freshness of her complexion and the smile on her mouth. For where cunts are concerned, I can find enough with lots of women, if I were to ask. This is why I prefer the mouth I often kiss to the cunny that kills desire."

So there it is: the exaltation of desire that motivates action and that gives the lover his power. And thereby is the justification for the modesty required in any and all amorous relationships engaged in by the lady with her knight-priest. It is a question of ritual, let us not forget, and all rituals aim at attaining harmony between above and below. Evil is in violence, vulgarity, and lack of discretion. The good is in loving *honestly*. It so happens that the *Art of Loving* attributed to Andreas Capellanus is primarily an "art of loving honestly." Hence the necessity of a code that guides behavior but respects the liberty of each individual.

The Discovery of the Rules of Love

In the second book of his *Art of Loving*, the author employs a fable to present and justify the rules of courtly love. The subject of this fable is borrowed from the normal paraphernalia of the Arthurian romances.

Historians have been quick to call this Arthurian fable a skilled plagiarism of Chrétien de Troyes's work. Although it is true that Andreas Capellanus's Latin text borrows a certain form of psychology that is dear to the heart of the author of *Le Chevalier à la charrette*, the framework of his story actually belongs to a much more archaic patrimony. It derives both from oral folktales and from that variant of Celtic myth whose legacy can be found in the Irish epics coming out of the high Middle Ages. To trace it all back to Chrétien de Troyes reveals an absolute misreading of the Western tradition. The Champenois poet and romancer, heir himself to countless traditional sources, is in fact the transcriber of heterogeneous elements that he manipulates with ease and integrates perfectly into the mentality of his time. But he never invented anything outside of the art of storytelling, and it is solely on the literary plane that he can be considered an innovator.

Having said as much, the fable told here with so much courtliness is far from devoid of interest. By itself it forms a veritable initiatory code that allows for a better understanding of the *rules of love*, which are then enacted for the use of he who would enter the knighthood of love. "A medieval text should never be read on its own," writes Charles Méla in his remarkable essay on the queen and the Grail.[6] "What it conceals can be surprising. A meandering course is as necessary for critics as errantry is for knight adventurers." This apparently didactic tale intended as an introduction to a code of love belongs to that category of texts that make constant references to other contemporary or earlier analogous tales and that cannot be explained save in terms of other narratives of the same type.

The hero of the story is a Breton knight whose name we are not told. We meet him while he is riding through the forest seeking the way to King Arthur's court. He meets a young girl who tells him that he will never find what he is seeking without her help. Intrigued, the knight asks her to explain. She answers: "You have pleaded for the love of a lady from Brittany; she has said she will never grant you her love unless you bring her the victorious sparrow hawk that sits on a perch in Arthur's court."

This is already extremely revealing. The knight has set off on a *love quest,* and in order to carry it out successfully he must go through adventures his beloved has assigned him by virtue of her right as an initiator. In this way she can assess her suitor's true worth. He will not be able to return to her until he passes her test, and it is no easy task. We find here a theme that appears frequently in numerous Celtic mythological tales, principally the Irish, but also in the Welsh version of the quest for the Holy Grail, the anonymous story of *Peredur.* It is a matter, in fact, of the obligation to go off in search of a treasure or a marvelous object belonging to the Otherworld, the classic model of the genre being Jason's quest for the Golden Fleece. But for the Celts, this quest for an object from the Otherworld is not prompted by the hero himself. It is not his lust or desire to excel that is taken into account. On the contrary, it is a magical obligation called a *geis* by the ancient Irish, which is something absolutely impossible to overturn.[7] This magical obligation could be caused by vengeance, as in the case of Tuirenn, whose sons were sent by the god Lugh in search of objects that were impossible to find in order to compensate for Tuirenn's murder of Lugh's father. Such an obligation could also be caused by a woman's amorous passion, as in the case of the young Grainne, who by this method forces the handsome Diarmaid—who does not love her—to run away with her. The case of the Breton knight belongs to this last category: the lady he loves has tossed him some sort of magical challenge, bring back something impossible to obtain. And if he succeeds his lady will grant him her love with no reservations and with no loss of rank, because the one she has chosen has shown himself worthy, having proved with this success that he belongs to the knighthood of love.

We should not assume that the quest is an easy task or that it is without danger. This is where the idea of initiation emerges. The hero can never succeed unless he is helped, *guided,* by a superior being—human or divine—or by a spiritual entity cloaked in a variety of appearances. This theme is widespread and often tied to shamanic initiation. Within the ecstatic trance phenomenon that is the journey of the apprentice shaman in the Otherworld, the neophyte is always watched over by a master who shows him the way and helps him avoid falling into the dreadful snares of the phantasmagorical universe. If he did not have this surveillance, this "help," the apprentice shaman could not successfully conclude his wandering and in all likelihood would not return from his journey but would instead sink into madness or death.

The theme of the guide can be found time and again in the oral folktale tradition. As a rule these stories concern three brothers who in turn leave their family and set off to seek their fortunes. In a forest they each in turn meet an old woman who is having a hard time carrying firewood and who asks each of them for assistance. The two elder brothers refuse or insult the old woman, who curses them. But when the younger brother comes along, he carries her firewood and the old woman reveals to him all he must do to succeed in his undertaking.[8] Sometimes she is a sorceress who takes the form of an animal and follows the hero in his wanderings in order to advise him and pull his fat out of the fire, when necessary.[9] Or sometimes there are animals the hero has spared that come to his aid,[10] or even the soul of a dead person whose abandoned body the compassionate hero has buried.[11] In any event there is an exchange between the hero and the man or woman he meets, the model of the genre being the famous Koadalan from the Breton legend who delivers a fairy mare from a sorcerer's diabolical grasp and in return receives all the signs permitting him to attain a true initiation.[12]

The essential thing is not for the initiator to perform the initiate's acts for him, but to clearly indicate the various stages he must go through and the dangers he must avoid. On his own the hero is incapable of spotting and recognizing the signs he encounters, although they are right before his eyes or all around him. The initiator's intervention consists solely of opening the hero's eyes to a profound vision of the universe, but at no time is the free will of the hero put in jeopardy: it is always up to him to know what he wants or does not want, what he sees or does not see, what he does or does not do.

In this particular instance, in the Chaplain's tale, the role of initiator is played by young girl of very great beauty. She is obviously a fairy, one of the aspects of the feminine deity whom the hero wishes to reach, her double in some way but still wanting in comparison to her knowledge. This is the role played by numerous "maidens" encountered by Lancelot and other knights of Arthur's when they set off on perilous adventures. We are given the feeling that without the aid of this young initiator the Breton knight will fail his test of bringing the sparrow hawk away with him from King Arthur's court. And the young girl does, in fact, reveal to him how he may gain possession of the bird: "You cannot obtain the sparrow hawk unless you have first proven by combat within Arthur's palace that the lady you love is more beautiful than any who dwell within Arthur's court. And you may not enter the palace unless the guards have shown you which is the sparrow hawk's gauntlet. But it will not be possible for you to obtain the gauntlet itself until you have triumphed in single combat against two valiant knights."

There is a part of Chrétien de Troyes's *Erec et Enide* that is equivalent to this, to wit, he who brings back the head of the White Stag will earn the right to a kiss from the most beautiful maiden in King Arthur's court—as well as the right to her hand. "The election of the most beautiful girl in Arthur's court," says Charles Méla, "involves the honor of the Arthurian knights; she calls them back to the obligation *to make their valor equal to their love.*" Thus the test required of the hero is in absolute conformance with the fundamental rules of courtly love: one cannot love someone who is unworthy. And "the custom of the White Stag and the custom of the sparrow hawk speak the same language: they satisfy the condition placed by the fairy, encountered in the land of adventure, on her offer of love."[13]

Because, when all is said and done, the lady to whom the hero owes his obedience—mirrored in the form of the young girl encountered in the forest—is a *fairy*, that is to say, the image of the divine woman, of a veritable goddess to whom he must devote his time and actions.

Before his encounter with the young girl, the knight recognized the *sense* of his mission. Now he knows its *sénéfiance* (a fairly untranslatable medieval term probably better rendered by *significance* than by *signification*). To use a terminology borrowed from Stéphane Mallarmé and further developed by Charles Méla: "In the literary treatment of signification, the signs are deprived of their proper signification and occupy, what we need a metaphor to describe, the forefront of the scene in order to play a role that is no longer simple representation."[14] We are within the framework of a literary narrative, even if the format has been borrowed from an ancient oral tradition, and the hero is no longer visible outside his literary context. This is exactly where our author was trying to bring us: to let us see that the signs everyone encounters on life's pathways are just so many snares one needs to dismantle as quickly as possible. The reader of a text like *De Arte amandi* (and the same holds true for every Arthurian tale) seeks only the *sense* of the hero's adventures. It so happens that the hero is merely seeking the signs that will aid him to achieve his objective. The difference is enormous. Again we should make quite clear that Andreas Capellanus's readers, like all people of the Middle Ages, were not looking for a meaning to this story, but simply for signs they could use in making their own way. This is why the Chaplain's text is primarily initiatory. The critical logic of our century perverts the message by rationalizing it, something medieval people had absolutely no need to do. In this case the literary game fed and enriched itself with new elements (although absurd in appearance, they are convincing on the level of the phonetic Kabbalah, or on that of the "correspondences" Baudelaire spoke of well before Jacques Lacan declared himself the evangelist of depth psychology). At this moment, "the Swan [*Cygne*] is elevated to Sign [*Signe*] for the *gaze* that knows how to capture it but which nonetheless is not irrevocably ensnared by it, for the Sign does not become exalted except through the Swan's frozen fate."[15]

There are as many metaphors as there are signs. And the extremely beautiful young girl who appears to the hero is both a *swan* and a *sign*, but also a dispenser of signs scattered along the difficult, winding path traced by the swan over the slumbering waters of a lake. The mystery persists through its ambiguity.

The hero feels this ambiguity perfectly: "I see that I cannot succeed in this enterprise without your assistance," he says. It is an appeal for help to this young girl emerging from nowhere and everywhere, this swan who is the symbol of beauty and perfection. And the hero is quite aware of the conditions imposed upon this aid: "I submit entirely to your will. In a word, demand that I undergo all forms of torture that I may obtain your help." He could not be any more direct, nor declare in any clearer fashion that the signs he has referenced, thanks to the appearance of the swan, have not a shred of signification, or at least not one bit of significance. It is easy to list the stars, to classify them according to their brightness or weight, but still have no idea as to their true purpose and whether they have any influence over our lives. They do not come with directions. And the hero in his ardor, his desire to rejoin the lady he loves, is ready to make any sacrifice provided he can manage to identify the goal of his action with the meaning he had given it when setting off on his quest.

Nevertheless, it is a serious matter to tell a young girl, even a very beautiful one, that you are ready to undergo any torture it pleases her to command. It is not only the lady who is considered a cruel and demanding goddess, but all ladies, in other words Our Lady, the unique yet multiple eternal feminine, as well. The logic of courtly love leads to a very strange metaphysics. This is where the concept of the tyrannical lady whose knight is her lover-priest comes in.

We should not mistake the meaning of the word *tyranny*, however. Its current connotation is clearly pejorative, but originally the word derived from the name of an Etruscan goddess, *Turan*, whose Indo-European root word meaning "to give" is still recognizable in the Greek word δωρον. And if the historical tyrant was a truly cruel and bloody despot, the same undoubtedly did not hold true for prehistoric times, especially if the tyranny was wielded by women. In the same manner that the Celtic king was a king of a moral order, whose duty was to unite the members of the community and provide them with food and prosperity, the mission of the queen-tyrant of certain archaic societies with gynecocratic tendencies was also to give: to give life, of course, but also to provide food, drink, prosperity, love, happiness, also death (in that, in the natural order of things, one begins to die at the moment of one's birth).

The request of the Breton knight, which consists of accepting in advance any and all tortures the young girl wishes to inflict upon him, is a reference to this concept of the queen-tyrant. Without her the knight can do nothing. But it is in fact an exchange. He wishes to obtain everything from this fairy girl; consequently, he must give her everything. A subtle psychological game is then established between the knight and this initiator, a game that leads into the greatest ambiguity: "in such a way that, in return for your total dominion over me, I may boldly inscribe the name of my beloved as the most beautiful of all women." We can see that the image of the lady he loves and from whom he wishes to obtain love is never absent from the discussion. However, the young girl, after having accepted the knight's request, concludes with him a veritable love pact: "She then gave him the kiss of love, showed him the horse she had been riding, and exchanged it for his mount."

Here is something that seems incomprehensible. The young girl gives the knight the kiss of love. This would appear to be an act of betrayal by the knight, who just a few moments before was declaring his love for his currently absent and somewhat unreachable lady, unless it is necessary that he go through the love of the young girl to reach that of his lady, in the same way as the mystic troubadours sought God's love through that of woman. Or it may also have concerned an initiatory stage similar to those found in Indian Tantric practices, in which one cannot have sexual relations with the woman one loves. The beloved is too remote, too pure a being; the slightest carnal caress causes her purity to be lost. Thus it requires the embrace of another woman, of lower caste (or a priestess appointed for this purpose), in the actual or fantasized presence of the beloved.

This attempt at an explanation does not hold up in the framework of Andreas Capellanus's tale. The young girl is merely the "revealer of signs" and as such constitutes a step on the knight's path. In fact, she teaches him love so that he may know later exactly how to behave in the presence of the lady he loves. This same method appears in the Breton tale *Koadalan:* the hero frees the fairy mare from her diabolical prison, and in return this fairy gives him the means to attain a princess who will become his wife. In a somewhat similar vein, the various "maidens" who offer themselves to Lancelot of the Lake in both Chrétien de Troyes's romance and the long thirteenth-century prose tale do not cause the hero to forget his obsession with his image of Guinivere, who is his one and only tyrannical lady. A trio is not created: the young girl who gives the Breton knight a kiss of love is not his mistress, she is only his guide.

The relationship established between them is an important one, however, and goes quite far—as is shown by their exchange of horses in addition to the kiss of love. In other analogous cases there may be an exchange of bracelets, rings, or even clothing. This exchange is a symbolic gesture whereby the virtue of one person is passed over to the other. It is a pooling of their mutual energies. The individual is no longer alone, and a still imperfect couple is formed. In short, the young girl is only the projected image of the knight's lady, its temporary fantasized realization that provides the means for the actual lady to emerge from the shadows—or in other words, the unconscious.

The pooling of mutual energies leads the knight to exceed himself in a certain way, which is all the more pronounced as the beauty of the young girl prefigures the even more extraordinary beauty of the beloved lady. Let us not forget that the knight, by undertaking his lady's quest, has gained entry into the knighthood of love. "Nature—the 'civil servant' of God, who, surpassing itself, creates the 'ladies,' who produce in the aristocratic man and all chivalrous society universal models of humanity conforming to the will of God—institutes, at the same time an unassailable morality. Extreme beauty implies an extreme moral value. Woman's mission in courtly society consists of actualizing the essential laws invested in the nobility by nature, laws that are 'reasonable' to the highest possible degree. *Natura* is identical to *ratio,* feudal virtue is identical to natural law of which it is the supreme accomplishment."[16] And more than ever, in her beauty as a white swan the young girl encountered in the forest, the feminine symbol par excellence, is the sign (and in some way the *statue*) whereby the man—the knight, in this instance—will recognize the goal that God has assigned to him. Furthermore, there is an alarming element about the intrusion of this young girl, whose appearance allows no doubts concerning her connection to Faerie. As Danielle Régnier puts it so well, she is one of those

> singular female figures who never appear as fairies but as feudal ladies, the mistresses of lands and castles who promise and provide gold and silver, goods and clothing, sovereignty and immortality. Singular female figures who possess every power, especially that of fulfilling the feudal world's most utopian dream of wealth, everything that may procure for the hero the admiration and allegiance of others. . . . Delicate and ephemeral administrators of the feudal order, restorers of the broken order, imperious seductresses for the Beyond, would one not be led to read between the lines the outline—prudent, certainly, to permit the reinvestment of mythical motifs—of a matriarchal and one could say archaic world, but which perhaps picks up some of the most seductive fantasies of the Middle Ages.[17]

Henceforth, all is clear to the knight. The young girl still grants him a little more advice, notably concerning the gauntlet that he must win by defeating two knights. "Once you have won, do not take the gauntlet they are holding, but the one you see hanging from a gold column." The universe wherein roam the Knights of the Round Table is often deceptive, and the signs discovered there are sometimes illusions due to the irrational functioning of the imagination. Thus put on his guard, the hero undertakes the second part of his quest. He will find there the classic paraphernalia of Arthurian fiction, the mythological paraphernalia conforming perfectly with that found in folktales from the oral tradition.

After the forest, there is "a wild and forsaken land." This is the famous "crossing of the desert." And of course he will collide with the barriers of a reality that his sensibility does not yet recognize as illusion: "He arrived at a river of incredible width and depth over which passage was impossible for any man, so steep were its banks." He has to find a place where he can cross. After traveling along the river the knight finds himself by a strange bridge: "The bridge itself was made of gold and both ends were fastened securely to the banks, but the middle of the bridge was partially underwater and often swaying so that it appeared to be completely submerged by the waves." This is reminiscent of the Bridge of the Sword and the Bridge under Water whereby one enters the land of Gorre in Chrétien de Troyes's *Le Chevalier à la charrette*. As the bridge is a mythological symbol, the sign of a difficult journey to an Otherworld, it can only be extraordinary. And of course this bridge has a guard, "a warrior on horseback of ferocious aspect."

This arrangement is shamanic in essence. Combat at the ford or at the entrance of a bridge is a symbolic element of the crossing through a stage of evolution in which one must show proof of one's vigilance and bravery in order to attain a higher plane. Of course, the Breton knight who is our story's hero, after a courageous battle, defeats the ferocious-looking man and intends to cut off his head. But as a good courtly knight, he spares his foe's life. In this way his adversary can attest to his generosity, which is essential for the knight's reputation as well as for his membership in the knighthood of love.

But the story is not over yet. On the other side of the bridge awaits a guard just as dreadful as the first, who bars the knight's way, shaking "the bridge with such force that the bridge often appeared to be no longer hidden underwater." The water theme is well known in all initiatory tales: water is the natural barrier between the two worlds; it prevents the spirits from breaching the boundaries of their domain. In reality it concerns a remembrance of the amniotic fluid, which separates the fetus—a potentiality of being, a nonbeing but already alive—from the concrete world of the living where the process of death takes place. The fetus belongs to a paradisiacal world, a world where the real is unknown, a world where only fantasies have any reality. The fact is that for the Breton knight—as for Lancelot seeking entry into the kingdom of Gorre to free Guinivere, or for Percival before the castle of the Fisher King, or even for the Welsh Peredur at the famous Ford of Souls, where half the Tree of Life burns, in the border zones of two worlds—to cross this large river guarded not only by nature but also by some formidable warriors is to undergo a second birth. The hero must destroy the pouch within which he is enclosed. Then the tumultuous waters will spread. This cannot happen without combat against the angel.

But whereas Jacob was fighting to force the divinity to grant him divine blessing, the Breton knight is fighting to discover the object that will be the key to the tabernacle wherein lies the woman he sees in his dreams. The courtly hero is more of a priest than Jacob was. We know that in more archaic times priests, like chiefs, battled among themselves so that the divinity could select the best and most faithful, the most zealous and the most apt at ensuring the act of supreme love. For, when all is said and done, if the superior deity is an entity that has assumed a feminine form, the priest most capable of ensuring her service and taking on her worship would be a man capable of overcoming all obstacles and making love fully with this female deity. Sex and worship are indissolubly linked. It is enough to recall the image—legendary or historical—of Saint Bernard de Clairvaux in the presence of the Virgin Mary, and to overhear certain words spoken by this historical figure who succeeded in making hysteria into a kind of saintliness: "Lewdness reigns everywhere. It is within this vice that perhaps appears that hidden abomination Ezekiel speaks of, and which we could not see without trembling if we were given the power to pierce the walls of hearts and to gaze upon the horrors that soil the tabernacle of God. Beyond fornication, adultery, incest, the passions of many descend to the very depths of turpitude and ignominy."[18] We should read between the lines, though: what the monk of Clairvaux reveals to us are the consequences of an action that should be an act of love. The virginal yet maternal appearance of Mary hides the erotic image of a woman, in reality the goddess of ancient times. She offers herself naked in front of the tabernacle, or even emerging from this tabernacle, to the lust of the priest who adores her and is waiting only for the supreme moment of bliss inside her and beside her.

In fact the supreme instant is after the seven veils of Isis have been unfurled from around the body of the goddess, the nudity seen by the priest, or the courtly lover if you prefer. The knight knows quite well that the lady-goddess is to be found on the other side of the river, on the other side of the water, and that if he manages to surpass the priest responsible for her worship—that is to say, her lover—it is he who will be admitted into the holy of holies, and he who will be authorized to perform her worship. An infernal worship, of course, and perfectly in conformance with the concept of the "infernal couple" who stand out with regard to courtly love.

Through the first warrior vanquished before the bridge and the second who shook the bridge there emerges the double image of the lover-priest who must be supplanted. The figure is the same on both sides of the bridge. Borrowing Freudian terminology, we could call this a case of the father's obsessive need to oppose, with violence if necessary, the son's reptation toward the maternal vagina. The father here is purely symbolic. All it takes is a transgression of a taboo of an obviously inces-tuous nature to unblock a situation bogged down in routine, that is to say, in nonaction. The situation is quite clear, even when considered as the supreme sacrilege: the Virgin Mary allowing herself to be kissed by her knightly lover, that is to say, the priest.[19] Of course this is a forbid-den union, but it is also a marriage of sense and essence. The problem is to determine who will best be able to carry out the lover-priest's duties to their fullest extent.

This is where courtly love, in both its theoretical formulation and its fictional adaptations, penetrates to the heart of the matter. Whatever the exact nature of the warriors guarding the bridge, it is obvious they are symbolic representations of the other lovers of the lady whose love the hero wishes to obtain. They form the major obstacle. The place is taken. And if the knight wants that place, he must supply proof that he is better. Now, being better means eliminating the troublemakers. The professed goal of courtly love is to emphasize prowess, the only way to procure the love that is the goal of the quest. So we know the guards of the bridge are the lady's lovers; they have concluded a pact of love with her.

> The fairy's love is furnished on one condition: a *convent* ("accord") has been established between them. If he remains with his Fairy Lover, the knight must defend the right of way against all comers. If he does so successfully until the appointed time (here just one year, but sometimes as much as seven), he will earn a reputation as the best knight in the world and will enjoy his lover's undivided favors. . . . The value is therefore a promise of bliss, which finds itself immediately compromised in such a way that the barely won felicity is once more at stake. This is the meaning of the pact concluded between the knight and his lady. If the most beautiful is offered as a reward, as "battle prize," to the best, the latter will not be able to stop making payment for his possession: its very value forbids the very possession it obtains.[20]

For the essential thing to ensure is the lover's service, whatever the cost. The equilibrium of courtly society—and thus the universe, because courtly society is the reflection of an idealized universe—is at this price. How many knights are fit to take on fully such a formidable task?

In the story told by the Chaplain, the hero, despite the difficulties, succeeds in crossing the bridge. Once on the other side he takes hold "of the one who shook the bridge and propelled him in the water." This was the best thing he could have done. Having thus eliminated his predecessors he continues on his way, passing through "extremely beautiful meadows," which are paradisiacal images prefiguring the delights promised him once he has won through to his lady's side. This image is followed by another meadow resembling Klingsor's enchanted gardens, "fragrant with the sweet smell of every kind of flower."

So he is now before the palace that was his destination. But there is no apparent opening. It is, according to the well-known alchemical formula, the search for "the open entrance to the sealed palace of the king." Before he can find this entrance, he must undergo another test: "In the field he found silver tables covered with uncommonly white tablecloths on which all manner of food and drink had been placed. In this pleasant field he found also an extremely clean silver basin containing enough for him to feed and water his horse." This is a widespread motif in Celtic tradition. In both Irish and Welsh stories heroes are often discovering fully prepared meals in empty castles. But woe betide anyone who takes a seat at such a table!

For it is a trap, to be exact, the snare of desire. The hero—he who desires a faraway love, as the troubadour Jaufré Rudel put it—in his symbolic oral stage cannot control himself when in the presence of his lady's nudity (her complete nudity obviously, which emphasizes the "forbidden" regions of the female body). So we find ourselves witness to another transgression of a prohibition achieved by the hero. The reaction is not long in coming.

Indeed, from the moment the Breton knight begins greedily to devour the food that has been prepared, "a door suddenly opened, making such a fracas in doing so one would have thought it was the rumble of nearby thunder. Immediately emerging from this door was a man of gigantic stature, bearing in his hands a copper club of immense weight, which he brandished as if it were no more than a piece of straw." This character emerges straight out of Celtic mythology. He is the god Dagda, wielder of a massive club that can kill with one end and restore life with the other. He is also the Ogre from folk-tale tradition, another face of a Gargantua turned literary.

The duty of this god is to apply censure. He begins by giving a good scolding to the hero, who is guilty, in the giant's eyes, of sitting at the king's table without authorization—this table is reserved for those knights who have supplied proof of their abilities. This is another typically Celtic motif. In epic Irish mythology, when the god Lugh wanted to enter the royal palace of the Tuatha Da Danann, he had to provide proof through his art that he was worthy of doing so. He eventually convinced the porter by listing all the qualities that made him a Samildanach, a "master of all the arts" or, if you prefer, a god of no single duty who assumes all duties. The same motif appears in the Welsh tale *Culwch and Olwen,* when Arthur's companions are seeking to enter the castle of the giant Yspaddaden Penkawr, or when the hero himself, Culwch, wishes to enter Arthur's castle. The gigantic figure with the copper club is the doorkeeper of ancient epics; he represents all the taboos that oppose the realization of desire.

The Breton knight of course replies that he has a perfect right to take a seat at the feast table: "I have the right to participate in all that is reserved for knights, for everything concerning chivalry is my sole concern, and it is my role as a knight that has brought me to these lands." By doing this the knight is bragging about privileges he does not possess, and he draws this response from the giant: "Not just anyone can sit at this royal table, only the inhabitants of the royal palace." That is no obstacle! The hero is ready to become an inhabitant of the palace, but in this case he must first "have fought and defeated the guard of the palace." Under a courtly form quite in keeping with the tone of twelfth-century feudal society, we see the same initiatory trial that in archaic Celtic epics consisted of proving one's skill in the arts—and of course the crafts as well, since the same word accounts for both.

After speaking of his desire (that is, to find the gauntlet that will allow him to grab the sparrow hawk), the Breton knight engages the giant in combat. This is a brutal event, as it should be, and only with great effort does he manage to defeat his adversary. He is about to make a killing blow against his foe, and the victim has his life spared only because he leads the knight to the object he covets. "The guard led the Breton inside the palace, to the spot where stood a very beautiful gold column, which supported the entire palace and from which the desired gauntlet was hanging."

It is obviously an enchanted—or at the very least magical—palace, one of those revolving castles that abound in the Arthurian romances and can even be recognized in a *chanson de geste, Le Pèlerinage de Charlemagne.* We could make extensive analysis of this motif, the revolving palace that is supported and spun by a single column, usually of gold, that implies not only magic rites but also construction based on a zodiacal design. It is actually an indication of the analogy between a king's residence and the entire universe. Numerous examples of fortresses, temples, and royal dwellings have been constructed on this principle. They can be found in Greek and Roman antiquity as well as in the high Middle Ages of both the Byzantine and the Western worlds. In some way, and on a purely symbolic level, it is the hero's task to pierce through the complex workings of the universe and gain an understanding of their function. Perfection is a prerequisite if he is to win his lady. Physical strength is not enough; science is an indispensable requirement for the man who is proclaimed the best knight in the world. In this way the hero gains possession of the gauntlet, but his trials are far from over.

He remounts his horse and crosses other meadows as heavenly as the first. He comes to another palace, "admirably constructed of gold, six hundred cubits long and two hundreds cubits wide; the roof and outer walls of the palace were silver, but the inside was entirely of gold adorned with precious stones. The palace consisted of a large number of beautiful rooms, but in the most beautiful King Arthur was seated on a golden throne. Very beautiful ladies as well as many splendid knights surrounded him." Before he can enter this room, however, the hero must face twelve knights. He shows them the gauntlet and they let him pass. He goes forward to pay homage to the king and one of the knights asks his reason for being there. He answers that he desires possession of the sparrow hawk. When asked why, he replies: "Because I have the good fortune to love a lady more beautiful than any in this court," an answer that obviously is taken as an insult by everyone assembled there. He must defend his words or be punished for uttering them. And the sole means of justifying these words is to enter in courtly combat with one of Arthur's knights. The judgment will be in God's hands.

So he begins the fight, which is long and difficult. Finally he gains his victory. He approaches the "extremely beautiful golden perch on which the desired sparrow hawk is resting, and near him two chained dogs sleeping." His reward prompts no murmur from those in attendance, as he has been judged worthy by God to take the bird. "He then took the sparrow hawk, as well as the dogs, at which time he saw a written parchment attached to the perch by a golden chain." He asks what it is and is told: "That is the parchment on which are inscribed the laws of love that the King of Love himself has decreed for lovers. You must take them and communicate them to lovers if you wish to take away the sparrow hawk in peace."

In short, the Breton knight cannot obtain total victory—the acceptance of his love by his beloved—unless he spreads the rules of love that are inherent therein. His experience is as valid for him as it is for the group to which he belongs. He will be the messenger of the god of Love for all those henceforth seeking to set off on this adventurous quest for the lady. This conforms to the general scheme of courtly knighthood, in which the individual (although perfectly recognized as such) is still a full-fledged member of a group with responsibilities toward his companions. This is how the "knighthood of love"—a brotherhood or, rather, a kind of fraternal community in which each member must commit to respecting the rules of the game—justifies its existence. And this obviously allows our hypothetical author to present his *rules of love* as if they were precious relics from that ideal society, King Arthur's court, a privileged universe apart from the world of the living but one in which, as in the universe of Plato's archetypes, everything works perfectly and in harmony so as to guide the actions of humanity. Laws of any kind must come down from on high, and it is preferable that they come from an enchanted or divine world; thus they only gain in value and it does not occur to anyone to dispute them or call into question their fundamental principles.

So the hero has made off with the sparrow hawk and the parchment. He returns to the maiden of the forest and gives her an account of his mission. The young woman maintains her role as initiator. She gives him her permission to leave. Let us not forget that she and the knight are bound in a kind of amorous pact, and she alone can give the knight back his freedom: "I ask that you do not find our parting too grievous, for anytime you return here alone, you will find me." This is almost exactly the same as the fairy mare Téreza says to Koadalan in the Breton folktale. The young maiden of the forest is a sort of tutelary deity who protects the lover, allowing him to fulfill his destiny. And so ends this fable, in authentic folk-tale fashion. It serves to justify the rules of love to which those seeking membership in love's knighthood would henceforth be subject.

The Code

Theoretical rules are necessarily simple, even simplistic. But they must also remain sufficiently vague so as to allow their eventual application or nonapplication to specific situations. Imprecision is often essential, because a code is only a framework around which each individual must structure his choice, which does not always happen without fumbling or getting the details wrong.

The code of love consists of thirty-one rules, of unequal importance and presented in somewhat disparate fashion. Some of them simply restate various precepts of love. Others are repeated two, even three times. Two rules are openly contradictory, at least in the way they are formulated. Taken in their entirety they give the impression of an artificial assemblage of rules then in circulation in polite society, which the author was content to harvest in bulk without the slightest intention of subjecting any to critical judgment. Actually, as these rules were intended for an audience that already believed, any kind of critical judgment of them is useless. The code is purely and simply a catechism for thirteenth-century lovers. A catechism is never questioned but is applied blindly, even if it is wrong.

The first rule of this code is essential, but it constitutes perfect ambiguity: *"The pretext of marriage is never a legitimate excuse against love."* On the surface the meaning is quite clear and has been repeated often enough with regard to the courtly system: love is incompatible with marriage. One may thus love a married woman, and this married woman may not refuse her love to another man. By the same token a married man may be loved by a married woman or a young girl. Love is a free emotion whereas marriage is a social and economic institution. It remains to be seen if all of this is compatible with the Christian morality of the time.

There has been such a strong desire to consider courtly love the exaltation of a purely "platonic" feeling (or passion) that the casuists may easily discover such a compatibility. After all, this sublimation, this transcendence of love, is it not the application of the fundamental principle presented in the Gospels: to love one's neighbor as oneself, for the neighbor is always in God's image. In this reading, courtly love is foreign to the idea of marriage because it does not entail any sexuality; it is not an attack on the institution of marriage but an extension of love toward the whole of humanity.

This idealist conception of courtly love is, however, totally unacceptable when we take into consideration the courtly literature, the poems of the troubadours, and also the sociocultural context of the time. It is nothing more than the daydreaming of nineteenth-century puritan scholars. Because courtly love, although clearly transcendental, although linked in numerous ways to mystical love, and although perfectly "platonic" in numerous cases, is irredeemably carnal as well as spiritual, the people of the Middle Ages refusing to create a dichotomy between two aspects of one single reality. Under these conditions it is impossible not question how compatible courtly love was with the Christian morality of that era.

To tell the truth, this morality is far from clear even if rules for life had been established, in theory, by the Church Fathers, various popes, and numerous councils. Contrary to general belief, morality is not actually a part of religion. Morality in any given time is always a compromise, a sort of poorly cut coat stitched together from theological principles and the situation of the social group in question. In any case it is an abuse of power when the clergy erects morality as a basic principle that influences religious life itself. It so happens that in the eleventh, twelfth, and thirteenth centuries the Roman Catholic Church practiced—in the domain of marriage, love, and sex—what one might easily call pragmatism, but what might really be a very clever use of intellectual fuzziness.

Christianity's beginnings were marked, in Rome and especially within Roman society, by an in-depth examination of the subject. Marriage, an indispensable act for society, became in the new Christian doctrine a merely *tolerated* act, although its value was enhanced by preaching its indissolubility. Marriage was really only a last resort, an outlet for sexuality and a necessity for procreation, and Saint Paul, the true founder of Christianity, clearly expressed his preference for abstinence. In fact, if we are to believe the Gospels, sexual relations outside of marriage were never even mentioned by Jesus. Jewish law required virginity for girls but not for young men. In the new religion young men were not allowed to spend time with virgins, married women, or prostitutes, who were rejected and repudiated women. Chastity was their only option. Of course, masturbation was passed over in prudish silence. This was the beginning of asceticism, with its emphasis on the renunciation of the things of this world and on universal love of all people and things.

It was only much later, in a decadent Roman empire where the number of Christians had increased significantly, that sexual repression was resorted to. The Romans then sought out the old "demons" from Mazdean Persia, prompting a strict division between Spirit, the embodiment of purity that issued from Christ, and Flesh, impurity itself, which issued from Satan. Original sin was no longer, as in the ancient tradition, the sin of knowledge and competition with God (which is clearly the upshot from the text of Genesis), but instead the activity of flesh itself. Thus the transmission of life became a veritable hereditary sin and suffered as if it were a real curse. And hence began, in the framework of Christian society, the era of sexual prohibitions and the association of metaphysical fear with carnal desire. The immediate result of all this was the reinforcement of family ties and the exaltation of marriage, in whose framework woman played a great role.

Of course, if one studies what really happened during the first centuries of the Middle Ages, one can see that a great gap existed between theory and practice. In actual fact license and incoherence ruled supreme. The clergy itself did not escape from these problems. During the first three centuries priests were allowed to marry. The seventh-century Council of Trullo allowed them to continue living with their families, but if they were appointed to the rank of bishop their wives would be cloistered, and following their ordination they could no longer marry without being excommunicated. In 1055 Pope Leo IX decreed that chastity was a duty for all members of the clergy. Finally, in 1073, Gregory VII solemnly declared that any sexual activity was incompatible with the religious life. This scarcely prevented the clergy from practicing concubinage over a long period of time, including the bishops and the princes of the Church as well as the more modest religious servants of the parishes. It even reached the point where parishioners preferred their priest to have a concubine than to be living alone: the thinking was that the priest would thus not seek to seduce the women of others. This is a good indication of a certain kind of mentality, as well as a great deal of license in social custom.

Courtly love—introduced onto the top of this social foundation, which was already shaken by various impulses—claims to codify amorous relationships in terms of marriage or on the outside of marriage. The situation is simple in feudal times: might makes right, and in this instance it is a matter of the might of man. Woman, magnified by Christian marriage but only as a *mother* (hence the rise of the Marian cult), is more than ever an object of economic or political exchange. She is wed in aristocratic society to gain possession of her domains or her fortune, in peasant society to have children and to work the earth. Woman submits to marriage as she submits to rape, depending on the case, or else to survive she must resign herself to accepting marriage or concubinage from whomever. Courtly love as a doctrine claims to remedy all this by proposing a new definition of the couple—a couple that in this case cannot exist without a mutual accord between two individuals.

But the social weight of marriage being so heavy, it was unthinkable to imagine any kind of freedom within the very interior of the indissoluble ties of this marriage. Love was therefore proposed as a natural feeling, escaping all constraint, which fully justified the first rule from the code of love. It hardly matters whether this love is uniquely spiritual, "platonic," or carnal; the question never even arose in the minds of the theoreticians. To the extent that it breaks with the inherent legality of marriage, however, this love becomes tinged with hellish elements: the couple formed this way, doing without marriage, can be only an infernal couple, and a love that would be only platonic cannot escape from the sin of intention, a sin that in Christian casuistry is just as serious as the one that is acted out. The heroine of Marie de France's *Lai du laostic*, content merely to see and speak with her lover at her window at night while her husband is sleeping, is just as guilty as Iseult, who profits from the absence of King Mark to welcome Tristan in her bed. Or else we must fall into the smoothest form of hypocrisy and refuse to see the carnal component existing in every so-called mystical attitude, and that constitutes the very basis of the impulse turned desire.

The formulation of this first rule is ambiguous to the extent that nothing is made explicit. If marriage is no obstacle—for a married woman to have an amorous relationship with another man and, conversely, for a married man to have a relationship with another woman—there is nothing to say that a married man and woman cannot experience a great love together. This summarizes the theme discussed by Chrétien de Troyes in his romance *Cligès*, and especially in his *Erec et Enide*, where this perfectly natural and free, although conjugal, love collides with the outside world, in this instance with the very principles of the chivalrous adventure. Chrétien de Troyes skillfully shows, by following the stages his hero goes through, that sincere love, though stained by "conjugality," can lead a knight to surpass himself and to achieve the most audacious exploits. It is true that Enide does not remain outside these exploits; she intervenes at opportune moments to aid or save her husband in situations that threaten to turn tragic. But the essential thing is safe: the woman remains the motivating force behind masculine activity. Erec sets off on endless adventures—as much to prove to Enide that he is capable of doing all for her as to prove to the world that he is capable of feats for the love of his wife. In the final analysis, it hardly matters whether they are married or not; it is love that leads hearts and souls to go beyond themselves, marriage being but a stage along the way, an absolutely secondary circumstance. What was important was to state it clearly.

Marriage was no longer considered the universal panacea, the unique and necessary outlet for sexuality, but as one of several operating modes in use. This is all, and it is already saying a lot. As for knowing whether the Church, during the courtly era, tolerated or did not tolerate the nonconformity involved in love and in marriage, this is irrelevant. The Roman Catholic Church never took a clear position because, in the marriage celebration, the priest is content to be a mere witness of the sacrament between the newlyweds.

Each side has therefore made its case. In the framework of the refined and aristocratic society that imagined courtly love, love and marriage are two different things with no natural points in common and can come together only when necessary. Everything else is just literature or subject matter that is of interest only to the casuists.

The second rule proposed is not of either a sociological or a religious order. It touches the very heart of amorous psychology: *"He who does not feel jealousy cannot love."* And since this observation does not seem enough, it is summed up again in the twenty-first rule: *"True jealousy always causes love to grow";* in the twenty-second rule: *"A suspicion about your lover causes jealousy and ardor to increase";* as well as in the twenty-eighth rule: *"The smallest supposition compels the lover to imagine the worst about his beloved."* Thus the code underlines a theme that has, for all ages, been essential to the problematic of love—jealousy. It follows that we must now understand what is meant by this *jealousy*. When the troubadours complained of the jealous *(gelos)* who spied on lovers and stood ready to denounce them, they were talking about the *envious,* people who could not stand the happiness of others or who wished to be in the same place as the happy lover. The jealousy we are concerned with here, in Andreas Capellanus's code, is one of the components of love or is at any rate presented as such. The term therefore designates the feeling of exclusiveness that one can have when one loves and is loved, and this feeling is obviously at the very boundary of the instinct of possession.

Total, absolute love, if it implies exclusiveness, cannot escape a certain constraint: the two lovers belong to one another. It is far from being a game, it is a reality; hence the suffering of the lover who sees his lady sharing her favors with another and that of the mistress who knows her lover is deceiving her with another woman. There is a risk that this jealousy will become intolerable, and it often provokes tragedies, perhaps in the form of desperate attitudes, suicides, headlong flights, so-called crimes of passion. In fact it is not the possession of the lover or the mistress that is flouted but the exclusivity, the privileged rapport one has established with a chosen individual.

Certainly, this jealousy is not felt the same way in all societies throughout history, nor the same within individual cases. So it would not occur for a lover to be jealous of his mistress's husband—at least not in the specific framework of courtly love, which denies any importance to marriage in the amorous process. By the same token, in this same framework, a husband could not be jealous of his wife's lover as he is merely the head of the family, having married his wife for reasons other than love. But if we examine the same case in another framework, one that does not have this somewhat feudal relationship between the lady and her lover, there is a risk of things being perceived quite differently. This said, and even within the courtly context (as is shown by the copious literature on the subject), masculine jealousy quite pure and simple exists in the case of a husband who has been defied. King Mark takes it very badly when he is betrayed by his wife and his nephew. Arthur mounts an expedition against Lancelot, even though he had clearly been an accomplice in his knight's adulterous affair with the queen. The husband of the heroine in the *Lai du laostic* kills the nightingale his wife claims to listen to at night, out of pure jealousy. And let us not even mention the theme of the eaten heart, so widespread in medieval literature, wherein the husband kills his wife's lover and tricks her into eating her lover's heart. This goes a long way back to the Celtic tradition, which seems to be at the source of this odd courtly trio of king, queen, and knight. In the Irish texts we see King Aillil, a cuckolded king by virtue of his role, in some strange way, who finds it difficult to put up with his wife, Medbh, lavishing a little too much of *the friendship of her thighs* on the warriors needed by the realm. It even happens that Ailill displays his bad mood by killing one of his wife's lovers.[21]

We should not believe, however, that jealousy in the framework of courtly love was exclusively the prerogative of the husband. It can also happen that the lover is stricken with jealousy toward the husband, and in a very negative manner. To be jealous of the woman one loves, because it assumes a permanent interest of the lover for his lady, is one thing, and it is somewhat legitimized by the code of love. But we are stepping onto shaky ground when we analyze the jealousy of a lover who, deprived of his lady, cannot accept the knowledge that she belongs to her husband, or grants her favors to someone other than himself. The example of Tristan and Iseult is revealing.

We know that the first French tellers of the legend gave a limit of three years' potency to the famous philter that the two lovers drank. But during these three years, the magical effect of the "herbed wine" resolved all difficulties.

> The philter had rendered the lovers not only impervious to physical ailments, but impervious to sufferings of a moral nature as well, especially those caused by jealousy. Tristan and Iseult do not suffer once from the pangs of this affliction during the three years they remain under its spell. . . . In dividing herself between Mark and Tristan, Iseult is unfaithful only to her husband, she is not cheating on her lover, thus giving him no cause to be jealous.[22] . . . In his exile to Brittany, Tristan is obsessed by one torturous image, that of the blond Iseult finding complete happiness in the arms of King Mark. This image causes him even greater suffering by the contrast it makes with his solitary life in a foreign land, occupied ceaselessly by the tasks of war and deprived of the joys of love. He begins imagining that Iseult . . . has gradually forgotten him. Why should he continue to pride himself on his vain fidelity and impose sacrifices upon himself that his beloved has refused to make?[23]

In this way the idea forms in his mind to wed the daughter of the duke of Brittany, the beautiful Iseult of the White Hands, who has the same name as the Other. This is, of course, a case of transference.

There is something else: "Tristan knows full well that Iseult the Fair does not really love King Mark with all her heart. For her it is simply a matter, according to the expression of Thomas, 'of experiencing pleasure without love.' By the same token, he will avenge himself on his beloved by following her example and giving her a kind of lesson in infidelity by marrying Iseult of the White Hands. This subtle maneuver is prompted by jealousy as a way to punish the supposedly unfaithful lover and bring her back to her one true love."[24] The experiment is conclusive. On one hand Tristan proves incapable of having sexual relations with Iseult of the White Hands; he is struck down with impotence because of the strong presence he carries inside him, the exclusive image of Iseult the Fair. On the other hand Iseult the Fair is terribly unhappy when she hears the news; she feels she has been abandoned and betrayed. Hell now gapes before the two lovers, who truly form the most characteristic infernal couple in all literature. Devoured by agony and "exhausted in the long run by feverish jealousy, they do not recover their serenity and peace of mind until they seek joint refuge in the arms of death."[25]

But it is impossible for jealousy to be a negative force. In the framework of the rules that form the code of love, jealousy would instead be an extraordinary driving force behind the ardor of love. This squares with the popular aphorism that states you can only be jealous of the one you love. To keep ceaseless watch on one's lover or one's mistress is also a permanent discovery of the other, the observation of the other's slightest desires, the fulfillment of those desires from fear of being supplanted in that service. From this perspective, it is undeniable that the feeling of jealousy—perfectly selfish in origin—is transformed into an altruistic attitude directed toward the beloved, which seeks to attend to his or her every need. In short, a well thought out jealousy is the best remedy against lassitude and indifference.

Furthermore, jealousy for the person feeling it acts as a powerful force toward personal accomplishment, toward surpassing the current situation. Out of this constant fear of seeing himself supplanted or of seeing someone else preferred, the lover strives to be the best, the most courageous, the most attentive, the most caring: in this way he commits himself to a perpetual struggle against the laissez-faire attitude that kills love by drowning it in habit and conformity. So the lover's watchword should be a constant self-renewal in order to astonish even more the person whom he loves. As we know, astonishment leads to admiration, and admiration is one of the mandatory components of love, especially when this love is considered on the plane of value.

All of this does not transpire without suffering. It is true that the troubadours were always complaining about suffering, even if the love they felt for their lady was reciprocated. It leaves the impression that the happiness of loving goes through a series of sufferings that it is important never to master but to accept. For what is suffering in comparison to the absolute happiness represented by the lady of courtly love? This goes to emphasize, once again, the ambiguous relationship that exists between pain and pleasure. The fact that the lady is always cruel, that she must be watched over ceaselessly because she is the most beautiful and consequently necessarily the object of other men's desire, that at the bottom of all male individuals there exists a certain distrust of the feminine sex considered as incomprehensible, fickle, if not downright hypocritical or diabolical, all of this procures, we should say, certain unmentionable pleasures to the one who loves in total sincerity and total exclusivity. But the lady who has doubts concerning her lover can also experience the same troubled sensations.

Thus there is the absolute necessity of being jealous in order to love. For the theoreticians of courtly love, a love without jealousy is not worthy of the name. And modern psychologists are not far from expressing the same thing, even though our era denies jealousy in favor of practices of collective sexuality or by displaying great moral tolerance.

This fundamental principle of jealousy is propped up by another rule, the third: *"No one can have two love affairs at the same time."* This is the principle of exclusivity. It is reinforced by the twelfth rule: *"The true lover desires no other embraces than those his beloved gives him."* There is no room for discussion here, on condition of course that marriage is not considered a liaison. In any case, the husband and wife who have sex out of obligation and not free feelings of love cannot be considered lovers. Marriage is not a liaison; it can become similar to a liaison only if the married couple renounce their obligations to each other in order to sincerely follow the dictates of their feelings for each other.

Under these conditions, from the perspective of courtly society, they are no longer considered a married couple but as lovers. Otherwise, as Marie de Champagne said in a verdict that has since become famous, "love cannot extend its rights over a married couple. In fact, lovers see eye to eye so completely and with such freedom because obligation has no role. The married couple, on the contrary, is obliged by duty to suffer each other's will and may never refuse anything to each other. Furthermore, if a married couple should treat itself to caresses in the manner of a pair of lovers, the value of neither partner would increase, and they would appear to be possessing no more than they had started out with." This gives us a good idea of the complete defiance toward marriage that was promulgated in the theories of courtly love.

It remains no less true that genuine love can exist only within a couple—whether it is (as in some cases) a married couple or the exemplary but somewhat infernal couple presupposed by the relationship between the lover-knight and the mistress-lady. All third parties are excluded in advance; the legitimate husband or wife is purposely left out of the game. And courtly love is also harsh regarding "false lovers," the deceivers who abuse those who love them. This is a sacrilegious crime against the god of Love himself.

The most beautiful example from the courtly tales on this subject is the episode of the Vale of No Return included in the great thirteenth-century prose text concerning the Arthurian legends. The "Vale of No Return," the "Perilous Valley," or the "Vale of False Lovers" is a valley within the Brocéliande Forest, which was enchanted by the fairy Morgana, sister of King Arthur and disciple of the wizard Merlin.[26] Morgana, deceived by her lover Guyomard, had decided to avenge herself against all those who had been unfaithful to their mistresses. She devised a spell whereby any unfaithful knight who wandered into this valley would not be able to leave again. Imprisoned by his illusions and fantasies, which prompted him to see the sides of the valley crowned with unbreachable walls, flames, and monsters, the knight would then lead a half-tone existence on the shores of a lake called the Fairies' Mirror, inhabited by dreams each more disreputable than the last.

Morgana had decreed that the spell would not be broken until the day a knight who had committed no offense against his lady entered the vale. But this knight was slow in arriving at the vale, and it filled up with all of Arthur's knights, Gawain himself the most illustrious among them. Of course it was Lancelot of the Lake who braved the interdiction and freed all his imprisoned companions. For not only was he the best knight in the world, he was also the only one who had remained totally faithful to his lady, who happened to be none other than King Arthur's wife, Queen Guinivere. Here we have the most characteristic example of the courtly concept of fidelity. The liaison between Lancelot and Guinivere, even though adulterous, is a single liaison that, according to the code of courtly love, the queen's marriage does not stain with any irregularity.

But this code of love is not as clear as we might be tempted to think. The thirty-first rule sounds a false note: *"Nothing forbids one woman from being loved by two men, nor one man from being loved by two women."* We have to keep in mind, however, that a person can be loved without responding to that love and conduct herself in a passive manner toward someone she does not love. This is the case with Queen Guinivere, sincerely loved by Arthur but herself in love with no one but Lancelot. This is the case with Tristan, sincerely loved by Iseult of the White Hands, his official wife, but himself in love with only Iseult the Fair.

Then another dissonant chord is struck by the eighth rule: *"No one should be deprived of the object of their love without sufficient cause."* In this case we have to admit that Arthur was deprived of Guinivere, and Iseult of the White Hands was deprived of Tristan. But there was sufficient cause: in these instances Arthur was the husband and Iseult of the White Hands was the wife and this was reason enough. In addition to which, a subtle casuistry was being roughed out in those famous courts, presided over by the great ladies of the time, a casuistry that foreshadows the great Pascalian developments of necessary reason and sufficient reason, which subsequently became the source of so much joy for the apostles of the dialectic.

We can find an excellent example of this in the verdict reached by a court presided over by the countess of Flanders. The case was as follows:

An utterly dishonest knight, whom all women disapproved of for that reason, had sought the love of a certain lady with such audacity and persistence that she relented and granted him reason to hope that his love was returned. Through her advice and conversation, as well as her caresses and kisses, this lady had so strengthened the character of her lover that, thanks to her, he became an honest man of good morals. It was at this point that another lady offered him her love. He accepted her offer, thereby forgetting the generosity of the first lover, who had been responsible for the betterment of his character. The countess of Flanders responded: "Everyone must agree that the first lover has the right to forbid her lover from accepting the caresses of any other woman. Indeed it was through her application and effort that a dishonest man was made honest and courteous. She has right and reason on her side against that man whom she transformed from a person of no integrity into an honest and highly moral individual through the pains she took and her solicitude." If our understanding is correct, it was then justifiable for this lady to deprive her lover of his new lover, and at the same time deprive the other woman of someone she no doubt loved as sincerely as the first lady did. In any case this shows that courtly love was not an unbridled passion that overcame lovers but was, to the contrary, a maturely considered love, subject to a fine-toothed examination by reason. It is in this measure that courtly love appears as an invitation to surpass and transcend oneself. If we devote a little analysis to the legend of Tristan and Iseult, which historians have tried at all costs to pass off as a story of mad amorous passion, we might be surprised to observe that in every version, including the Irish archetypes, reason never surrenders its rights.

For the avowed goal of this subtle play, at the same time sensual and intellectual, that makes up courtly love is to provoke the transcendence of the lovers, knight as well as lady. The knight goes through a series of steps that bring him in some way to an equal standing with a lady who previously had been untouchable by virtue of her more elevated, quasi divine position. The lady, through the test she gives her lover and the benefit she draws from it, attains fullness of being and personality. None of this can happen without desire, and the ninth rule declares: *"No one can truly love without being pushed by hope for love."* This is evidence that scarcely needs demonstrating. No human action can be undertaken without there being an objective to be reached, and this objective, in principle freely chosen by the human being, must lead him or her to a certain satisfaction. What is the good of loving or trying to love when there is no hope of being loved in return?

This type of evidence is encountered several more times. The sixth rule explicitly states: *"A man cannot love until after puberty,"* which can have the air of a mere truism but does in fact emphasize the clearly sexual aspect of courtly love. Likewise the seventh rule establishes: *"At the death of his lover, the survivor will wait two years,"* which simply corresponds to a period of mourning. And let us not mention banalities such as that of the fourth rule: *"Love must always be either growing or declining"!* We must mingle in a few clichés with the more subtle research that aims at the creation of an ideal couple.

For we are certainly dealing with a couple, and not the individual taken in his or her singularity. An entire series of rules denotes this loss of individual identity for the benefit of a new identity, formed by the fusion of two individuals. Accordingly, the fifth rule declares: *"There are no saving graces to what the lover obtains without the accord of his lover,"* whereas *"Every action of the lover terminates in the thought of his lover"* (twenty-fourth rule), *"The genuine lover finds nothing good in what has not pleased his lover"* (twenty-fifth rule), *"The lover can never be sated with his lover's pleasures"* (twenty-seventh rule), and *"The genuine lover is always obsessed with the image of his beloved"* (thirtieth rule). We can regard all this as a kind of amorous coquetry, a parlor game in which it was considered good form to appear very much in love with a person of higher rank as was later the case in the time of mannerism. But it is nothing of the sort. The exaggerated or ineffectual aspect of these rules must not make us forget that in the tales concerning Lancelot of the Lake—Chrétien de Troyes's as well as the later texts—the hero cannot make a move without the image of Guinivere entering into it. In fact Lancelot never acts on his own behalf, or on behalf of the Arthurian community (of which he was actually never a member, although he contributed greatly to its blossoming), or obviously on behalf of King Arthur, or even on behalf of Guinivere herself, who is the objective to be won. He acts always and only on behalf of the ideal, prodigious, adulterous, infernal couple he forms with her.

This is, in fact, the great lesson provided by courtly love: the surpassing of the selfish and egotistical stage of development in order to create a symbiotic state with the unique individual one has chosen. It presupposes a total renunciation of the temptations of the ego. Hence the apparent depersonalization of Lancelot, ready to do anything in obedience to the queen's desires. At first glance this seems to be a kind of servitude whose ridiculous aspects have all too often been placed in the foreground. But in the final analysis, we can see that Lancelot's value and power exist only as a function of this renunciation. Furthermore, in the curious story of *Perlesvaux*, Lancelot himself confesses as much to a hermit who reproaches him for sacrificing the quest of the Grail for the quest of Guinivere. Lancelot makes a significant comparison between the image of Guinivere, the perfect woman and model of all the virtues, and the Grail, the divine symbol of perfection. For Lancelot the Grail is Guinivere, with all this entails regarding the deification of woman. What counts most, however, is not so much the Object to be attained but the quest itself, which is action and metamorphosis. And just as the Object is always modified by the action of the Subject, we can say that Guinivere loved as we know she is by her knight-priest is no longer the young queen she was before meeting Lancelot. Guinivere no longer exists without Lancelot. Lancelot no longer exists without Guinivere. We have here, both on the plane of myth and on the plane of literary expression, the example that best conforms to the theories of courtly love.

This fusion with the Other explains fairly well the attitudes claimed by the code of love to be those of the genuine lover: *"He who is dying of love's passion neither sleeps nor eats"* (twenty-third rule). Love must imbue his entire life, each second of his existence, because love is perpetual renewal. The fifteenth rule states: *"Every lover must grow pale when in his beloved's presence,"* which can seem an exaggeration, but which is actually the obvious transposition of an internal movement, because, as said by the sixteenth rule: *"At the sudden sight of his beloved, the heart of a lover should tremble."*

In short, love according to courtly theory is not a state but an action. Moreover, it is for this reason that marriage is automatically not included, because marriage is a way of making love safe and secure. Now, love can never make the person experiencing it feel safe and secure. This is peremptorily stated in the twentieth rule: *"Those in love are always fearful."* In fact there is a constant fear of losing one's lady, losing one's love, losing one's reason to live. Jealousy, in the noble sense of the word, is ever present, as is the fear of displeasing one's lady. The pains taken to respond to the desires of one's lady spur one's action, and everything must be brought into play so that the couple becomes the union of two beings isolated on this earth, thereby re-creating, although they may not know it, the famous dyad, the sacred couple, the mythical androgyne, which some feel may have been the very origin of life. The lover's fear concerning his lady is more than mere psychological fear; it is a genuinely metaphysical fear: the entire world risks toppling if the ideal couple loses its balance, since this infernal couple of courtly love is the reflection of a world that each individual is attempting to restore to its original grandeur and purity.

Furthermore, it is in this restoration of the original divine couple where the miracle is to be found. It is a miracle because this restoration is fragile, but also because it is possible. The individual's deepest impulses necessarily lead to this fusion. It is reminiscent of the time from once upon a time, it is a nostalgia for our origins. But to recover these origins, we must not go backward; rather, we must proceed forward, wandering along the deceptive footpaths of the Brocéliande Forest where traps have been laid to eliminate impostors. First of all, in order to evade these snares, the polarity must be reversed and the *signs* decoded. No one has provided a better depiction of this quest—which cannot be undertaken without a complete reversal of values—than the troubadour Raimbaut d'Orange:

Voici qu'éclot la fleur inverse
sur les rochers, parmi les tertres.
Fleur de neige, glace et gelées,
qui mord, qui resserre et qui tranche.
Meurent chansons et meurt qui siffle
dans la ramure et sur les tiges.
Mais moi me tient vers l'allégresse
quand je vois sèche la bassesse.

Car tout ainsi pour moi s'inverse
et les plaines me semblent tertres,
la fleur jaillit de la gelée,
le chaud dans la chair du froid tranche,
l'orage devient chant et siffle
et les feuilles couvrent les tiges.
Si bien me lace l'allégresse
qu'en nul lieu ne paraît bassesse.

Aille mon vers de sens inverse
au-delà des vals et des tertres
là où on ne connaît gelées
et ne se peut que le froid tranche;
pour ma dame je chante et siffle
clair. Sur le coeur frappe la tige
s'il ne sait chanter qu'allégresse
et de son chant bannit bassesse.

Très douce Dame, l'allégresse
nous tient unis malgré bassesse . . .[27]

Here blossoms the flower upside down / upon the rocks, among the mounds. / Flower of snow, ice, and frost / that stings the flesh, and hurts, and cuts. / Dying are songs and dying are those who whistle / in the branches and among the stems. / But me I hold toward delight / when I spy the withering of baseness. / For everything for me also turns upside down / and the plains appear to me as mounds, / the flower blossoms from the frost, / the warmth cuts through the flesh of cold, / the storm becomes a song and a whistle / and leaves cover the stems. / So well does delight hold on to me / that no place anywhere seems like baseness. / May then my verse go upside down / over and beyond the vales and mounds / to where they know not frost / and the cutting cold has lost its sting; / for my lady I sing and whistle / clear. On his heart strikes the stem / if he knows to sing only of delight / and to banish all baseness from his song. / Very sweet Lady, delight / holds us together in spite of baseness.

Once the signs have been decoded and the traditional values turned upside down, there is no reason for "baseness" to exist. Courtly love is, in short, a rule for life that allows one to go from low to high; it is in this regard that Catharism has often been mentioned in connection with the poetry of the troubadours. And it is a fact that the renunciation of baseness and the exaltation of the primordial couple, freed from the illusions of this world, and also the attempt to overcome the ego in order to attain a perfect fusion are all familiar themes of the Cathars. It might be stretching a point, but we could reasonably claim that the difficult journey of the courtly lover is the reascension of the Fallen Angel toward the Divine Light. In any event, this interpretation does not contradict the intent of establishing new relations of an affective order between men and women, such intent seeming to be the fundamental element of courtly love. The appeal made to a value shed of all base elements and washed clean of all that encumbers it—that is, free from diabolical illusions (enticements of gain, desire for power, pride) and false interpretations (in which appearances supplant the essence)—is an invitation to achieve a genuine catharsis through which one can claim to have become "perfect." After all, is the lady of courtly love not the symbol of perfection in every domain?

It is because his lady is Perfection that, as stated in the twenty-sixth rule: *"The lover can refuse his beloved nothing."* We rediscover here the

conception of the "tyrannical" mistress, reverting to the original meaning of the word *tyrannical* as "one who gives." The legend of Tristan
sheds a good deal of light on this point. Tristan, before his encounter
with Iseult, had led an ordinary life, even a plantlike life, we might say.
He became conscious of himself as an individual only through Iseult's
love. This is because Iseult the Fair—as shown by her Irish archetype,
Grainne (whose name is derived from *grian*, "sun")—is the representation of the sun, whereas Tristan is the moon (and Mark the night). The
anecdote of the philter, supposedly poured in error because of the ignorance of Brangwain (a Celtic goddess of love), should not cause us to
forget that, in the archetypal tale, Grainne spoke a dreadful *geis* on the
man she had chosen to carry away with her. Thus, Iseult-Grainne claims
complete power over Tristan-Diarmaid, but in doing so, in becoming
tyrannical, she gives of everything and assumes her solar role in providing strength, consistency, and light to the moon roving in the night, that
is, in the shadow of his uncle King Mark. Tristan can no longer live
without the light of the sun since symbolically he is the moon. And in the
prose version of the legend, it clearly states that Tristan must have sexual
relations with Iseult at least once a month or else he will waste away. So
it is normal that Tristan, following his separation from Iseult, would
return to her each time his desire for her reappears. His desire for the
beautiful Iseult is perhaps in conformance with the rules of courtly love,
but for Tristan it is also a vital principle. The troubadours are saying the
same thing in their poems when they implore their beloved for a look or
a smile. The rays of the sun (and metaphorically the "eyes of the lady")
cause the revitalization of the lover-moon, who is nourished by this
divine warmth and light, at least for a certain period of time (the duration of a lunar cycle), and it is necessary for this solar-lunar encounter
to recur periodically. This is shown quite clearly by Tristan's tragic end:
it is not his poisoned wound that actually kills him but the fact that
Iseult, delayed by a storm and then the absence of wind, did not arrive
in time to infuse him with new warmth and life. Tristan remains the best
example of the lover who cannot live—or survive—unless his "tyrannical" mistress gives him everything. Thus it could be claimed that Tristan

was a courtly antihero, because he really did lie carnally with the wife of his uncle! And the same holds true for Lancelot of the Lake, who would not exist if Guinivere, who is his joy if not his love's bliss did not give him everything. And if she gives him everything, it is because she is a tyrannical mistress.

The more tyrannical the mistress, the more the initiation process of the courtly lover is accelerated. *"An easy conquest strips love of its charm; a difficult conquest enhances its value."* Those who consider Lancelot's attitude servile and grotesque in *Le Chevalier à la charrette*—he obeys Guinivere's every whim, allowing himself to be beaten shamelessly when she asks, climbing into the hangman's cart and being reviled like the worst criminal—have not comprehended the profound significance that should be given to this behavior, which borders on the abnormal. Guinivere destroys Lancelot's ego with her tyranny. And contrary to what one might think, it is not Guinivere who emerges the victor of this trial, but, rather, the couple she forms with Lancelot. This is the essential thing here. By refusing his beloved nothing, Lancelot loudly proclaims the superiority of the one he loves and the difficulty it took to win her. But in doing this, he transforms himself. Guinivere has taken everything he has; she has also given him everything. The exchange is perfect. We now have the new couple—the ideal, infernal couple that takes possession of the world for its greater glory, since in reality the Arthurian world as dreamed by the authors of the courtly romances is maintained only by the cohesion of this fundamental couple. This can be seen when Lancelot retreats back to his own domains and Guinivere is carried off by the usurper Mordred, Lancelot's dark double.

Considered from this angle, the code of love takes on a value that goes far beyond the petty amorous strategies of the drawing room. This value is first psychological, then sociological, before becoming metaphysical and ultimately a matter of pure religion. It is pure and simple the reascension of the Light Being, who had been momentarily deceived by his illusions, back to the repose he ought never to have left. This perhaps may be a Cathar theme, but it is also a human and universal one. The twentieth-ninth rule, slyly lost in among the others, gives us the key to the system that has been put in place: *"He whose lust is too great does not truly love."* This could be taken as a rejection of sexuality and a platonic interpretation of courtly love. It is nothing of the sort, as the terms are clear and precise: it is only too great a lust that should be avoided, not lust itself. This simply implies that lust is not an end but a means, a sort of operating method (ultimately comparable to mathematics) that permits the accentuation of man's awareness of the reality that surrounds him and, consequently, the taking into account of this reality in a metamorphosis of the world. This consideration can, furthermore, appear to be close to contemporary conceptions centered on entropy, which pose as a principle that the universe is under construction and that human beings have a certain role to play in that creation. In fact, this is nothing other than an updated version of the Druidic doctrine whereby God does not exist but is found in a state of perpetual becoming. This is not quite the same as the static formulation of the so-called revealed religions, particularly Christianity, especially since it was subverted by the Church Fathers, who were fixed on the defense of the human institution to the detriment of its divine message.

Lust is part of the universe. The religions of India are living proof of this. Lust is one of the means to attain Knowledge (which includes the biblical form of knowing). The intimate relationship that develops between the lover-knight and his mistress-lady necessarily happens through sex. But here the sex is not a final end but a necessary method of acting in order to gain awareness of an Elsewhere that is in a constant process of unfolding. Is orgasm not considered a "little death"; are its gasps of pleasure not similar to the rasps of dying? Orgasm is only a form of passage. The key thing is to foresee where this passage can lead those audacious souls who condescend to take the plunge.

Dangerous? Perhaps. Some never return from their journey through Hell. The courtly couple is an infernal couple to the extent that it appears at the clash between laws and customs, and it attempts to regain the original, paradisiacal condition at the dawn of time, when the antinomies were not perceived as contradictory. But the path of the courtly couple, whatever one may think, leads them through the hell of sex.

TWO

L∙VE in QUESTI∙n

The elaboration of a code of love assumes from the start that the route to the realization of that love is scattered with pitfalls often difficult to discern. To love is not a simple matter. After all, what does the verb *love* actually mean, what does the substantive *love* mean? Certain terms are sometimes used in such a way, often in a derivative or completely wrongheaded sense, that it is difficult to avoid confusion when seeking to define them with precision.

It should not be forgotten that the medieval term for courtly love was *fin'amor:* It was thus a question of a *fine* or *refined love,* and also (if we have understood it correctly) of a love pushed to its farthest extremes. And this would not happen without a certain *finesse,* or without a certain end [*fin*] in mind. *Fin'amor* can thus be understood as an organized amorous activity with an objective.

The word *amour* ("love") is confusing in the French language. Originally it defined the attraction one could feel toward a physical object. The word comes from the Latin *amor,* which has undergone the same semantic evolution, starting from the material to end at the spiritual, but it was just as confused in Cicero's language. The first Christians were not fooled. They resorted to the ancient Indo-European root *car,* which can still be seen in the adjective *carus,* from which they made *caritas* ("spiritual love"), which we have transcribed since the sixteenth century as "charity" but only by shifting the word from its original meaning. Making charity is not making love and yet. . . . The Indo-European root *car* can be found in Gallic and was preserved in the Celtic languages. The Germanic language used another root word, which gave us the German *liebe* and the English *love*, but the English language makes a distinction between loving a thing, "to like," and loving with love, "to love." The French language systematically commingles the two, accentuating the physical aspect in the use of the expression *faire l'amour* ("to make love") when it concerns only a sexual embrace where genuine love does not necessarily have a part. Furthermore, when the Latin word *carus* was adapted into the French language, it was as the root of an equally ambiguous adjective. We can have a relationship with a dear person *(une chère personne)* and we can call just about anyone a "dear friend" *(un cher ami),* but the semantic evolution of the word also entailed a more material signification: this object costs dearly *(coûte cher).* What an arduous task, to translate the concept of love into the French language!

It is not completely unproductive to recall the major difficulty entailed in providing a conscientious definition of love, all the more so when it concerns *fin'amor* as formulated in French. Medievalists who have sometimes delved happily into the theme of courtly love have diverged wildly in their opinions—some regard it as a simple social game, others consider it an attempt at spiritualization, others have seen it as the symbol of Cathar asceticism, and still others as the result of platonic theories in Christian thought. The least that can be said, in any case, is that the problem of courtly love is not a simple one. Even during the eleventh, twelfth, and thirteenth centuries, courtly love was discussed and dealt with in various manners, according to circumstances and the people implicated.

The Courts of Love

A tenacious tradition tells of courts held by the great ladies of twelfth-century society, actual tribunals where verdicts were returned concerning cases of love brought before them. The general belief is that these somewhat exceptional court sessions were held primarily in Poitiers, at the court of Eleanor of Aquitaine; in Troyes, at the court of Eleanor's daughter Marie, the countess of Champagne; as well as in certain courts in Occitania.

Scholars from the nineteenth and the first part of the twentieth centuries have gone to a great deal of trouble to affirm or deny the historical existence of these love tribunals, but in truth debates of this kind are utterly irrelevant. Whether courts of love actually existed or are merely a matter of legend, some judgments were written down and remain to constitute undeniable documentation of the interest inspired by questions of love in the refined and cultivated aristocratic society of that era.[1] We can thus assess the pains taken to formally record this or that difficult case and the enthusiasm generated for finding a solution to each case. By the same token, these judgments reveal the existence of a codified courtly law even before *De Arte amandi* was written down, which everyone in this courtly milieu knew and strove to respect.

The philologist Raynouard in 1817 was the first to supply evidence for the existence of the courts of love. In his words: "These tribunals, which were more stern than fearsome and in which beauty itself exercised a power recognized by courtliness and opinion, pronounced judgments over the infidelity and inconstancy of lovers, and over the strictness of their ladies' whims and, through an influence that was as gentle as it was irresistible, spurred on and ennobled, to the benefit of manners and civilization, a chivalrous enthusiasm, that tender and impetuous emotion which nature grants man for his happiness but which almost always is the torment of his youth and all too often the source of life-long unhappiness."[2] This was written at the onset of the romantic era, when it was good form to go into ecstasies of amorous passion. Stendhal remembered the courts of love in his treatise *De l'Amour,* in which he pertinently analyzes the mechanics of amorous behavior and added the code of love as an appendix. But Raynouard, with every chance of being right, went on to analyze the composition of these courts, which generally consisted of a "great number of ladies" and were presided over by an important lady of high rank. Sometimes parties or their representatives appeared before these courts to plead cases. Sometimes the ladies discussed cases among themselves and returned judgments on the petitions or simple questions brought before them, all in an impassioned but thoughtful atmosphere. An amusement if you like, these courts of love, but even if their number and importance have been exaggerated, they made a considerable contribution to the study of the workings of love. They also provided us with a fairly exact depiction of what the members of high society were thinking at the time.

Twenty-one judgments from these courts of love remain in our possession, judgments delivered and explained by such great women as Eleanor of Aquitaine herself; Marie, the countess of Champagne; Elizabeth de Vermandois, the countess of Flanders; Ermengarde, viscountess of Narbonne, as well as Alix de Champagne, third wife of Louis VII.* As Gaston Paris wrote: "the names of the great ladies cited by Andreas Capellanus are those of the principal patrons of amorous science. Eleanor's court was no doubt a model that was quickly imitated, and other great ladies aspired to the glory of becoming doctors and jurists of love. . . . In this way a jurisprudence supported by the authority of illustrious names was established next to the fundamental laws that the god of love himself had revealed to a Breton knight."† And this jurisprudence, although preaching the determinative role of women in all matters of love, constitutes astonishing documentation of the way the code of love was really lived—always within the framework of high society, whose members had the time for reflection.

The themes are as varied as the cases, but their constant concern is the delicate relations within a couple. Everything proceeds as if support was sought from an exemplary case, in order to establish a general rule that would allow lovers to model their behavior on a consensus everyone found satisfactory. Because, even more than before, lovers are not alone in the world: this "world" watches them and judges their actions in accordance with their conformance to current custom and, if need be,

---

* *Translator's note:* The twenty-one judgments can be found in an assortment of medieval records as well as in *The Art of Love* by Andreas Capellanus.

† *Translator's note:* Gaston Paris was a nineteenth-century French scholar who wrote a number of books on medieval literature.

helps these lovers to overcome any difficulties they may encounter. The courtly couple, although utterly illegitimate with regard to the morality and the social structure of the era, thereby acquired a curious sort of legitimacy within this intellectual elite, a legitimacy that actually constituted an antiworld or, rather, an ideal world parallel to that of everyday life.

One knight had an excessive passion for a lady who persistently refused to share his love. Eventually touched by his perseverance, she offered him the *hope of love* on condition that he swear to a solemn agreement: "You will obey all my orders and if you fail a single one, I will deny my love to you completely." Of course the suitor gave his oath, and the lady then commanded him to no longer concern himself with her love nor sing her praises anymore in public. Her smitten admirer was thus caught in a trap. However, he put up with this irksome situation until the day he overheard someone speaking ill of the lady he loved with such passion. He was unable to contain himself and refuted the lies against her and praised her in ringing terms. This came to his lady's ears, who declared that she would henceforth deny him her love because he had disobeyed her orders by singing her praises. The matter was brought before the countess Marie de Champagne, and the judgment she handed down was as follows: "This lady's requirements were too strict. In fact she had no fear of resorting to an unjust decision in order to circumvent someone who had delivered himself entirely to her will, and to whom she had given hopes of her love by binding him with an oath. This is deceit that no woman can be permitted to indulge in without a serious motive. The lover in question committed no fault in seeking to convince his lady's detractors of their errors. Indeed, if he made such an oath it was in order to obtain her love more easily. It seems unfair that the lady then ordered him not to trouble himself anymore in pursuit of the subject of his love."

Another knight had a woman friend whom he loved and who loved him in return. One day he asked for a kind of "discharge," permission to establish ties of love with another woman. His request was granted. The knight left and remained away a month. Then he returned to his first lady, saying he had never taken any liberties with the other woman and in truth had never desired her but had only wished to test his lover's faithfulness. His lady took this badly. She rebuffed him for being unworthy of her love, saying that the freedom he had requested and been granted justified denying him her love. Queen Eleanor sat in judgment on this case and responded: "It is quite common in love for lovers to feign that they desire the caresses of another, to better test the fidelity and faithfulness of their beloved. Thus it is an offense against the supreme nature of love for the lady to cite this reason to refuse her lover the caresses he is accustomed to or to refuse him her love, unless there is proof that the promised faith has been violated."

A young man of no honesty whatsoever and a very honest but married and hence adulterous knight were pleading for the love of the same lady. The young man claimed he should be preferred over the adulterer, for if he obtained the love he sought he would be able, thanks to that love, to mend his ways, and this would be a great honor to the lady for having thereby contributed to making an honest man of a dishonest one. When consulted on this matter, Queen Eleanor responded: "Even though a dishonest young man may be elevated to an honest one by virtue of the love of a sagacious woman, it is not the same thing when a woman prefers to love a dishonest man, especially when her love is sought also by an honest man of fine moral qualities. In fact, it could happen that, because of the dishonest man's behavior in spite of the good and desirable things he has received, his flawed nature might find no cure because the seed that is sown does not always bear fruit."

One knight was once unknowingly involved with a lady who was pregnant. Once her pregnant state became obvious, the knight requested his freedom. But the lady, who was very attached to her lover, made her claim upon his love, declaring that her fault was irreproachable as when she and her lover first began their affair she was not pregnant. This problem was also brought before Queen Eleanor of Aquitaine, who responded: "This woman pleads against right and justice for she is striving to preserve a lewd love under a veil of error. Indeed, we are at all times obliged to censure lewd and questionable actions, which are, moreover, opposed by human law with the most severe penalties." Her answer is quite clear, but the case is not. By all evidence the lady in question was not under a husband's authority, for in that case her being pregnant would not justify her lover's jealous reaction. The more probable possibility no doubt was that this lady who sincerely loved her knight had a transitory affair with another man. In any event, there was no recourse but to find her guilty as, from the courtly love perspective, no one was allowed two liaisons at one time.

A young girl had broken with a lover who was most respectable in order to marry another honorable man. She wished to have done with her former lover and refuse him all his customary indulgences, whereas he, still madly in love with her, ceaselessly sought their restoration. This case was judged by Ermengarde, the viscountess of Narbonne, in a manner that allows no evasion: "The unexpected event of a marital bond in no way excludes the rights of the first lover, unless the lady has determined to no longer trouble herself with love and to never love another individual." It could not be said any more clearly that marriage does not figure in questions of love. Furthermore, when this same Ermengarde de Narbonne was asked which feelings of love were stronger, those shared by a married couple or those shared by a pair of lovers, she responded no less definitely: "The affection between a married couple and the genuine love shared by lovers are shown by nature to be completely opposed and to have their sources in completely different movements [of the soul]."

There is an opposing view, however. A lady had first been married, but then she separated from her husband after their marriage was annulled, and her former husband still insisted she give him her love. This lady, not knowing what to do, asked the advice of the viscountess of Narbonne, who answered: "If two people have been joined and subsequently find themselves separated, for whatever reason, we declare that it is not the fault of the love they shared and that love is perfectly legitimate." Here is another assertion that marriage is nothing but a social contract with no connection to emotion.

Certain cases present complications, however. A lover already bound by a deep attachment to one lady who loved him dearly made earnest demands for the love of another woman as if he was currently free of any amorous ties. Following the dictates of his heart and through his persistence, he obtained all he was asking for. But once he got what he had desired so strongly, he returned to his first lover and asserted his rights to her love while contriving a quarrel with the second. A scandal ensued that was brought before the court of the countess of Flanders, where it was asked what punishment this man deserved, since he was incontestably guilty of having two love affairs at one time. The answer to this question is interesting insofar as it was a social punishment: the dishonest lover was actually banished from society. "This unworthy individual who was guilty of such serious betrayal, deserves to be denied the love of both women, and should not pride himself with the love of any other honest woman, for we can see that he is ruled by an impetuous hunger for the pleasures of the flesh that is the very enemy of love." Furthermore, this "excess of love" is emphasized as the opposite of love insofar as the carnal is the departure point of the spiritual.

Cases of absence and temporary separation were also the order of the day in the courts of love. The lover of a certain lady had long been absent on an expedition to a remote country, presumably as part of a crusade. As the lady had given up any hopes for his early return and everyone despaired of hearing any news of him, she wanted to take a new lover. But a confidant of her first love took exception to this as an offense against the one who had taken him into his confidence. He brought his opposition to the lady's desire for a new love before the court of Countess Marie de Champagne.

The lady defended herself in the following manner: "If a woman widowed by the death of her lover is permitted to love again after two years, that is all the more reason that a woman would have this right when widowed by a living lover from whom she has long been denied the pleasure of receiving a letter or spoken message, especially if he has had numerous opportunities to do so." The dispute dragged on, or so we are told, and it was necessary to submit it to arbitration by the countess, who concluded the debate as follows:

> A lover does not have the right, under the pretext of her lover's long absence, to break with him without obvious proof that his love has

failed or that he has violated her trust. This is especially true when a lover is absent out of necessity or his absence is due to honorable reasons. Nothing should bring greater joy to a lover's heart than news from afar concerning her lover's glory or learning that he is held in great esteem by the assemblies of the great. The reproach that he has neglected to send her messages or letters could be interpreted as proof of his great prudence, because his secret is one not to be entrusted to a stranger. And if he sent letters whose tone remained unknown to their bearer, the secret of his love could easily be divulged, either through his messenger's disloyalty or through his death during his journey.

As we have already seen, in accordance with the code of love, all precautions must be taken to prevent the revelation of a secret love.

Another problem concerns physical integrity, a very uncertain matter during those violent and warring times. In one case a lover had lost his eye or suffered the loss of some other portion of his anatomy during valiant combat. His lover then rejected him, saying his ugliness made him unworthy of her own beauty, and henceforth refused him the caresses she had previously granted. Ermengarde de Narbonne's judgment on this point was explicit: "A woman is deemed unworthy of honor if she decides to renounce her lover on account of an injury incurred in the case of war and of a nature to only befall valiant fighters. Now it is the audacity of a warrior that most excites a woman's love and increases her desire. For this reason a crippling injury that has been incurred in consequence of natural bravery in battle, should procure for her lover a compensation in love." This judgment is eloquent in that it permits a comparison between the attitude of the noble ladies of medieval aristocracy and that of a girl from any era when confronted by the prestige conferred by a uniform and the troubled desire awoken in her when she finds herself in the presence of a man who kills.

Outside of the husband, regarded as of no importance in the courtly scheme of things, a third party can sometimes become involved with the couple: the confidant. This too can provoke incidents. For example, a knight was in love with a lady, and as he had no favorable opportunity to speak with her and with her accord, he relied on an intermediary through whom each could learn more readily the wishes of the other and to whom they could secretly confide their own. Thanks to this confidant the love they shared could be kept a secret. But the confidant who had accepted this intermediary role did not live up to the trust invested in him and began at once to act on his own behalf, declaring his own love for the lady in question. This same lady made the unacceptable decision to respond in kind. Making herself his accomplice in deceit, she granted him her love and fulfilled all his wishes.

The knight soon learned of what had transpired and, deeply affected by this betrayal, denounced the affair in full detail before the countess of Champagne, asking that the case be judged by her and the other ladies of the court. The accused, once acquainted with this development, also accepted the countess's arbitration in the matter. Before pronouncing her verdict the countess summoned sixty ladies and concluded the affair in this manner: "May such a false-hearted lover, who has met a woman worthy of his merits as she felt no shame in consenting to such a crime, enjoy, if he so desires, the bliss of a love so poorly acquired, and may she justly enjoy the bliss of such a friend. But may both of them be forever deprived of the love of any other person; may neither of them henceforth appear at the assemblies of the ladies or the courts of the knights, for the lover has violated the faith of chivalry and the lady has acted shamelessly and against the modesty of ladies by granting her love to a confidant." Here, too, we find banishment from all society for a crime committed not only against the lady's appointed lover but also against the whole of love's knighthood, to which the lover now has no right to belong because of his abuse of authority.

A knight became enamored of a lady who was already seriously involved with another man. He obtained from her this hope of love: if in some future time she should be deprived of her lover, then she would grant her favors to this knight. Shortly thereafter this same lady married her lover. The knight then demanded the fulfillment of the promise she had made him, which the lady absolutely refused, claiming she had not been deprived of her lover's love. The case was brought before Alix de Champagne, queen of France, who responded: "We dare not contradict the opinion of the countess of Champagne who has set down a formal judgment that genuine love cannot extend its powers over husband and wife. Therefore our wishes are that the lady named make good on her promise of love."

This could not be any more straightforward. Once again we are shown that marriage is considered null and void in matters of authentic love. The lady who before marrying her lover had committed the serious error of accepting the love of another man must, now she is married, obey the promise she made her suitor—and moreover, this is as licit as can be. We are told by Marie de Champagne: "A precept of love informs us that no wife can receive the reward of the king of love without serving, outside the bounds of marriage, in the knighthood of love." This legitimation of adultery—whether actual (in certain precise conditions excluding normal coitus) or simply spiritual and moral—is one of the essential characteristics of *fin'amor*, that is, love considered as a means of achieving perfection, an operating method within the grasp of sincere lovers who wish to reach a higher plane of consciousness.

Debates Between Heart and Spirit

It is possible that the courts of love were theaters of impassioned discussions between poets debating certain cherished themes before a select audience. There was no better place than before an assembly of ladies for the troubadours, and their successors the trouvères of the north, to show off to advantage their talents as poets and dialecticians. The principal subject of the troubadours' poems was indeed love and all the joys, sufferings, and assorted other problems inspired by it. The chansons de geste that have survived into the present most often seem to be veritable illustrations of Andreas Capellanus's code.

This is particularly true for two poetic forms that were highly honored in the twelfth and thirteenth centuries: the *tenson* and the *partimen,* or *jeu-parti,* which are poetic dialogues using the voices of two or more real or imaginary characters. The *tenson,* which the northern trouvères called the *débat* ["debate"], consists of a discussion between two troubadours taking different sides of a single question. This discussion can center on any subject—religious, literary, political—but most often concerns amorous casuistry. Whereas the debate in the *tenson* develops freely, the questions in the *jeu-parti* are posed by one speaker to another as a choice between two hypotheses, obliging the latter to come up with arguments that the first speaker then tries to repudiate. These discussions always end with a judgment from an arbiter or arbiters selected by the two debaters. The arbiter is generally the lord or lady of the house. And it is quite probable that this method of doing things was at the origin of numerous legends concerning purely imaginary courts of love.

From what we know of the works of the troubadours, we can compile an actual list of the most commonly debated subjects. Each one stands on its own as an illustration of the code of love and has the added merit of stating in precise detail what is by nature a general rule. The problems raised are universal, as well. "What would be more bearable, the death of your mistress or her marriage to another?" It goes without saying that the response to such a question is a matter of individual sensibility, but we can confidently state that the one who chooses the second option (the marriage of his lady to another) displays a more complete and altruistic love than he who prefers his lady's death. In this way the man who chooses his lady's marriage to another transcends his personal selfishness and sets his sights above all else on the happiness of his beloved, even though it be the source of his own despair.

Here is another question that apparently has no answer: "Who suffers more, the husband whose wife is unfaithful or the lover deceived by his mistress?" According to courtly logic the husband has no grounds to be jealous of his wife, because jealousy should not exist within a married couple. Therefore it would be the lover who suffers more. But there are cases escaping codification, and medieval literature has many examples of husbands driven to extreme measures when tortured by jealousy.

Male boasting is also not overlooked: "Who is more at fault, he who brags of favors he has not been granted or he who makes public those he has actually received?" An absolute rule in the code of love stresses that lovers' secrets are never to be divulged. Therefore, it is quite obvious at first glance that he who makes public the favors he has received is more at fault. But if we think further on the matter, the man who brags of favors he has never received is equally at odds with the code of love, for the considerable damage his lies could cause the reputation of the woman who he alleges granted him love's indulgences. It is fairly common knowledge, in any case, that the person who brags loudest about his success with women is usually the one who actually has the least success. Hence the contempt generally inspired by this kind of person.

Sometimes the casuistry goes right to the heart of the matter: "If you had a rendezvous at night with your mistress, would you rather see me leaving as you are arriving or see me arriving as you are leaving?" The problem of jealousy is largely surpassed here. It is simply a question of knowing what gives the lover the greater satisfaction, being first or following after another man. Vanity would dictate the first option as it is always more flattering to come after: it is proof that the other did not provide satisfaction. But where, in this dilemma (which occurs more frequently than one might think), is there a place for the true love that does not permit of sharing?

In any event, this kind of debate comes close to defining love, without ever quite succeeding. "You are given the option of sleeping with your beloved for just one time, but on condition you never see her again for your entire life, or else to see her every day without ever obtaining anything from her: Which would you choose?" True love, which transcends the sexual impulses, would be inclined to favor the second option, and the troubadours did not fail to develop this theme, falling into ecstasy on seeing their lady pass by, whose sight allowed them to go on living. But the first option emphasizes another well-known theme, that of the "brief encounter," a theme that has been exploited countless times in literature and even more so in film. It is, in fact, possible to live out an entire love that has no tomorrow in the space of several hours, because eternity perhaps may be the possibility of seizing happiness in the sparkling of an instant.

The debate can even have bearing on questions of pure technique: "Two people who love one another are sleeping together and restricting themselves to modest caresses: which of the two is making the greater sacrifice?" This is obviously a trick question, in that we are not told who took the initiative in restricting themselves to modest caresses. From what we know, anything was permissible between courtly lovers on condition that the rules of the game were respected and that one did not seek to obtain everything at once, with the fundamental restriction concerning coitus itself, normally out of bounds for reasons, moreover, that had more to do with magic than morality. Under these conditions there is no possible answer to the question, whose sole merit is to demonstrate that the lovers' pleasure must above all else be the respect for each other and the desire not to exceed each other's desires, and this all in perfect agreement between them. Again it is the couple that counts, not the individual.

Other subjects for discussion seem pointless to contemporary mentality: "Who is the happier, an old woman who becomes the beloved of a young man or an old man who has a young lover?" As for knowing whether it is "better to have a woman or a maiden for a mistress," in the context of courtly love it is definitely preferable to have a married woman for a mistress, as this establishes between her and her lover the same kind of tie that binds a vassal to a suzerain. Another question asks: "Would you prefer a mistress of mediocre beauty but very wise or a mistress of mediocre wisdom but very beautiful?" But this can then lead us to ask what has become of the lady of courtly love in this question, as she is necessarily the most beautiful, as well as the most intelligent and the wisest woman of all.

Other questions are not lacking in perversity: "What is preferable for a woman, to have an experienced lover who has already known pleasure or a young virgin boy who has not yet known it?" On the majority of occasions this kind of problem will unleash the troubadour's enthusiasm, and things quickly take a turn to the crudest form of obscenity. By way of comparison we find tales of the misadventures of young men, such as in this chanson de geste from an anonymous troubadour: "The other day, I thought I had a lover, the best I'd ever seen, and also the most beautiful; she was an old woman to make one ashamed, poor and badly-dressed. . . . She came in the dark of night in the place of my beloved. She was partially holding up her dress. I raced to her side, only to find her head was bald, her throat wizened, her shoulder sharp, her breasts hanging and empty as a shepherd's purse, her chest bony and flat, her belly wrinkled, her waist scrawny, her thighs rough, her knees hard and swollen. When I uncovered her, was I ever depressed: I immediately took to my heels and did not stop."[3]

A much more serious tone predominates in the debates offered us in the *jeux-partis*. The starting point is often a seemingly frivolous problem upon which are grafted speculations that border on a very skilled application of depth psychology, even sometimes a metaphysics of love. "What makes a lover happier: the hope of sexual bliss or the actual sexual bliss itself?" It is obvious that the hope of sexual bliss is a powerful motivation, which can hold back intense moments of happiness. In any event, it is not so much the goal that matters more in every quest, although it is of interest in the strict sense of the word, but the actions that lead toward this goal. I am sure readers will agree with this if they care to analyze the numerous rebounds occurring in such tales as *The Quest of the Grail* (in any and all of its variations). In the context of the genuine quest of love proposed to any knight seeking membership in the knighthood of love, the lady is thus the goal to be won, but the steps leading to her form the heart of the matter. Furthermore, it should again be emphasized, it is not the individual at work here but the couple. This debate on the relative value of the hope of experiencing sexual bliss compared with the actual experience of sexual bliss goes much further than simple amorous casuistry in that it sheds light upon man himself, who, when confronted by a certain obvious goal such as death, manages to go beyond it thanks to the activity he engages in every moment of his life.

In addition, if sexual bliss may perhaps be dazzling, like a lightning flash or even an "illumination" in the Buddhist sense of the word, it borders too close on the theme of the "brief encounter" not to also prompt speculations of a metaphysical nature. The problem posed here concerns the relationship between the individual and time, considered as an absolute, not as a duration. Did the troubadours who posed this question perceive how it touched upon theological discussion? Perhaps they did, and if this is the case it is no doubt appropriate to bring up the obscure but tenacious Cathar presence that lurks behind all literary manifestations of medieval Occitania. Whatever the case may be, the debate between the hope of sexual bliss and the actual experience of sexual bliss cannot be considered closed by any one single answer, because it inspires many more questions.

This is the proper metaphysical and theological perspective from which to examine certain other subjects of *jeux-partis:* "Who makes better use of his time, the man who pursues a worthy woman with hopes of sexual bliss or the man who loves a fool with whom he actually has sexual relations?" The theme here is clearly a Cathar one. The fool represents the Roman Catholic Church, which, with its paraphernalia of sacraments and ceremonies, offers an immediate sense of security to the faithful, whereas the worthy woman is the Cathar Church, or at least the Cathar faith, which in extremely rough conditions, surrounded by perpetual dangers and torments, allows for the hope of the reascension of the Angel of Light to the heavenly abode. The same is equally true for another popular subject of debate: "Which is preferable, the love of a pitiless woman or the favors of another woman whom you do not love?" The allusion is clear. But the Cathar interpretation is not completely incompatible with understanding on a more primary level, which fits more within the context of amorous casuistry. Let us simply say that the troubadours quite often made use of popular literary themes to transmit a message they could not reveal openly. And it is quite certain that genuine love, whether sentimental or sexual or even mystical, could not content itself with the indulgences that came from a "fool" or from a lady who does not truly love. Neither human nor divine love will permit mediocrity. And in the same way that, for the Cathars, the world will not become again the kingdom of Light until the last human soul has been saved, for the zealots of *fin'amor,* the kingdom of Love will not see daylight until there is no longer even one false lover on the face of the earth.

Speculations of this kind make the phenomenon of courtly love an enthralling subject, and we can now see just how far we have come from the definition of sterile social games that is the widespread opinion of medievalists on this topic.

This desire for purity in love, this thirst for the absolute that characterizes the quest of the inaccessible lady, explains the troubadours' frequent tirades against the faithless, against those who pervert the very meaning of the quest. It inspired the poet Marcabru to unleash some veritable curses: "He who hesitates before doing his utmost seems perverse. . . . Love was once straight, today it is chipped and twisted and is so flawed—listen to me—that where it cannot bite it licks more fiercely than a cat. . . . He who joins with false love traffics with the Devil and has no need of any other switch to beat himself with—listen! He will feel its effects no less than someone who scratches himself so much that he skins himself alive." Sometimes they go so far as to accuse women of being responsible for this betrayal, in misogynist tones one would hardly expect to hear in courtly poetry. "They possess so fine and noble a heart for deception," says the troubadour Peire de Bossinhac, "you cannot find a single one among them who can fool her companion. Then she laughs and scoffs when she witnesses him commit follies. . . . They will make you hate what you cherish most, and love what, in a thousand years, will never bring you joy. He who thinks to find fidelity among women thoroughly deserves reproach. I say personally he will be looking for lard in a dog's kennel." Is this the troubadour taking note of a decline in morals, or just his observation that the code of love has not been applied? The troubadours' view of their society can sometimes be quite pessimistic, witness this text of Peire Cardenal: "Falsity and immoderation have waged war against truth and integrity, and falsity has won. Disloyalty plots against loyalty and greed lays hold of generosity; the traitor prevails over love, perversity over worth, the sinner crushes the just and the false the innocent." It is true that all this is symbolic: the quest of love goes through storms that are necessary for it to face, otherwise its victory will be of no value.

This is why, according to the code, "the lover is always fearful" since "merit alone gives worth to love." He fears the worst because the worst can always happen. "A lover enjoys his mistress; another loves her as much as he and has hopes of enjoying her charms soon. If she were to die, which of these two men would feel the more grief stricken?" This question appears insoluble. "Would the perfect lover desire to follow his lady into the grave or survive her?" If we are to believe the legend of Tristan, it is impossible to survive the death of the one you love. Marie de France said in her *Lai du chèvrefeuille* ("The Lay of the Honeysuckle"): "neither me without you nor you without me." A couple may not be destroyed by death, because death does not yield to the whims of lovers. So we could easily ask the question, a popular subject of the *jeux-partis:* "Is it through the eyes or the heart that love is best upheld?"

All these discussion topics prove that courtly society knew full well that love was a constant battle, one that did not take place without continuous joy and suffering. But would we ever be able to know joy if suffering did not assume the role played by silence in music? Furthermore, who among us is able to declare precisely what the limits of joy and suffering are? The same holds true for love and hate, which may well be two separate faces of one reality: "Is a woman who refuses her favors to her lover and yet forbids him from courting another woman motivated by love or hate?" And again: "Is it better to love the one you hate or to hate the one you love?" There were so many debates with which to spark alarm and uncertainty in people's souls.

The main thing is not to be deceived about the person who is to become the privileged being, he or she with whom the individual will form the ideal couple. Without falling back on vague notions of fate or any other sort of predetermination, the troubadours and the great ladies of the courtly era all insisted it was necessary to make the right choice. Love is not the fruit of chance—from which there came certain cases of a very precise nature, which do indeed smack of the greatest frivolity: "A knight who long made his entreaties in vain to a lady redirects his praises toward another lady who grants him a rendezvous. But the first lady, informed of this, also grants him one for the same time. Which of these should the knight go to?" This indecision is a long way from the philter that was drunk "in error" by Tristan and Iseult, but we should point out that this famous philter actually arranged things very nicely in that it provided a convenient way for the heroes to avoid any conscious choice. At least this is how the medieval text makes it appear.

Oddly enough, the courtly couple is truly defined only within the context of *a trio.* If the lover has the wife of a lord for his mistress, it is the best of all possible situations. If the lover must choose between two ladies, the situation is not identical but it is still possible for the couple to extricate themselves. For these are tests, and tests are necessary in order to make a choice. A famous *jeu-parti* among the troubadours Savaric de Mauléon, Gaucelin Faidit, and Uc de la Bacalaria provides an excellent illustration of the difficulty of making a choice in a test that resembles more a parlor game than a hard-fought battle out in the field. The subject is clearly set out by Savaric de Mauléon: "A lady has three suitors, and she is so tormented by their love that when she finds herself in their presence, she gives the impression of loving each of them. She gives one a loving glance, gently squeezes the hand of the other, and smilingly nudges the foot of the third. Through these actions, tell me, to which of the three is she showing the greatest love?"

The chief characteristic of this kind of debate is that there is never an obviously satisfactory solution, which allows for all manner of discussion and possible interpretation. Gaucelin Faidit, however, did not show a moment's hesitation. For him the lady exhibited the greatest favor toward the one she gazed at so openly, "with no deceit in beautiful eyes that were filled with grace." He accorded no importance to her squeezing of the other suitor's hand, "for it is common for women to perform such gestures out of simple friendliness." As for the nudging of the third suitor's foot, this proved nothing. Uc de la Bacalaria categorically rejected the lady's glance, "because if her eyes were looking at one suitor, they were also looking elsewhere, as that is their sole power. But when that lady gently grasped the hand of her beloved with her own fair, white, and ungloved hand, her love was coming from both her heart and her spirit." Savaric de Mauléon had but one solution and defended the nudging of the foot: "So I say that her playing footsie was a pledge of open friendship, not witnessed by talebearers; and it obviously seems, since the lady had recourse to this expedient of laughingly pressing the foot of her friend, that this lady's love was free of all deceit." Of course none of the troubadours was willing to admit defeat, and each decided to submit his case to a female arbiter.

The arguments of the three troubadours are valid insofar as they take into account the apparent reality of a situation they had not personally experienced. The three of them are at the stage of *playing*. However, the problem they pose is far from boring; in truth it concerns the knowledge necessary to reveal genuine love within a worldly context where every gesture can lend itself to ambiguous interpretations. And through the application of courtly logic, it would seem clear that the man whose foot was brushed by the lady was the one she favored most, for a very simple reason. Courtly love regards discretion as an absolute rule, and of the lady's three gestures the nudging of her lover's foot is the one that remains the most secret. It is the one gesture that concerns solely the lady and the knight who was her definitive choice, a choice made in the most subtle fashion without anyone else's knowledge.

Furthermore, all these gestures can basically be counted as forming an integral part of love. A passage from the Occitan romance *Flamenca* presents an excellent description of the amorous behavior of a lady and her knight when they are joined by this purified yet impulsive passion that constitutes *fin'amor* in the minds of the theoreticians. "She kissed his eyes and face and looked him in the eyes so tenderly that all suffering was driven from his heart; and the Love he saw in her look gave him such rapture he no longer felt any pain in any part of his body. . . . Love's power is so great that it makes two souls live as one. Each submits to the other. This gentle pleasure is so sweet there is no word in our own time that can communicate it perfectly. It is with great difficulty that our comprehension might understand it better, that understanding which is alone in perceiving lots of things that the ear cannot hear and the tongue cannot name."[4]

The essential thing is the fusion of the two individuals, the creation of a new, infernal, ideal couple in which all the phenomena of consciousness come to a halt before the profound reality of sense. This reality is ineffable, inexpressible, also incomparable and incomprehensible for anyone who tries to explain it rationally. A popular Irish saying claims that the eyes of cats are doorways to the Otherworld. The eyes of lovers could well be something quite similar. But only those who are in love have the power to return the *penetrating* gaze.

"When two pure and sincere lovers look each other in the eyes as two equals, they are feeling, to my knowledge and according to genuine love, such joy in their hearts that the gentle feeling that is born there reanimates them and nurtures their entire heart. And the eyes through which this tenderness passes back and forth are so loyal that neither of the two lovers can hold anything back for solely their own benefit." Individual self-centeredness has been surpassed. Joy, which when all is said and done is the ultimate objective, is the metamorphosis of individuals into another, amalgamated entity that has nothing more in common with what people willingly say about procreation. For courtly lovers there is no need to extend love into a third flesh-and-blood being such as a child. In truth children are completely excluded because the courtly relationship is adulterous, or at the very least extramarital, and procreation is the exclusive domain of marriage. To a certain extent courtly love resolves the problem that results from the confusion among sexuality, love, and procreation. The new being created by the merging behavior of the lovers is a spiritual, subtle being who develops outside of all contingencies. And there is neither mother nor father—as this sexual differentiation would presuppose different roles—but two parents of the same nature and absolutely equal.

This is how the power of the gaze is emphasized. It is the first sign of love sought by the lover when he undertakes the quest of his lady. This can even go so far as voyeurism, if we are to believe certain tales of the troubadours' lives, such as the *Vie de Raimbaut de Vaqueiras,* for example, which informs us why the poet gave his lady the *senhal* (or nickname) of Beautiful Knight. "Raimbaut had the good fortune of being able to see Madame Beatrice when he wanted, provided she was in her room. He used to look through the cellar window and no one was any the wiser. One day the marquis, on returning from the hunt, came to her room and placed his sword next to her bed; then he left. Madame Beatrice, who had remained in the room, took off everything but her underclothes. She then took the sword and girded it around her waist like a knight; then she drew it from its scabbard and brandished it in the air. . . . And Raimbaut de Vaqueiras saw everything I just described to you through the cellar window." This concerns only what one individual saw, of course, but how many courtly lovers would not have tried to see their lady in similar fashion? It corresponds to mute worship. Next comes the search for the other's gaze, the other's response, the reward for the lover's faithfulness. Finally comes the merged gaze, the first stage toward the fulfillment of the couple.

The second stage is the kiss. According to the *Flamenca:* "During a kiss the mouth cannot stop from keeping for its own benefit a little of that sweet flavor before it allows anything to make its way to the heart. And the kiss the mouth takes is a guarantee for each of the lovers: it feels the sincere joy that love brings." But this second stage, from the properly courtly perspective, can cause *fin'amor* to deviate. Because those who "can take a kiss whenever they please . . . next turn to removing their ladies' belts." The spiritual union becomes a carnal one, something the author of the *Flamenca* regards as deviance: "He was one of those who could not forget the joy of love that enters through the eyes and not by the embrace nor the kiss." Let us remind ourselves, though, to refrain from considering courtly love as solely spiritual, as placing a barrier between *fin'amor* and vulgar love. It was not that simple. The anonymous author of the *Flamenca* can insist all he wants on the incomparable value of the gaze; he knows full well that the gaze constitutes the first door to be opened. And it is only the first door that is difficult to open: "The kiss is the veritable sign of the perfect Love brought by the eyes, which it uses as a clear, pure, and luminous doorway in which it sees and mirrors itself often as it comes and goes in and out from one heart into the other. And it makes both these hearts so full that each of the lovers thinks they will swoon when the other is absent if one does not see the other immediately in that mirror where their desires bring them to embrace, kiss, caress, and take such subtle joy that they forget all their thoughts and cares as long as their pleasure endures. We have to believe that anyone who doubts even a little that our lovers feel such joy will ever be lucky in love."[5]

All this is presented in the polished language that conforms so well to the refinement of high society at that time. But let us not entertain any illusions here: the troubadours' poems are often filled with word games involving *cors* ("body"), *cor* (*coeur*, or "heart"), and *cor(n)*, ("anus," or "horn" in the obscene sense of the word). Certain poems are constructed in a thoroughly ambiguous fashion on the following theme: "The Lady will bestow her heart *(coeur)* if one blows on her body or ass with his asshole," a theme that is obviously scarcely compatible with the beautiful theories of the code of love, and which risks pulling the rug out from under the purely platonic interpretations of *fin'amor*. None of these obscene poems makes any allusion whatsoever to coitus, which, I repeat, was forbidden within the strict framework of *fin'amor*.[6] The stages here are perfectly established in conformance with courtly code: the gaze, the kiss that causes one to forget oneself, the embrace that could be qualified as "reserved." This is how morality—courtly morality—is preserved.

The forthrightness of some of the troubadours' remarks must not hide from us the reality of their erotic language with double meanings in works considered "serious" or in "good taste." Do not be fooled; the modest and precious description of "love's joy" given us by the author of the *Flamenca* is in fact an astonishingly clinical study of orgasm. And the same could be said of the majority of troubadours when they launch into their ecstatic evocations of their ladies—real or imaginary—in which a moment necessarily arrives when they "score," all in terms that even a prudish author would not disown, and which, curiously enough, are also to be found in the writings of the great mystics, particularly women, such as Saint Theresa of Avila and Catherine Emmerich.

This proves, in any event, the importance taken on by these erotic questions in the eyes of educated people of the courtly era. If we can doubt the widespread occurrence or even the very existence of the courts of love, we can nonetheless remain certain that these questions were widespread and the subject of lively discussion. A lay assumed to be Breton from the beginning of the thirteenth century, the *Lai du lécheur* ("The Lay of the Licker"), shows how even highborn ladies were not loath to look the truth in the face and give it a name. This lay concerns an assembly convened at Saint Pantaléon, somewhere in a fictional Brittany, that consisted of the most beautiful girls and ladies of the land. The custom of this assembly was to compose a lay on a debate topic. One of the most noble of the ladies in attendance suggested a topic close to her heart: what is the reason knights achieve so many feats of prowess? The argumentation is quite adroit:

> What is it that makes knights so daring? What is the reason behind their great love for tourneys? What makes the young men preen? Whose is the love they are so noble for, and so generous of heart? What pushes them to avoid doing ill? What is the purpose of their love for embraces, kisses, and words of love? Is there any other reason if not this one same thing? We can make all the handsome speeches and beautiful phrases we want before replying, but when all is said and done it is always one thing we come back to, the thing we are looking for! This thing is at the origin of great declarations of love, and the reason so many feats of daring are accomplished! Many men have been improved and sought renown and merit, who otherwise would not have been worth the price of a button, were it not for the desire of cunt! On my faith I guarantee that the most beautiful face in the world would not earn a woman a lover or a gallant if she had lost her cunt! Since all these splendid actions are accomplished because of it, let's not seek any farther: the new lay will be composed in its honor and it will please all who hear it.[7]

We can continue, as it was put so perfectly, to beat around the bush all we want; we will always and every time end up in the same place in matters of love or eroticism (the one does not come without the other).

The female sexual organ crystallizes impulses and desires by its mystery, by the fear it can inspire, by the memories of birth or the intrauterine state it prompts, by the symbolic aura developed around it in all traditions including religious traditions. The highborn ladies gathered at Saint Pantaléon were no fools. All they expressed was what all of humanity has felt, even if this humanity most often prefers to bury this disturbing reference in the darkest regions of the subconscious or in the quagmires of the unspoken.

It is to the honor of the authors of the courtly epic that they lifted the veil, even when they did so in refined terms. They sought to show the importance of love, true love (which in French is a feminine word), by restoring to it all of its significance and power. And woe betide anyone who has not worshiped the god of Love!

Another lay, also dating from the thirteenth century and which is not very well known, the *Lai du trot* ("The Lay of the Trot"), provides a clear warning on the subject of love. The story is a simple one: a young knight of King Arthur's court, a certain Lorois, has ventured into the forest and suddenly comes across a group of eighty courtly and beautiful maidens:

> They were extremely well dressed. They wore neither coat nor coif spun from cloth but had their heads covered with crowns of roses and eglantine, putting out a sweet aroma. The weather was mild and they were wearing only tunics. . . . They were all mounted on white horses, which advanced with such gentle steps it was impossible for the rider to tell if they were moving forward. . . . At their sides, mounted on war horses, were their lovers, elegant, charming, and praiseworthy, cheerful and singing with all their hearts. . . . Their pleasure was unblemished, they were all with their lovers! Some were hugging and kissing, others remained locked in each other's arms, still others were talking of love and of prowess. Their lives seemed full of pleasures!

The knight Lorois was still trying to make sense of this sight when another hundred maidens emerged from beneath the forest foliage, which had begun to echo with piteous lamentations. They were mounted on "black pack horses that were thin and worn out. They arrived at a good pace, alone, without the company of any man, and their torment seemed great. . . . Not a one had stirrups, nor did any have any shoes or stockings, their feet were bare. Their feet were all ruined and cracked, and they were clad in black trousers; their legs were bared up to their knees, and their clothing only covered their arms to their elbows in very pitiful fashion. They were plunged in a great distress. Over their heads snow fell and thunder rumbled, the storm was so violent that nobody could bear to cast a single glance, even for a moment, at the great sufferings and pains they were subjected to day and night." The knight also saw a hundred men plunged in the same sufferings, then a single lady "seated on a pack horse whose gait was so painful it caused its teeth to chatter so much they seemed in danger of breaking." The knight, understanding nothing of the spectacle before his very eyes, decided to inquire of the lone woman. She told him a deplorable tale:

> Those preceding me, the ones at the very front, display such joy because each is bringing with her the man she has loved most in life. She may, as she pleases, kiss him, embrace him, and feel him near her. They are those who served Love faithfully during their lives and have borne great love for their beloveds. They have faithfully followed the precepts of love. And this is how love rewards them, by letting them feel naught but happiness. . . . Those who follow behind them, to the contrary, who lament and sigh without cease and are subjected to the painful gait of their horses, who suffer such torment that their faces are pale and discolored, who ride ceaselessly, deprived of the company of a man at their side, are those who have never done anything for love and have never deigned to love. This is how love has caused them to pay dearly for their great presumption and arrogance. Alas! Just as I have paid, being afflicted so sorely for not having loved. For no season will bring us any ease or relaxation, and there is no escape from our endless suffering. We are born under an evil star because we did not

devote ourselves to love! If a lady hears tell of us and listens to the recounting of our misfortunes and if she herself does not love during her own life, she will be obliged to join our company and her repentance will come too late. For, as the peasants say: "he who delays closing his stable door will lose his horse and find it extremely aggrieving"![8]

The moral of this story, clearly inspired by the code of love, is the essential rule of courtly love, that is, the *obligation to love*. But let there be no mistake, it is not just any kind of love. It is not marriage. It is, pure and simple, *adulterous love*, within the infernal couple of *fin'amor*. Outside of this *fin'amor* there is no salvation. Such is the warning posted by this *Lai du trot*.

The Heroes of the Romances

Every intellectual fashion, when it has gained a certain audience, finds illustration in the literary and artistic works of the time. We have already seen that the troubadours' poems, which were in turn quickly picked up and passed on by the trouvères of the north, formed a solid framework for the code of courtly love, even if this code remained rather vague in people's minds and open to frequent discussion, witness the judgments delivered by the courts of love as well as the various *tensons* and *jeux-partis*. But it is especially in the plot of the romance that this amorous behavior was to find its most perfect expression, benefiting from the multiple possibilities of description and analysis provided by that literary form.

In truth, what we call the courtly romances were not created with the intention of illustrating themes then in vogue. The topics presented had been lingering in memory long before anyone thought to formulate precise rules for amorous behavior. The various writers who undertook the composition of courtly romances did so using fictional elements borrowed from numerous sources; they were content to tailor for contemporary tastes plots that owed much more to Greco-Roman culture and the oral folk traditions of western Europe than to their own imaginations.

It has been said that Chrétien de Troyes invented the French romance, or at least was the first romancer worthy of the name to write in the French language. There is some truth to this assertion, if we think in purely literary terms, but the matter becomes much more complicated if we take all his works and place them back in their original context. Then we must note that Chrétien de Troyes is the ideal transcriber of legends belonging to the Celtic tradition of Great Britain and Brittany. His principal merit is that he knew precisely what to make of these legends, how to express them in language appropriate for his twelfth-century milieu, and how to integrate within them all the issues of *fin'amor*.

Truthfully speaking, he was the best placed of all the writers of his time to accomplish this task. We know very little about his life. His name Chrétien (Christian) leads us to think he was a converted Jew and thus heir to the great Hebraic tradition that had been preserved in Troyes. But he was a cleric and perhaps a canon. He was a member of the entourage of Countess Marie de Champagne (in fact her protégé), for whom he wrote *Le Chevalier à la charrette*. By virtue of this he found himself at the very heart of courtliness. It is probable that he also frequented the court of Eleanor of Aquitaine in Poitiers, a crucible that combined various traditions—Occitan, Latin, and Celtic—throughout the entire twelfth century. Chrétien de Troyes offers us a perfect example of the learned cleric formed in the classic monastic schools, which were nevertheless open to the oral Celtic traditions that were beginning, through the channel of Breton and Welsh bards, to invade continental Europe.

He was certainly the first of those "men of letters" who made the Middle Ages such an extraordinary era of culture and research. He may even be considered the first of the "moderns," in that he caused the romance to evolve in a direction this literary genre would never leave again.* In fact, before him what was called the romance—which originally concerned a fictional account written in the Roman language—

---

* *Translator's note:* The French use the word *Roman* for the medieval literary "romance" and also for the "novel," its successor.

barely managed to distinguish itself from the epic. The epic concerns the community rather than the individual, whereas the romance applies more to individuals. In the twelfth century the romance is thus a new and modern genre, a work that no longer owes anything (except its subject) to the oral tradition. The romanesque narrative is based on a precise outline containing events relating to the destiny of an individual. In the traditional epic poem, neither the subject nor the object of the plot (which remained general and typical) existed outside that plot, and experience had no importance.

Henceforth, in the romanesque work, these elements became separated. The subject of the action, these will be the circumstances recounted, infinitely variable, even if they are borrowed from the oral or simply epic tradition. The object will now be a character presented within his daily existence, whom the reader will strive to follow step by step while analyzing his thoughts and feelings. This is why the romancer generally chooses to present his hero—who can be only a noble knight because he is necessarily a model—in the heart of a courtly world, in the situation that is the most appropriate to bring out the value of all his aspects, in other words, the "quest of love." And, of course, facing the hero will be the lady, the supreme goal who motivates his behavior, which will lead to the supreme importance of the woman in all the so-called courtly romances.

Chrétien de Troyes wrote a lot, but a portion of his work was lost, namely a tale concerning the legend of Tristan and Iseult. Enough remains, however, for us to appreciate his talents and to think that the Champenois romancer belongs, by literary right, to that knighthood of love they were endeavoring to create on the marginal boundaries of aristocratic society. He also composed several adaptations of Ovid's *Art of Love*, which gives a definite clue to his central interests. Drawing liberally from classical memories and a foundation of Celtic tales, he wrote a series of Arthurian romances that are particularly precious because they provide an excellent view of how the twelfth century interpreted a mythology that was not Greco-Roman and that had nothing at all to do with Christianity. What is more, Chrétien de Troyes, taking to heart the courtly problematic, devotes himself to a study chock-full of manifestations of amorous feeling, which allows us to understand a little better the thinking that presided over the courts of love.

It is surprising, however, to observe that all of Chrétien's romances except one *(Le Chevalier à la charrette)* sing the glories of conjugal love, apparently in contradiction to the courtly theory then in vogue, which claimed that true love could exist only outside the confines of marriage. This even constitutes a sort of taking sides, on the part of the Champenois romance writer, as if he sought to find a solution between courtly adultery and Christian marriage, not of compromise but of synthesis, thus restoring to marriage an affective nature by ridding it of its sociological weight.

The story of *Erec et Enide* starts with a marriage. The knight Erec, who in the initiatory hunt for the White Stag has proved he is the most valiant knight, marries the beautiful Enide. But she is poor, from a family of minor nobility, and this does not conform with the rule that knights must love ladies of higher station. It does not matter in the least, for if Enide prevails over all others, it is by her beauty and virtue. Chrétien seems to be trying to prove that high social rank is not enough to merit "nobility." In any event, it is not Erec and Enide's wedding that interests us here but what follows after.

In fact, once married, Erec finds the company of his wife such a joy that he forgets his obligations as a knight. He no longer participates in the tourneys or the masculine activities of the court, to such an extent that his fellows start whispering he is a *recréant,* that is to say, someone who neglects feats of prowess for acts of love. The chivalrous ideal intends for love and prowess to be linked intimately and interdependently. These whispers reach Enide's ears. They affect her terribly: has she married a man unworthy of her, a man who prefers the soft life and easy living to creative activity? A woman, just as much as a man, can sink by loving someone of lower quality. Enide skillfully arranges for Erec to find out what the rumors are saying about him and, without seeming to do so, provokes him.[9] We do not have long to wait for Erec's reaction: he drags his wife along into a series of chivalrous and marvelous adventures in which he acquits himself with honor, but *with the help of Enide,* who is now even more omnipresent as "lady" and "mistress." In all, it matters little that Erec and Enide are married. The essential thing is that man can transcend himself thanks to woman—and woman thanks to man—in the perfect fusion exemplified by the courtly couple: prowess and love are tied together, and the theory of *fin'amor,* although not respected on the level of the situation (marital, not extramarital), is nonetheless respected on the level of social behavior. The artistry of Chrétien de Troyes is that he passed on this message by using both a traditional framework and the essential structures of *fin'amor.*

In his second romance, *Cligès,* the situation is quite different. First of all, the subject is not Celtic, and the Arthurian framework is merely a simple decor provided by circumstance. Next, there are two adventures recounted in one story. Finally, the respect shown toward sacrosanct Christian marriage pushes the very limits of what is tolerable. The story concerns a certain Alexander, son of the emperor of Constantinople, who has covered himself with glory among King Arthur's knights and who has married Queen Guinivere's maid of honor. During his absence Alis, Alexander's younger brother, has usurped his power. Alexander leaves him the throne on condition that he does not marry and that he take as heir Alexander's own son Cligès. But Alis breaks his word and marries the beautiful Fénice, of whom Chrétien gives us an enthusiastic description. She is truly the courtly heroine in all her splendor. And as the young Cligès is also the perfect model of the courtly, handsome, sensitive, and intelligent knight, the inevitable happens: a great love unites the two young people. The problem is that Fénice refuses to play the role of Iseult to Cligès's Tristan: "Better to be dismembered than for Iseult and Tristan's love to be remembered because of the two of us." The upshot is a situation in the style of *fin'amor:* the two lovers love each other, but their love is only spiritual.

The same situation can already be found in a work that is generally classified as a chanson de geste, but which is of a different nature— *Girart de Roussillon,* dating from around 1150. Here we see the beautiful Elissent, daughter of the emperor of Constantinople and wife of

Charles the king of France, who is in love with Girart, to whom she had been promised before. Not wishing to transgress the prohibition weighing on her and on Girart, Elissent takes the initiative of joining with him in a solemn ceremony: she swears before God and several witnesses to a sort of amorous friendship with Girart de Roussillon, which by its very nature can not cause alarm either to her husband, King Charles, or to Girart's wife, who is also present. "Thus their love will endure forever, pure of all evil thought, and with nothing more between them than good intentions and a secret understanding." René Nelli, who has closely studied this kind of *affrèrement,* writes in this regard that Elissent "believes in good faith that her feelings for Girart are of the same nature (but deeper) than those she feels for her father or for her husband. It is because she does not know how to define—other than in terms of kinship or of friendship—carnal love cut away from its carnal foundations." But, René Nelli adds, "contrary to the view sometimes put forth, it is absolutely impossible to assimilate this erotic *affrèrement* to the courtly ceremony of engagement (which, however, derives from it). The lover here does not become his lady's subordinate, like a vassal to his suzerain. It would be almost the contrary. . . . If Girart responds to this 'love,' it is done freely and in the strictest equality. On the other hand, there is not a trace here of the carnal preoccupations that act as the trigger for courtly love, even in its purified form."[10] Elissent's situation quickly becomes intolerable, however.

Let us go back to Cligès. Since marriage is a sacred thing, it is not a appropriate to openly scorn it. But there are always accommodations that can be made with Heaven. Thanks to the ruses of Fénice's lady-in-waiting Thessala, who is a skilled magician, Fénice will drink a drug that will make her appear dead. Thus, once her name is somehow struck from the civil registers, she can give her love freely to Cligès. So Fénice lies buried. Everything would be going just fine and in the purest hypocrisy. But luckily, the husband has the excellent idea of dying: Fénice can then marry Cligès, who ascends the throne of his ancestors. All's well that ends well, and most important, Christian morality is spared.

It has been said more than once that *Cligès* was an "anti-Tristan." This is not certain. It is no fault of the lovers that the situation unfolds so favorably for them, and Fénice's ruse corresponds purely and simply to adultery before God, if not before society. One has the overall impression that Chrétien de Troyes, not lacking a sense of humor, had quite a good time writing this romance. And in doing so he had the merit of again throwing out all possible questions on courtly love. In this way he followed the wishes of his patron Marie de Champagne.

In his *Chevalier au lion* ("The Knight of the Lion"), Chrétien once more poses the problem of the couple, but this work concerns the conjugal couple again. Here the outline is purely Celtic, with connotations that have nothing in common with courtly customs.[11]

Chrétien makes brilliant use of this inheritance in order to study the amorous psychology of his heroes. The starting point is the magic fountain of Barenton in the Forest of Brocéliande.[12] This is the "Fountain That Makes It Rain," a folkloric element that masks an older reality—the tradition of a sanctuary in the heart of the forest, the Gallic *nemeton*, the ideal site where heaven and earth meet. In this instance the clearing of Barenton (formerly Belenton, and still visible today) is a sanctuary dedicated to the god of light: Belenos, "Brilliant or Shining One." One custom maintains that whosoever draws water from this fountain and sprinkles it over the steps surmounting it will unleash a storm that would devastate the entire countryside. A knight, Yvain, the son of King Uryen, one of King Arthur's regular companions (but also a historical figure of the British in the northern British Isles), is trying out the experiment with the fountain. A black knight, who in Chrétien de Troyes's story has the name Esclados le Roux (Esclados the Redhead), comes to chastise the audacious young man and provokes him into fighting. Provoked by Esclados le Roux, Yvain fights him and wounds him mortally. Yvain pursues Esclados to his fortress, where Yvain manages to get himself out of trouble with the complicity of the lady's maid Luned, a mysterious individual who is certainly a fairy. Having fallen in love with Esclados's widow, the beautiful Laudine, Yvain wins her hand in marriage and himself becomes guardian of the fountain. But King Arthur and his knights appear on the scene and, after receiving a cordial welcome from Yvain, they take him along with them into a series of new adventures, tourneys, and various courtly games. Yvain has been granted a leave of one year by Lady Laudine, which she bestowed with no problem. But caught up in his knightly activities, he completely forgets the time limit imposed upon him and a messenger from Laudine arrives to shame him before all of Arthur's knights.

We see that the matter of *recréance* has appeared again as a necessary topic of discussion. As a knight, Yvain cannot refuse to accomplish feats of prowess whose glory falls as much upon his lady as upon himself. But in disobeying his lady Yvain has deliberately made himself an outlaw, having broken his word to his mistress (in the full sense of the word), who is also his legitimate wife. Laudine, the Lady of the Fountain, is in fact the most perfect image of the lady of courtly love, and it is not the least of Chrétien de Troyes's merits that he succeeded in making her Yvain's wife. For all this, the courtly scheme of things is not undermined: the knight always returns to his lady because she represents—whether she is wife or lover—the perfection to which he must attach himself or risk demeaning himself and being considered disloyal.

So here we have Yvain rejected and shamed by his lady. He roams the forest like a madman or, rather, like a wild beast. He saves a lion from a snake, a symbolic combat if ever there was one, and befriends the lion, an animal of exemplary fidelity. He accomplishes numerous feats, even managing to save the lady's maid Luned from an impossible situation. And in the end it is she who sets things right. She tells Yvain to lurk near the fountain every evening and sprinkle water over the steps. The storms brewed by this action ravage Laudine's domains. It is then an easy matter for Luned to reveal to Laudine that the only man who can pull her out of this trouble is the mysterious Knight of the Lion. But, Luned adds, it is all to no good if Laudine does not undertake to reconcile this knight with his lady. Caught in the trap, Laudine can do nothing but accept this solution, and when she sees that Yvain is the knight in question it is too late, she cannot go back on her word. So we now have Laudine and Yvain reconciled and once more forming the ideal couple.

Certainly, as in *Cligès,* Chrétien de Troyes must have enjoyed himself immensely recounting the adventures of these lovers—and married couple—who could find their balance only via the trial. This was already the meaning of his story *Erec et Enide:* it is not enough to be married to form an ideal couple; it is necessary that both members of this couple display uncommon qualities. If not, what is the point of talking about them? The couple formed by Yvain and Laudine is, in the beginning, a legitimate couple in the eyes of the law and Christian morality but not in the view of the code of courtly love. All the adventures Yvain is subjected to in the second part of the romance are therefore necessary, proving that he genuinely belongs to the famous knighthood of love, outside of which it is impossible to be a hero. Chrétien de Troyes's opinion thus rests on the spirit of the courtly code, even if circumstances make his heroes a married couple. Moreover, it is actually stated in the rules of love that two married individuals can maintain a passionate amorous liaison: the sole condition being that this liaison is a matter of free consent for both of them and in no case liable to marital obligation. Hence the momentary discord between Yvain and Laudine, a kind of temporary divorce, that serves as a test. Laudine can no longer refuse to reconcile with Yvain because he has satisfied the essential obligations of the courtly lover. And it is as a lover and not as a wife that she reintegrates him into the ideal—and infernal—couple she forms with him.

Chrétien de Troyes's dialectic is subtle because it seems that Christian morality, and consequently social morality, which is identical, is respected. There is none of that adultery to shock the decent people of society, even if everyone knows it is not complete adultery. There is, on the other hand, the exaltation of a total union, a merger between two beings who have sought one another for a long time and who rediscover each other at the end of a long series of complicated trials for the greater good of love and prowess. It is still in this sense that the courtly couple may be defined as the infernal couple: it escapes from contemporary classifications and presents itself as utterly marginal with respect to the customs of the time. We can indeed imagine the bizarre structure of the couple formed by Yvain and Laudine: born from the necessity of ensuring the protection of the Lady of the Fountain's domains, the couple is reconstituted at the end of the adventures by this same necessity. And this necessity appears to justify the love that in fact unites the knight to his lady. For how can we explain Yvain's relentless determination to achieve his feats of prowess other than by the love he bears for Laudine? How else can we explain Yvain's madness and breakdown when he learns his lady has rejected him? How to explain Laudine's patience and final indulgence if not by her very deep love for this man, although he is so undisciplined, the man who mocked her commands, who did not return at the time she set?

So would this prove that a masculine revolt has surfaced within the framework of courtly love in answer to the tyranny of the lady? This has been the claim. It has also been claimed that Chrétien de Troyes laid it out this way for Marie de Champagne, who had obliged him to write *Le Chevalier à la charrette,* the perfect illustration of the lover who submits entirely to the will of his beloved.

For it is *Le Chevalier à la charrette* that most clearly displays the code of love, following its discussion and analysis by the great ladies of the era, of whom Marie de Champagne, like her mother, Eleanor of Aquitaine, was one of the most central intellectual figures. On his entrance into the game, Chrétien de Troyes clearly announced his intentions and duties: "Since the will of my lady of Champagne is for me to undertake a story in French, I will place great heart into the task, as one so entirely devoted to her in all he writes in this world without any intention of flattery." He also freely admits where the subject of the story comes from: "The countess has generally presented him with the material and the main idea, and he shapes it in his fashion, adding little but his work and application."[13] This shows that Chrétien did not consider himself the author of the book but simply the transcriber of a subject that had been imposed upon him.

Chrétien de Troyes is, however, the one responsible for the introduction of Lancelot of the Lake into the Arthurian legend. Originally the tradition of Lancelot appears foreign to Great Britain, land of King Arthur, and must be sought in Armorican Brittany, particularly the land of Vannes.[14] Lancelot of the Lake is "already mentioned in *Erec and Enide* as the hero of an Anglo-Norman poem known only in a translation in middle high German as *Lanzelet*, but most probably earlier than *Le Chevalier à la charrette*, and in any case independent of it, . . . and belonged to Breton subject matter before Chrétien write his first Brittany romance."[15] In any case, one thing is certain: Chrétien was the first to make Lancelot the lover of Queen Guinivere. Jean Frappier adds:

> We can easily guess the essential transformations he had to make to the original plot, partly on Countess Marie's instigation. To Arthur's detriment,[16] he makes Lancelot the liberator of the queen, thereby illustrating the doctrine of courtly love and the *fin'amor* sung of by the troubadours. The knight-lover prevails over all others in prowess and valor because he is guided by love, the infallible deity and ennobling virtue, and he submits obediently and joyfully to every desire and whim of the desired and adored lady. It is in this concept that the sense or spirit of the romance resides. It leads to a new religion of love, with its duties, tests, mystical enthusiasms, graces, ecstasies, and rewards outside the rules of social law and ordinary morality, even above chivalrous honor, as is so wonderfully demonstrated by the symbol of the hangman's cart.[17]

The subject of the romance is borrowed from Celtic mythology. The queen, symbol of the community, is carried off by a god from the Otherworld, in this instance Meleagant (whom the Welsh texts call Maelwas). In the name of the king and the community, a hero will undertake perilous adventures, also borrowed from Celtic mythology, to free the queen and bring her back. On this traditional outline Chrétien de Troyes has traced the courtly quest of the lady by infusing in each event a particular resonance that conforms in every way to *fin'amor*.

Guinivere is thus kidnapped by Meleagant, who is the anticourtly lover: he does not wait for the woman to respond to his love; he makes the first move and uses violence. This is something that cannot be tolerated in courtly society. The seneschal Kay, the expression of this society, attempts to free the queen but is vanquished, wounded, and held prisoner. One may ask why King Arthur did not become involved. But the Celtic kind of king does not take action because, on one hand, he is content just to be present in order to ensure the balance of the social group and, on the other hand, he is the husband, so he does not count from the particular viewpoint of courtly love. It is thus Gawain, the king's nephew and presumptive heir, who sets off in quest of the queen in the name of the social group for which he is the most faithful representative. As for Lancelot, it is on his own behalf that he sets off on this adventure, because he is the lover—it so happens that the lover is always jealous, and in this instance he is jealous of Meleagant. Therefore he must wrest Guinivere away from Meleagant, who is a potential lover, and neutralize him. But, let me repeat, Lancelot—who is the image of the multi-roled Celtic god Lug given the qualities of a hero—does not belong to the Arthurian community; he is only allied to it and thus retains all his autonomy, a privileged situation for one who is the queen's lover. This detail therefore allowed Chrétien de Troyes to charge this individual with a delicate and exemplary mission, that of becoming *the one* priest-knight of the cult of the lady.

Not just anyone who wishes to can become a priest-knight. Formerly, when a priest said the standard mass he began by kneeling at the foot of the altar before climbing the stairs leading to the tabernacle. A posture of humiliation is necessary before arriving at a victory. The same is true for Lancelot, who will be confronted with the most serious kind of humiliation: to be taken for the basest of criminals.

This occurs in the famous episode of the hangman's cart. Lancelot is on foot, he has lost his horse, and he does not know which direction to take to pick up Meleagant's trail again. He sees a cart driven by a dwarf, but it is not just any cart: "Like the pillories, this single cart was shared by felons, murderers, those found guilty in trials by combat, thieves who made off with the goods of others by ruse or force in the woods. The criminal caught in the act was placed in the cart and led up one street and down the next. Every last shred of dignity was stripped from him. From then on all courts refused to listen to him. Gone are all signs of honor and welcome! This was the sinister significance of those carts in those times."

Lancelot asks the dwarf if he knows anything concerning the queen and her abductor. The dwarf, in diabolical fashion, answers him: "If you would climb into the cart, before tomorrow dawns you will know what has become of the queen." This puts Lancelot in a perplexing situation: "Woe on him that he hesitates, woe on him that shame keeps him from leaping immediately into the cart. What a punishment he will undergo, far too cruel for his liking! But Reason, at odds with Love, urges him to refrain from taking such a leap and lectures him and instructs him to undertake nothing that will attach opprobrium to his name. Reason has no home but on his lips and takes great risk in speaking to him in such a way. Love is in the enclosed heart, it gives an urgent order. He must climb into the cart with all haste. Love wishes it, the knight leaps in. What does shame matter to him, since this is love's command?"[18] This is the essential phrase: for the love of his lady all must be overcome, with no restrictions whatsoever. Lancelot's hesitation, as we know, will earn him the queen's harsh reproaches, but stifling his shame the knight consents to disgracing himself. So he finds himself in the cart, dragged through towns and villages, generously heckled and jeered at. During this time Gawain, who refused to climb into the cart, is content to follow on his horse:

> In other words, and Gawain is incapable of understanding this, the knight has wished on himself the tragic fate of his degradation; his adventures have led him precisely to this place, the source of all reasons to hate his life, to be at war with himself, to commit insane acts. Because his infamy gives him access to the impossible aspect of his bliss. But if he has chosen this path, what is the cost so that he can stand it, without succumbing to his temptation? The shame appears profoundly ambivalent because Lancelot has chosen it just as much as he has been subjected to it: if it arranges for desire to be transgressed, it no less maintains the hero in retirement with respect to himself. Ecstasy or irony. Without the shame, Lancelot would not have experienced the first nor played with the second. The lover's immoderation is equaled only by the perfect moderation of the knight.[19]

All the necessary conditions for amorous desire to exert itself in its largest dimension are brought together: the absence of the beloved lady, the danger represented by the rival Meleagant, the atrocious jealousy that grips Lancelot, the materially impossible situation he finds himself in with no horse to take him to his lady. The debasement and shame he accepts, not without a certain inner debate, and finally finds the courage necessary to confront a jeering crowd, the renunciation of his rank of knight: he undertakes all this rather than lose Guinivere. The lover here is more submissive to the lady than ever, or at least to the image he has of her. But after all, Guinivere's reality is quite fragile: would she exist outside of Lancelot? It is here the question of the couple comes up again. And we quickly come to realize that the man and the woman have no real existence apart from each other: the man exists only with regard to the woman he loves, and of course the woman exists only to the extent that she is desired and loved by the man. Lancelot, in the cart of disgrace, is on the point of losing his individuality and his honor as a knight in order to become one of the components of a couple. We understand now that this breakdown was necessary: it was indispensable in order to obtain the emptiness that will inevitably prompt the appearance of the new being, the couple.

Therefore the cart represents a significant test, as will also the crossing of the Bridge of the Sword later. To enter the city of Gorre, that strange Otherworld "from which none may return" and where Meleagant holds Guinivere prisoner, one must cross a dangerous turbulent river by one of two ways, a bridge underwater or a bridge above the water that consists of a gigantic sharp sword placed between the two banks. Whereas Gawain chooses the bridge underwater because it seems more reassuring, Lancelot chooses the Bridge of the Sword, the way that is more dangerous, more rapid, more direct, which conforms perfectly with his loving ardor. And he is wounded atrociously. This is where the symbol of love's wounding appears; it must be bloody because it puts the entire individual at stake, body and soul. Moreover, we should recall that the crossing of the Bridge of the Sword actually does not cause a new wound. This wound has already been in existence a long time, ever since the queen first set eyes on Lancelot. The theme of eyes that mortally wound the lover—like the rays of the sun, which can also be murderous—is well known by all the troubadours, but the baroque poets of the sixteenth century were particularly skilled in its use and in outfitting it for contemporary tastes. In any case, Lancelot can reach Guinivere only as one who has been shamed and wounded. He has to strip himself of everything and in some way become virginal again: Her Ladyship the Queen demands it. This is the price he has to pay in order to enter the paradisiacal orchard where the goddess waits with the greatest impatience for the lover who will be her equal. And in this respect the Bridge of the Sword is just as cruel as the climb into the cart:

> What strange and wonderful behavior: he takes off the armor covering his hands and feet. He will not reach the end of this test unmarked and unscathed. But upon this sword sharper than any scythe, he will firmly anchor himself on his bare hands and feet, because he has kept on neither toecaps, boots, nor leggings. He can spare scarcely a thought for the injuries this will cause his hands and feet. Better to maim himself than to fall from the bridge and take an unintended bath in water from which he would never escape. Through the suffering prepared for him, he manages this dreadful crossing. Blood pours from his hands, his feet, his knees. But Love is his guide and it gives him balm and healing. For this reason he finds his martyrdom sweet.[20]

So now it is in his flesh that the lover is suffering. He is ready to accomplish the final action, that is, to present himself before the lady to whom he has provided proofs of his love: he has gone all the way both physically and morally.

At least this is what should have happened. But the object of his devotion is forbidden as long as the abductor—the rival—holds her in a prison, which bears a strong resemblance to the lower depths of the unconscious. Lancelot still has to fight Meleagant and vanquish him.

Meleagant's father, the good king Bademagu (another mythological fig-ure, one with features in common with the Saturn of Rome's golden age), intervenes in his capacity as one who maintains the equilibrium of the world and halts the fight, obliging Meleagant to return Guinivere. After which Bademagu leads the victorious lover into the presence of the queen; he is convinced he is about to receive his just reward.

He receives nothing of the sort. The queen, in superb fashion, turns her back on him and ignores the presence of the man who has under-gone so much to free her. So what is this all about? Guinivere says noth-ing. Bademagu finds her attitude utterly incomprehensible. Lancelot has a confused idea that he may not have been the perfect lover but does not know what he did—or did not do—to earn the queen's displeasure. He sinks into despair. Guinivere's image haunts him, and the longer and more pronounced the queen's absence becomes, the greater grows his desire for her. This is the law of love. As the code of love says: "An easy conquest strips love of its charm; a difficult conquest enhances its value." But this same code adds: "The lover can refuse his lover nothing." Clearly, Lancelot must have denied Guinivere something. But what? This is something we will learn later.

In the meantime, through the play of circumstances (something Chrétien de Troyes arranges so well, allowing him to shuttle the plot back and forth through numerous twists and turns), Lancelot ends up presumed dead whereupon Guinivere sinks into despair. She realizes she has acted unjustly toward him. In truth, she even feels responsible for his death. "I believe that none but myself could have inflicted the mortal wound. . . . Yes, my refusal to speak even a word to him ripped out his life together with his heart in the space of a moment. . . . Alas, how I would now find salvation from despair if I had just held him in my arms but once before he died. How? Ah, yes, I would be naked against his nakedness, so I might know greater happiness."[21]

If our understanding is correct, Guinivere's reaction is best explained because everything that has happened up to this point has been per-fectly futile. Lancelot's long quest for Guinivere's love, a painful quest if ever there was one, has served no purpose for it was not crowned by the intimate union of two individuals. This is Guinivere's recognition of a stalemate, but a stalemate that concerns her just as much as it does Lancelot. Hence her other question also conforms to the code of love: "Now that he is no more, only cowardice prevents me from flying into the arms of death." Should one, in fact, survive the death of the person one loves? Guinivere, tortured by doubt, arrives at the most logical solution. "The beloved who prefers death to enduring pain for her lover is of little worth. It is my whole wish to suffer the weight of my grief for a long time. It is better to live and suffer the harshness of fate than die and find eternal rest." The heaviness of their guilt weighs constantly on the infernal couple formed by Lancelot and Guinivere. This guilt exists as part of the very nature of the couple, because the couple is adulterous, but it is further reinforced by the fact that a sin committed by one lover is reflected on the other. Guinivere, feeling guilty of Lancelot's death, must expiate it, and to do that she must survive him. This is one possible answer to the rational system of *fin'amor*—but it will be noted that in a similar situation, with evidence to back it up, Iseult did not hesitate a single second to join again with Tristan in death. The debate that rouses Guinivere does not trouble Iseult, nor does the idea of culpability. This is to say that the couple formed by Lancelot and Guinivere has not yet reached its final phase, where, fusion having been attained, only death can satisfy a desire that no longer can be made manifest.

It would be a good idea at this point in the discussion to make a slight digression concerning the desire that motivates lovers. This desire can be carnal as well as intellectual and spiritual. For Guinivere, being naked next to her lover simply means the complete merging of two individuals into one. If we see any sexual allusions here, it is because we are looking at it from the dichotomic angle toward which the Roman Catholic Church has steered us by integrating the work of the flesh into a context of procreation or, in the final analysis, the idea of guilt. Any work of the flesh that is not followed by procreation is an insult to the divine work, thus a sin. But Guinivere is not discussing sin. She is talking about realization. And if she has doubts, it is because she is convinced that neither she nor Lancelot has gone all the way to the end of their desire. So something is lacking. Or, rather, there is a feeling of frustration: what good has been served by their mutual extended wanderings, which have ended in unlived experience?

In any case, this proves that Guinivere's and Lancelot's love has not attained the point of no return indicated by the very strange and beautiful Japanese film directed by Nagisha Oshima, *In the Realm of the Senses*, in which—on a purely sensual level—the upsurge of desire leads to death. This, on a different scale, is the conclusion called for in the story of Tristan and Iseult, even though during the course of the story no emphasis is placed on the sexual component of their relationship. In the case of Lancelot and Guinivere, the author just tells us their relationship has not yet reached the point of no return that demands death, hence Guinivere's questions and her final decision to live on, allegedly to expiate her sins but in reality because she still nurtures a wild hope that Lancelot is still alive.

And he actually is still alive, and he too is asking questions. The public rumor mill, definitely quite prolix, leads him to believe that his lady is dead. Despair and doubt seize hold of him and he prepares to commit suicide. Life no longer has any meaning. He is surrounded by emptiness, not that vacuum ready to be filled that he felt while crossing the Bridge of the Sword, because at that time by stripping himself of his armor and his shoes he was making himself available to receive the gift of Guinivere. What he feels now is no longer emptiness in the metaphysical and even Buddhist sense of the word, but a void, absolute nothingness. There are no expectations left.

Of course everything works out in the end. His companions rescue him from death. Has he merely been spared for the slow death he now sees before him? Fortunately the famous public rumor mill rectifies its errors. Lancelot learns that Guinivere is alive and well. Guinivere learns that Lancelot is still in this world. And Bademagu, bearing a yet closer resemblance to the good Saturn, king of the golden age, has not stopped in his efforts to reunite the lovers and effect their reconciliation.

What is more, they have no need for reconciliation in that the trial they have been through suffices to dissipate all doubts and false inter-pretations. Lancelot, however, needs to know why Guinivere showed such indifference toward him. He asks the queen, and she responds with a frankness that reveals as much naiveté as it does a firm belief in true love: "Have you forgotten how the cart caused you shame and great fear? You climbed into it with too much regret, did it not cause you a hesita-tion of two steps? This is the truthful reason I wished neither to speak with you or even look at you."

This could not conform any more closely with the rules of the code of love. It is clearly tinged with what now would be called sadism. Consequently, it is necessary to speak of the masochism shown by Lancelot—who, according to certain critics, tolerates absurdities here worthy of an age of obscurantism. This seemingly insignificant detail has been treated with derision, which also denounces the stupidity of a doctrine making submission to women an absolute rule verging on the irrational. This "hesitation of two steps" seems ridiculous and at first glance will give Guinivere the appearance of a cruel, vain woman—for having dared reproach for such a small fault someone who, despite all the dangers, saved her from a grim fate. This "hesitation of two steps" (that is, Lancelot's hesitation) is a primordial element, though, and it can lend itself to numerous observations for those few who care enough to really consider it in its natural context.

In Lancelot's interior debate, transcribed for us by Chrétien and prompted by the invitation to climb into the cart, reason wars with love. The use of allegories that will later be the joy of the authors of the *Roman de la Rose* should not conceal the reality of what is passing through Lancelot's mind. As a knight, climbing into the cart and shaming him-self is not only an act of individual consequence. It involves the entire knighthood to which he belongs; any shame that befalls him will fall on the entire group as well. Does he have the right to betray the group? On the other hand, Lancelot knows that if he does not climb into the cart, he risks losing the queen forever. The situation is somewhat Cornelian.*

---

* *Translator's note:* This adjective is derived from the name of the French playwright Corneille and usually signifies a conflict between love and duty.

Chrétien de Troyes makes sure to specify, however, that reason remains confined to the lips, that is, within the domain of words and speech alone. In contrast, love finds itself "enclosed" within the heart, in a more secret fashion that escapes all rational language but prompts and drives actions. And it is love that prevails, that is to say, nonreflection. There is a pedagogical intent behind all this: love—true love—is such a perfect state and represents such a surpassing of the self that reason no longer has any business there. We have reached the realm of pure emotion and pure sensibility. And it behooves us to note, as did Guinivere, that Lancelot had not reached completely this perfect state and surpassing of the self that is the equivalent of the total fusion of bodies and souls. Certainly this state is not too far away. All it will take is two steps. But in Guinivere's eyes, as in those of any impartial observer, Lancelot has not yet reached the level necessary for the antinomies to be perceived as noncontradictory. If he truly loved, he would not have debated the matter and thus would not have hesitated. Guinivere, strictly applying the law of love, cannot help but note the remaining discrepancy, hence her gesture of scorn and indifference toward him. She requires a perfect lover and will wait until that perfection is achieved.

Lancelot is more than willing to recognize his shortcoming. He knows that if the same circumstances were to present themselves again, he would not make the same mistake. The queen knows it, too; it has served him as a lesson. Guinivere can henceforth be generous and forgiving. It is also one of the rules of the code of love to be altruistic and to know how to show love to others. Forgiveness is a form of love. It is as if Lancelot were to be absolved by a court of penitence and the priestess of that court was Guinivere. What is more, he can now claim his promised reward.

What is this reward? In courtly terms it could be anything from a glance to carnal union. What Lancelot desires is to go all the way to the end. We do not know if the two lovers had gone all the way before this point, Chrétien does not tell us. It would even be in keeping with the logic of the situation that they had not reached that point until this moment, and that the saving feats of prowess achieved by Lancelot would thereby take on their full initiatory value. Moreover, the climb into the cart and the crossing of the Bridge of the Sword (like the different misadventures of Lancelot with the damsels who offered themselves to him)[22] have obvious sexual connotations that prepare the access to the ultimate stage. The queen knows full well what Lancelot desires, all the more as she desires the same thing. But an equally absolute rule of the code of love insists that *fin'amor* be realized in the greatest secrecy, protected from the jealous and the rumormongers. Never mind. Guinivere will instigate a ruse and, in so doing, will oblige Lancelot to pass through an additional test, as if she still seeks to avenge herself for his two-step hesitation, simply to have her lover make up for this delay.

The queen is in a room in Bademagu's palace, guarded by Meleagant and his men. What is more, the wounded Kay is stretched out on a bed in the same room. This chamber is thus prohibited. At least until . . . "Come speak with me at my window this evening when everyone else is sleeping. You must make your way here through the orchard. You will not be able to enter this home as if you were a guest invited for the night. You will not succeed if you try to get in. Nor will I be able to approach you, except through the words I speak or the touch of my hands." Their program is therefore fairly limited, but Lancelot refrains from voicing any complaint as he is overjoyed to have this chance to be in the queen's company at all.

So here is Lancelot, redeemed and radiant, flooded with the solar light that emanates from a beloved woman, making his way through the *orchard* and arriving at the *chamber*. These are the two sanctuaries of courtly love, and the troubadours never broke their promise of exploiting all their poetic possibilities. But as he draws near the chamber, the grille that seals the window reminds him that his place is not yet inside. Furthermore, it would hardly be a matter of triumph for a lover of his stature to find a window or a door deliberately left open. The ritual game unfolding requires certain complications: "The woman who has offered herself sexually to his desire has suddenly become, without his being able to tear his eyes away, a terrifying object. He is constrained to pursue the matter further when his quest is struck with impossibility. . . .

If the way appears clear to a lover, he has no choice but to invent an even more absolute interdiction. . . . On the very threshold of his satisfaction, events play out as if the lack itself were missing and he must, at all costs, restore it. He creates his own torture personally if the other forgets to be cruel. Such are the deepest truths attained in *fin'amor.*" As for the greatly desired woman, "she must be beyond grasp in order for the unforeseeable night to arrive that will finally deliver her into his arms. If she had sensed this and made herself his everything before he had even possessed her, all the eroticism of the troubadours would have been pointless and the cover of a complicit darkness would never have enveloped the queen's disturbing and wonderfully white shirt."[23]

"The queen appeared wearing a white shirt. . . . When Lancelot saw that the queen was resting her head near his upon the thick iron bars of her window, he spoke a tender greeting that she returned immediately, for they were impelled by the same desire, he toward her and she toward him."[24] This desire becomes imperious. The fused point of no return has been attained. Lancelot has passed the final test before reaching his objective. With an incredible show of strength, he manages to twist out the iron bars that seal her window. In so doing he wounds himself dreadfully, repeating the ritual gestures performed on the Bridge of the Sword. He is bleeding from countless cuts but does not even notice: "Iron bars cause only the blood of adultery to flow."[25] He has now managed to gain entrance into the chamber, the second and ultimate sanctuary of *fin'amor,* the most provocative image in the poet's arsenal, the perfect knot around which all fantasies are coiled. As the troubadour Arnaut Daniel sings: "When I am reminded of the chamber where I know, and this pains me, no one enters . . . there is not a part of my body that does not tremble, not even my nail, as the child shivers before the switch, so fearful am I that I will not possess her soul! May she receive me with her body and not her soul secretly in her chamber!"[26]

Lancelot is well aware that for all intents and purposes he is within a sanctuary. No matter how deeply he feels his desire, he respects the ritual: "He bowed before her and worshiped her, for he believed more in her than in the relics of the saints."[27] But the queen knows that her lover has made his whole long journey with the unique goal of forming with her the absolute, infernal couple that has been the long-standing wish of both of them. "She made him the most gracious welcome, with unrestrained ardor, because Love and her heart were inspiring her transport of joy." As for Lancelot, lost in his amorous adoration, "he tasted such happiness, born of kisses and the celebration of all the senses, that in truth a truly wondrous rapture came over him. Never again would such a marvel be heard tell."[28] In some way Chrétien de Troyes, who treats the physical details of this embrace with discretion, presents it as the most totally successful outcome and the most remarkable result of an exemplary, unequaled *fin'amor*.

But their bliss is not without counterpoint. Lancelot's wounds have left traces of blood in Guinivere's bed. We see here a theme exploited in the Béroul version of the *Romance of Tristan*. Bloodstains are certain proof of adultery, and we must never miss an opportunity to recall that the Guinivere-Lancelot couple, like that formed by Iseult and Tristan, is an infernal couple. "While the lovers' games revealed to them unheard of pleasures, the bloodstains that inexorably spattered the white sheets silently transformed the bed of Wonder into the bed of Shame. These silent traces are, in the instant of drunkenness, like a note of infamy, the memory of the Law. The cut on a finger evokes the menace that accompanies every transgression in the direction of bliss. The marvelous joy of which they then have the privilege can not and must not be spoken of: it is the Impossible whose form will marry the Real! From this point forward, Lancelot's wounds are nothing more than senseless upside-down versions of that fabulous wound suffered by the Fisher King, stripped of meaning."[29] What Chrétien de Troyes clearly refrains from saying—but no observer from that era would have said it either—is that the attitude of Guinivere, crucified on the bed by Lancelot's presence and bathed by the blood of his wounds, cannot help but evoke, but in a horizontal manner, the attitude of Christ, vertical on his symbolic cross, covered with the blood of the wounds inflicted upon him by humanity and letting out a great cry at the moment of death. Guinivere's orgasm is a death. Christ's death is an orgasm. Do not be fooled; the equivalence is there, and let us not forget that for Lancelot, the Grail—which contains the blood of Christ—is Guinivere. Furthermore, Guinivere is the omnipotent goddess, mother of humanity, to whom Lancelot as a representative of that humanity wishes to devote a worship that is not at all idolatrous, because there at that precise moment Guinivere is not an absent image but a carnal and spiritual reality, for you cannot have one without the other.

This episode of the chamber is the most powerful part of the story. The rest of the tale just restates what has already been told in another form and specifies several points intended to emphasize the beauty and the cruelty of Guinivere as well as Lancelot's chivalrous valor. First of all, Chrétien de Troyes, who was a humorist, did not miss any opportunity to amuse himself, and he thereby established a kind of countertext to the serious, basically sacred episode he had just finished describing. The pretext for this humor are the bloodstains, which, however, as we have seen, are essential elements of the *passion* (in the Christian as well as the amorous sense of the word) recently experienced by Lancelot and Guinivere. That morning, after Lancelot has left (having put the bars of the window back as they were), Meleagant sees that the queen's bed is covered with spots of blood. Now, as the seneschal Kay—who had the steadfastness not to awaken during Lancelot and Guinivere's amorous play—had slept in the same room, it did not need much for him to be accused of adultery and felony, all the more as his own wounds were still bleeding copiously. The queen protested Kay's innocence and claimed a champion for a trial by combat. It is obvious that Lancelot will have to fight Meleagant once again, but this time in Kay's name and for the purpose of removing all suspicion from him. Furthermore, prior to this combat, Lancelot has no qualms about swearing on holy relics—holy relics to which he hardly accorded any faith (recalling Chrétien de Troyes's earlier remark)—that Kay was innocent of the crime he had been accused of. All this foreshadows Iseult's famous "ambiguous oath" in Béroul's romance, where she swears she has never opened her thighs to any man save her husband, King Mark, and the vagabond who had recently carried her on his back through a swamp. This vagabond was actually Tristan in disguise.

A good example of how authors, in the romances at least, dealt as they pleased with the strict rules of courtly love.

It is true that adultery is almost mandatory in courtly love, and a primary rule is that it remains secret, thus any means are good for ensuring the nondisclosure of a relationship, which is valid only in its negation of normal moral law. The Guinivere-Lancelot couple, which nonetheless gives Arthurian society its strength and balance (Lancelot, through his obedience to the queen, is demonstrably the most faithful member of the community she represents), is an unequivocally marginal couple whose survival and very nature require silence and shadow. The activity of this couple is pernicious, in that it takes place in private, out of the view of others. These others are the men, the warriors, who just have to say the word to get anything they want and yet who keep quiet, haunted as they are by the flamboyant image of the woman whom a demonic power has introduced into their ranks. This seems a strange way to act, or rather not act. "Courtly feudalism, a society of masters, has adorned the Lady with the attributes of omnipotence; through Her, the sole mistress, man, following the pull of his desire, caught a glimpse of another shore, not that of death, but a place where he discovers he is mortal, an unknown land that is home to a woman."[30]

Lancelot never ceases in his defeat of death. From combat to combat, encounter to encounter, sometimes even at the cost of the greatest of sufferings, he is the eternal Orpheus returning with the phantom of Eurydice. But are we certain it really is he who returns with Eurydice? Would it not, rather, be Eurydice who is returning with Lancelot, back to the land of the living?

Through the remainder of his story, Chrétien de Troyes still shows us Lancelot in combat. He takes part anonymously in a tourney, in the presence of Guinivere. She has him ordered to fight as poorly as he possibly can. And Lancelot obeys her command. He runs from the blows of his adversaries and behaves like a complete coward. In so doing he reenacts his experience in the cart of dishonor. He annihilates himself. He becomes pure emptiness. And all this because his lady, the tyrannical mistress he has chosen, has ordered him to do so. He fights the worst he can because she wants it that way. But when the command comes to fight his best, everything becomes clear. We see him the victor over all, and nothing can stop his triumphal, triumphant march through the tourney. Lancelot had to realize that he must withdraw into himself in order to jump off better, that he must create a void within himself in order to fill it later.

But fill it with what? The answer lies with Guinivere. Mysterious and inaccessible to common mortals, the queen is a goddess with many faces, who can herself survive only by virtue of the love she bears the one knight she has chosen from among all the world's knights to be her other *half*. The infernal couple is actually the reconstitution of the original dyad, and it is only with this dyad that a new world may be built.

The problem is that, before a new world can be built, the old one needs to be destroyed. This is of little concern to Chrétien de Troyes. In the story of *Le Chevalier à la charrette,* he has Lancelot imprisoned, through Meleagant's treachery, after he has achieved his victory. Once Lancelot has been locked up in a tower (a very eloquent symbol), Chrétien visibly loses all interest in the fate of his hero. He does not finish the romance and gives the cleric Geoffroy de Lagny the responsibility of adding an ending. We could simply regard this as a good example of literary collaboration. But the Middle Ages abounds in similar examples. What should we think about this one in particular? Probably that Chrétien de Troyes had fulfilled his contract with Marie de Champagne and had provided enough of an illustration of *fin'amor* to be allowed to back out of the assignment. Lancelot and Guinivere have now formed the infernal couple; what was the point of adding an epilogue concerning their subsequent fate?

Chrétien de Troyes had numerous successors. They benefited enormously from the character of Lancelot of the Lake and made him the pivotal figure in countless adventures largely recovered from Celtic legend. In decade after decade and tale after tale, the figure of Lancelot would expand to cover the vast grouping of prose works sometimes called *Lancelot in prose,* sometimes the *Vulgate Lancelot-Grail.* It is a sign of the times that Lancelot, the sometimes lover and the best knight in the world, would be sent off in search of the Holy Grail, which he would never find. The character would take on many different colorations, and his significance would evolve dramatically. Primarily, the serene amorality coloring *Le Chevalier à la charrette* would give way to an examination of sin: if Lancelot does not discover the Grail, it is because of the sin he committed with Guinivere, and if the Arthurian world teeters on the brink of the abyss, it is because Lancelot quarreled with Arthur over Guinivere and abandoned the community of the Round Table, whose faithful protector he had once been. The notion of *fin'amor* can scarcely be found at all anymore in these prose stories, although the Guinivere-Lancelot couple still forms the ideal example of the benevolent and malevolent infernal couple, dominating the plot and directing the course of events.

What happens is that the couple becomes more of a political symbol. It seems that the thirteenth century had resurrected the Celtic formulation of the king who is cuckolded by necessity. At the same time the problematic of courtly love, while denying the husband's role, had a tendency to isolate the couple within its social group without giving it any real importance over events. Certainly we still find, loud and clear, the lover's oath to his mistress, paralleling the knight's oath of loyalty to his lord. This even plays a fundamental role in the story of Lancelot's amorous adventures. When he first arrives at Arthur's court he swoons in ecstasy before the queen. But she is without cease wondering who Lancelot is. Their attraction is mutual; it does not seem that Lancelot has to undertake any kind of quest to merit a glance from his lady. On the other hand, at the moment he is dubbed a knight in Arthur's court, "Lancelot does not want to be made a knight at the hand of the king, but at the hand of another person, with whose help he hopes to better himself."[31] It is not hard to comprehend that this person is Guinivere. Thus Lancelot will be the vassal of the queen, not the king, and this with the blessing of Arthur himself, because, having noticed the young man's exceptional valor since Lancelot's arrival at court, Arthur has asked Guinivere to do everything in her power to keep him at court.

Thus we are in the presence of the classic triangle of courtly love.

Normally the husband takes no offense at all seeing a knight become his wife's lover—according to the specific rules of *fin'amor,* that is to say, excluding total sexual union—if that lover is to serve him with success. Arthur conducts himself as the perfect courtly husband. Lancelot conducts himself as the perfect courtly lover, at least in the beginning stages of his tempestuous passions.

It is later that everything will take another turn. From the moment when Lancelot truly becomes the best knight in the world, the couple he forms with Guinivere takes on a new dimension, picking up where the old Celtic myth left off and extending it in dramatic fashion. Queen Guinivere is no longer just the lady of a feudal society in the process of transformation; she is the very embodiment of sovereignty, as was the woman in the Irish tradition. Now this sovereignty, according to Celtic definition, can only be collective, and consequently Guinivere becomes the symbol of that collective entity. She *is* the Arthurian community that concludes a privileged alliance with King Lancelot, who does not belong to this community because he is a foreigner, proud of being so, and taking every opportunity to display his marginality. It is thus a kind of hierogamy that Lancelot and Guinivere form together, a hierogamy whose political ramifications do not hide its mythological origins.[32] And whereas its appearance might still conform with courtly theory, its spirit no longer does; for while it is not a question of denying the very real passion uniting the two lovers, it must be recognized that the consequences of their love go way beyond them to involve the whole of the community.

The prose stories of the classic *Lancelot* were written fifty years after Chrétien de Troyes. The evolution of manners and customs is quite evident in these works, and the profound motivations of *fin'amor* have been enriched with mystical elements that cause a shift from human love to divine love, as is shown in *The Quest of the Holy Grail.* It so happens that the great loser in this sacred quest is Lancelot, because of his *sin.* The Guinivere-Lancelot couple is therefore no longer just a marginal couple, tolerated by a feudal Christian society, but clearly becomes an accursed couple, an *infernal couple* that no doubt feeds countless fantasies and proves enchanting but is nonetheless still cast back into the shadows. It is because of Guinivere and Lancelot that the Arthurian world collapses. The Cistercian influence is more than obvious here, and the slightly sulfurous coloration previously given the couple of *fin'amor* has now become an unequivocal condemnation. But every sin can be expiated: Lancelot and Guinivere will come to an honorable end, both of them retiring to a monastery, after Arthur's disappearance, in this way reenacting on the fictional level what had been the authentic story of Abelard and Héloïse in the previous century.

It is certain that Chrétien de Troyes, when writing this beautiful story of *Le Chevalier à la charrette* on behalf of Marie de Champagne, had not foreseen such developments, no more than he had foreseen what would ultimately be done with the mysterious object he had named *a grail.* He had certainly not imagined that the *joy,* the ineffable joy (that is to say, sexual bliss pushed to its highest peak) experienced by Guinivere and Lancelot in the chamber of Bademagu's palace, in the city of Gorre (which is to say, of Glass, where all is translucent, where the winter sun gathers together its rays to *burn* the lovers), would become under the pen of the Cistercian monks or those inspired by the Cistercians the *bitterness of sin.* As Charles Méla said: "*Fin'amor* balances the strength of the prohibition by the outrageousness of the ideal. To mad love an excess of honor! As if one must be at the feet of the Lady in order to rise above kings. But exaltation skirts the abyss, or even, according to the symbols from the last part, 'the deep pit, black and hideous' follows the ivory throne and its rich golden crown."[33]

This bitterness of sin drowns the *Mort du roi Arthur* ("The Death of King Arthur"), the last piece of this immense fresco dedicated to Lancelot and Guinivere, in an unhealthy fog in which the tragic grandeur of the lovers is in proportion to their infernal nature. The *sin* is the *defeat.* But every defeat is a sin. The Cistercian monks understood this so well they did not dare follow this line of reasoning to its logical conclusion. To have done so would have led them to deny the Roman Christian definition of sin as being the disobedience of an established law. They would have been led to consider this sin, in fact, as the lack of power to go even farther, or even as an absence—a momentary absence—of good, according to Cathar thought, which on this point meshes quite neatly with the amorality of the Druids and their successors, the abbots of Irish Christianity. What a terrible dilemma! The Cistercian monks preferred to keep quiet and bury Guinivere and Lancelot in the deep well of opprobrium. All love is guilty, and all the more so when it claims to go beyond the primary level of procreation in order to redeem the individual and restore the wholeness that was lost when the Angel with his fiery sword chased Adam and Even from the fabulous Eden they never should have agreed to leave.

The weight of clericalism distorted every initiative of the Middle Ages. *Fin'amor* was one of these attempts to escape from Time. But the Roman Catholic Church had need of Time in order to drain human beings of their energies, to make them serve (in the strict sense of the word) the material interests of those who claimed to be the heirs of Christ. What is the purpose of power if one does not abuse it? Time disperses the energies and weakens the ardor that manifests in a single—and eternal—instant of love. To move the object of desire toward a promising beyond, or simply toward a tomorrow filled with song, this has been the achievement of the Roman Catholic Church over the course of the centuries, and especially from the eleventh to the thirteenth centuries. The Church has succeeded in its undertaking beyond its wildest dreams. The lady of *fin'amor*, remote, cruel, inaccessible? That is fine. But when Lancelot joins his lady in her chamber and there unfolds a veritable ritual of love, leading to ineffable joy, now this becomes intolerable. *It is a sin.*

This notion of sin seems absent, however, from the legend of Tristan and Iseult, the other love story recovered by the romance writers of the twelfth century, which proved more resistant to clerical pressure, probably because it could not be reduced to any particular Christian problematic. Tristan and Iseult never committed a sin, and "God protects lovers," as is so often repeated in the different versions of the legend. It is true that someone took pains to invent the famous philter "drunk in error" by the two heroes, which arranges everything so nicely: if Tristan

135

and Iseult fell in love with each other, it is not their fault. Now, if there is no sin of intent, then there is no sin at all; there are only unfortunate circumstances that in a pinch can give the neighbors something to yell about.

This perspective completely overlooks the origins of the legend, and especially its Irish archetype in which the young Grainne (meaning "sun") casts a dreadful *geis* on the man she has chosen for her lover. The heroine's responsibility is total, but from the Celtic perspective there is no question of imputing it to any kind of sin. Hence the serene self-confidence of the Anglo-Norman romance writers and their German imitators in denying any sin on the part of Tristan or Iseult. This goes a long way—as far as the famous *ambiguous oath* that Iseult swears before the entire earth, which, under the eyes of God (and thus with his complicity), will furnish unimpeachable proof that Tristan and Iseult have never had sexual relations. This is surprising, but there is no choice but to accept that the transcribers of the legend of Tristan have systematically glossed over any idea of adultery, whereas we are at the very heart of the problem.

It is true that the romance of Tristan, in all its different versions, has been claimed as being the model of the anticourtly work and that no one then should search for the slightest trace of *fin'amor* in it. This is easily said.

Moreover, the same commentators, happily erecting definitive criticisms, have themselves come around to considering two versions—both of a spirit that is different, even opposed, to this legend so incontestably of Irish origin, which has since spread widely throughout the world without any one inquiring of its profound significance.[34] The first version, represented by the fragments of Béroul's romance (circa 1165), is called the "common version" because it closely followed a lost original that could have been of inspiration also to Chrétien de Troyes's story *Yseult la Blonde* ("The Fair Iseult"), which he wrote at the start of his career and which has since unfortunately disappeared. The second version, reflected with well-known success in the work of the German poet Gottfried von Strassburg, is that of Thomas of England: this would be

the "courtly version," since the author's long psychological developments are not without connection with the casuistry of the troubadours
and the courts of love.

However, on first analysis, the issue raised in the story of Tristan and
Iseult does not concern *fin'amor*. It concerns essentially an immense and
fatal love, the result of magical causes, which is entirely irrational, a
source of public troubles and of a marked social decline, all things that
do not conform to the code of love. The pure or courtly lover chooses to
love without measure a lady whose grandeur and beauty are so many
motivations for his heroic actions, but this love is discreet, even shy, torn
between fear and hope, always secret for fear of scandalmongers and
public gossip. Moreover, the consummation of adultery is not inevitable
because passing to the act could well signify the end of desire. Now the
legend of Tristan is closer to a changing or moving reality, exalting and
difficult, loudly affirming the rights of a passion that is refined through
trial, supported by a carnal desire that is never denied, and perhaps
never fully satisfied.

It is, nonetheless, impossible to separate the legend of Tristan from
the courtly context that witnessed its writing. Furthermore, it does not
seem that the poets and romancers of the twelfth and thirteenth centuries were too much troubled by the characters they so quickly built
into models. Trouvères and troubadours made perfect lovers out of
Tristan and Iseult, lovers that people sought to equal; there are numerous references to this subject throughout courtly literature. In reality,
despite its uncouth character, wild flavor, and incontestably mythological origin (Tristan is the moon, Iseult the sun, and Mark the night), the
legend of Tristan offers, partly by chance and partly through the deliberate intent of its authors, the principal elements of the courtly system
of logic put into action through dramatic experience. All the traditional
elements of traditional courtly lyricism are gathered here: the orchard,
the chamber, the adulterous lovers, a deceived husband playing a very
minor role, the inevitable scandalmongers who spy on the lovers, the
jealous people who denounce them, the art of Tristan who "knows how
to harp so well," the suffering of the lovers, the ruses they employ to keep

their love a secret. It is true, everything is here. Tristan and Iseult are uncommon heroes, living in a time when it is the fashion to be super-human and even somewhat fairylike.[35]

Thus they are permitted to fulfill their love—and to do so without sin, as is constantly repeated by the authors—even if the torments they experience are of a similar size, that is to say, outrageously enlarged. The legend of Tristan could thus represent a variation on the exemplary case of a courtly love, fully realized through a series of material situations and characteristic morals. The courtly spirit here takes a detour through the legend in order to reach a reality that would otherwise be denied it.

This is obvious even in the so-called common version, represented by the Béroul fragments. Tristan's quest for Iseult, although situated on the level of the unconscious, leads to the maturation of the hero. From exploit to exploit he eventually reaches the inaccessible lady, who then, as if he is undergoing a second birth, reveals to him his true nature until then unknown to him. In any case, Iseult is the wife of Tristan's suzerain, and there is between Tristan and Iseult the same oath of interdepen-dence that binds any other courtly lover and his lady. The sanctuary where the love ritual is accomplished is still the orchard and the cham-ber, and it is not until the scandal erupts, through the fault of the jeal-ous or the scandalmongers, that the celebration of love moves into the forest, where the lovers are obliged to seek refuge.

There are also precise details. We know that, in Béroul's text, the philter's effects will last only three years. After this time, and after debates of conscience, the two lovers decide to reconcile with Mark so that the queen can once more assume her rightful place at court. This decision—according to the author prompted by remorse—is nothing less than a reintegration into the courtly social order. More than ever, Iseult will be the inaccessible, tyrannical mistress who condescends to receive Tristan in the secrecy of the night to grant him his desire, on condition, however, that he deserve it. In this way the indispensable trio is re-formed, without which there is no *fin'amor,* and which had been destroyed by the provocative and malefic activity of *lausengiers* and *gelos*. It is in this sense that we should understand the famous "ambiguous oath" with which Iseult, in front of the world, clears herself of the accusation of adultery. This adultery, even though its reality cannot be doubted, must be accomplished in the most absolute secrecy, hence the necessity of *publicly* proving the queen's innocence.

On the other hand, Iseult seems to be fully satisfied with this ambiguous situation, perhaps even more so than Guinivere. There is no political connotation in the couple formed by Tristan and Iseult, but it must be said that the queen occupies a privileged place at the heart of the trio. She is as much Mark's mistress as she is Tristan's insofar as she contributes to balancing an unstable situation that sets the youthful forces represented by Tristan into competition with the aging forces represented by Mark. In this way is affirmed the continuity of the group, for whom the individuals of the trio are the guarantors.

All this does not happen without ambiguity on the level of Iseult's psychology, either. She is desired as much by Mark as she is by Tristan, which is not displeasing to her and which constitutes a powerful leaven. On one hand she ensures her domination over her husband, who will always fear losing her and will refuse her nothing; on the other hand as Tristan's tyrannical mistress she instigates his prowess and heroism in every domain, and Tristan too can refuse nothing to the woman from whom he expects everything, even his own survival. This is shown clearly by his last wound: it does not kill him; he dies because Iseult arrives too late.

Iseult is playing a game that one could objectively qualify as disturbing or almost dangerous. From the opposition, even rivalry, between Mark and Tristan she draws considerable benefits on the moral as well as the material plane. We could even say this situation entirely justifies her existence. As Denis de Rougemont puts it so succinctly, it is not conceivable that Iseult should ever be "Mrs. Tristan." But on the other hand, it is absolutely essential that she be "Mrs. Mark," otherwise the subtle game of *fin'amor* would not be fulfilled. In fact, the more Tristan cannot stand sharing her—the presence of Mark (and this despite the devotion Tristan feels for his uncle) provoking in him atrocious feelings of jealousy (but all lovers *should* be jealous)—and the more Mark suffers (from the image of Tristan haunting Iseult and feeding Mark's fear of losing her), the more Iseult finds herself at ease. She can in fact allow herself to feel jealous of Mark, who must not prefer any other woman to her, and of Tristan (whose marriage with Iseult of the White Hands will feel like a wound to Iseult the Fair), who is bound by a tacit oath to be faithful to her on pain of being rejected.

Specifically, there are significant details in Beroul's text concerning the moment Tristan delivers Iseult to Mark, which reveal that the return of Iseult to the social group only refines and even makes sublime the love the two bear for each other. It is as if the life of the two lovers in the Morois Forest by softening their desire leads to a weakening, even a disappearance, of their love. Love has need of difficulties for it to feed itself. If there are none, lovers are forced to create them. If Mark did not exist, it would be necessary to invent him. But he does exist, well and truly, and it is enough to restore him to his proper place as a cohesive element of this decidedly and increasingly infernal couple. As much for Iseult as for Tristan, their reconciliation with Mark and Iseult's restoration to her rank as queen and wife no way involve a rupture between them. On the contrary, it is at the moment of their separation that they most strongly declare their mutual love and intention to meet each other again more or less regularly to commit this sacrosanct adultery that is truly the corollary of the sacrosanct marriage.

The text is quite explicit. At the very moment of their parting Tristan and Iseult exchange "pledges of love." Tristan gives his dog Husdent to Iseult. She gives a ring to Tristan, saying: "By the faith I owe you, if you do not send me this ring that you wear upon your finger, in such a way that I can see it, I will not believe a word of what your messenger tells me. But once I see the ring again, neither tower, nor wall, nor fortified castle will prevent me from immediately fulfilling the wishes of my lover, according to my honor and my will, provided I know that this is your desire." Are these the words of repentant sinners who have decided to break off their mad love affair in order to return to the path of duty?

In any case, in the long conversation of the two lovers before their separation, it is a question only of the love that unites them, the "loving present," the "mutual pledge of possession," the blind obedience to the desires of the other ("Whether they be wisdom or folly, whatever the cost, I will fulfill them . . . "). But this all stays well within the strictest limits of the code of love. And Tristan, sometime previously, has taken pains to state explicitly that he has never had "sinful relations that could have been a source of shame for him" (King Mark), adding that he is ready to fight in a trial by combat with anyone who dares "suggest that I have enjoyed your love in any dishonorable manner." What does this mean? Tristan has been accused of playing with words, but it does not seem that this is the case. The authors' determination to wash away all culpability from the lovers rests not only on the famous philter, itself a recollection of the magical action of the Irish *geis*. It is quite possible that Tristan and Iseult have integrally respected the contract of *fin'amor*, which is to say that their sexual relations, although quite real, have stopped before the final consummation of the act duly reserved for the husband.[36] This would thus justify Tristan's words when he claims he has never acted dishonorably regarding Mark; because he has not exceeded his rights, he has not deprived the king of his truly unique prerogative, the penetration of his wife during the sexual act. The joy of the lovers can be procured by many other means, sometimes much more elaborate and (to borrow a moralistic term) more "perverse." But what does it matter if immorality—with respect to the Christian doctrine—exists in the details as long as morality is spared on the essential level? By this reckoning, it is truly with a light heart that Tristan can part from Iseult. He knows he has not committed any sin. In the same manner Iseult can swear her ambiguous oath before Arthur, Mark, and all the Knights of the Round Table, declaring that no man but her husband and the vagabond who carried her across the swamp has ever adventured between her thighs. After all, "bestowing the friendship of her thighs," as is said in the old Irish texts, does not imply the authorizing of penetration.

These considerations are not futile because they shed light once again on Tristan's attitude regarding the guilt people wish to accuse him of and which he obstinately refuses. His attitude passes for hypocrisy: it is true in an absolute sense, but it is no more than a sincere protest if we take into account the true nature of the sexual relations he enjoys with Iseult. The authors were not fooled by this, and their goal was certainly not to "blacken" the hero's reputation by making him play the role of Tartuffe. Furthermore, "God's judgment" and the trial by combat were matters of too much consequence in the twelfth and thirteenth centuries for anyone to mock them in a shameless manner. The writers of the Middle Ages are sometimes very crude, but they never blaspheme, especially about matters as fundamental as a feudal type of oath. No, Tristan has never failed in his duty to King Mark, and the sexual relations he has enjoyed with Iseult are only those that are tolerated by the specific morality of *fin'amor.* This may also explain the "endless burning" experienced by the lovers, which compels them to reunite no matter the circumstances and no matter the enemies spying on them. Too bad if ordinary Christian morality reproves such manipulations. The knighthood of love, which has other requirements, has its own code of honor that does not concern the uninitiated. In this way "God protects the lovers" since they are not at all guilty.

That said, if Iseult seems to get accustomed very easily to this scabrous triangular situation in which she is the necessary pivot and the crystallization point of desires, Tristan takes a poor view of the matter. And he even asks himself some pertinent questions—if we are to believe the author of the courtly version, Thomas of England, who wrote for the needs of the refined audience of the court of Henry II and Eleanor of Aquitaine. "What is the point of remaining faithful to a love from which no good can result?" His suffering from Iseult's absence becomes intolerable and pushes him to imagine she has forgotten him. However, the power of their love is such that it is impossible she could have made a clean slate of the past. He does his best to convince himself: "I know full well that, if her heart had drawn away from me, it would have alerted my own heart. . . . How would she be able to change then? As for myself, I am unable to betray the love I bear for her." But he is ravaged by doubt, as any self-respecting pure lover would be; it is part of the nature of courtly love to incite jealousy, and each detail provides a pretext for a disturbing thought that is ultimately translated into a great and constant suffering. Tristan is not happy. His inner debate becomes violent. He becomes jealous of Mark, which does not conform at all with the rules of the code of love, because conjugal love is of no importance within the particular relationship of the *fin'amor* couple. He exclaims, however: "What is my love to her now compared to the joy she feels next to her husband?" There is a kind of revenge of fate in this, if we recall how King Mark, tracking the lovers in the Morois Forest, was himself the prey of a similarly atrocious jealousy. And slowly the idea of vengeance takes hold of Tristan's heart. Because Iseult has renounced love and sought pleasure in the arms of her husband, "I wish to renounce it as she has done with her husband. So how could I experience this, if not by marrying a woman?"

This step is dangerous, because it opens the way to all manner of experiments, especially to an escalating tit for tat. However, Tristan very prudently sets aside the hypothesis of this escalation: "I do not act this way because I want to hate her, but because I want to distance myself from her and love her as she does me, in order to know how she loves the king." If we understand this correctly, it is not spite on Tristan's part, nor is it a desire for vengeance, but quite simply the desire to know *how Iseult can love Mark*. It is an attitude of jealousy in its paroxysms, almost the attitude of a "voyeur" insofar as Tristan, eaten away by inner suffering, has to harmonize a suffering actually rooted in his imagination with a reality that escapes him, but one that he thinks he can attain.[37]

So Tristan is going to marry the daughter of the duke Hoël of Brittany, Iseult of the White Hands. "He believed he would find bliss there, not being able to find bliss where he would like to. In the young girl, Tristan took note of the name, the beauty of the queen. He would not have wished to take her because of her name alone, nor because of her beauty if her name had not been Iseult. If she had not been called Iseult, Tristan would never have loved her; if she had not possessed the beauty of Iseult, Tristan would never have been able to love her." So what we have here is a typical case of transference. But beware, the author warns us, "he wished to rid himself of his pain and in fact raised only new obstacles." This proves that something is not right in his reasoning, and that he is mistaken about the true objectives he is pursuing: *"To his own misfortune, he sought a vengeance that would double his torment."* That is the sloppy truth.

In fact, the night of his wedding with Iseult of the White Hands, someone takes from his finger the ring given him by Iseult the Fair. This is the straw that breaks the camel's back. Tristan finds himself again suffering all he had wished to escape. He is caught in the trap. Never has his love for Iseult the Fair been as strong, as *unique*. The beloved woman can only be unique, even when seen through a substitution object. (This, moreover, renders infirm all the hypotheses that have been made on the subject of the more or less direct relationship between the story of Tristan and Indian Tantrism.) In short, Tristan pretends to his wife that a painful wound prevents him from consummating their marriage. Iseult of the White Hands will remain a virgin; Tristan does not even touch her. And later, it is because the young girl, taking a walk with her brother Kaherdin, will laugh when splattered by water between her thighs, where no man has ever laid a hand, that Tristan's presumed brother-in-law learns that his sister's marriage is null and void.[38]

Tristan's voluntary impotence is an element of capital importance in the problematic of the infernal couple formed by Tristan and Iseult. Now the two lovers are equal because both are married. But whereas Iseult can respond to Mark's conjugal desire and at need provoke it, Tristan on the other hand cannot satisfy his wife's desire and has no desire to do so. Tristan is incapable of making love with any woman other than Iseult the Fair, no matter what his motives are: a desire for vengeance, an experiment, knowledge through comparison of what goes on between Mark and Iseult.

We find here the basis of the "triangle" problematic. Iseult the Fair can divide herself between her husband and her lover *because it is not the same thing,* but Tristan cannot divide himself between the two Iseults because this would be the same thing, but halved, which is impossible. Tristan reveals himself to be the absolute courtly lover, who can love only one woman.[39] Here is all the difference between him and his lover: Iseult the Fair, who truly suffers from their separation, is faithful only spiritually, whereas Tristan is faithful spiritually and physically. Ought we to conclude that, contrary to appearances and common assumptions, man is capable, when in love, of taking on more dreadful sacrifices than woman?

The myth transcribed in the romance about Tristan answers this question with a categorical yes. Yes, man can assume the more dreadful sacrifices. Yes, man can love desperately. And this is the very meaning of *fin'amor*: the lady is always a goddess, the embodiment of all beauty and perfection, but often cruel and always ambiguous, as are all divinities.

But the deity, completely ambiguous as she is, also cannot survive without the one she has chosen. For in no uncertain manner it is always she who chooses, as Grainne had cast the *geis* on Diarmaid. When Iseult arrives too late and Tristan has just died, she does not have a moment of hesitation: "Friend Tristan, as you are dead, it is fair that I should live no longer." Her choice has been made for a long time, ever since she asked Brangwain—in secret—to serve them the philter. And she remembers this as she lies down on Tristan's deathbed: "I will find my consolation in the same drink." Thus *fin'amor* can be fulfilled, love in its final phase, love that is eternal, the love of that ultimate, fatal embrace that leads the lovers to their victory. There is no question that Tristan and Iseult are certainly the most absolute representatives of the infernal couple.

THREE

Ambiguous Liturgies

It is from Chrétien de Troyes's pen, in the tale of *Perceval, ou le conte du Graal* ("Percival, or the Story of the Grail"), that we find the strangest eulogy, spoken by Gawain and concerning the *Domina* of courtly love, embodied in this instance by Queen Guinivere. "Not since the first woman was formed from Adam's rib has there been a lady of such renown. She fully deserves it, for just as the teacher instructs the little children, so Milady the queen instructs and teaches all those alive. From her descends all that is good in the world, she is its source and origin. No one leaving her may go away discouraged. Well she knows each person's wishes and what she should do to please him."[1]

It is surprising that it is Gawain who delivers such an homage to his uncle's wife, and not Lancelot. But after all, Gawain, the son of Arthur's sister, is according to Celtic matrilineal custom the normal heir to King Arthur. He is therefore Tristan's equivalent in the famous symbolic triangle we find in every courtly text. Lancelot is a foreigner, someone with no duties, who is introduced late in the game, even if he does take the place of the nephew whom he surpasses and eclipses. What is equally striking about this homage is the universality attributed to Guinivere. She is the source and origin of all that is good in the world, which makes her the equivalent of a mother-goddess, she who nurtures the whole of humanity by distributing food and wealth. We could get the impression we were reading a canticle in honor of the Virgin Mary, because the mother of Jesus is also the mother of humanity, and we know the Marian cult gained considerable popularity during the courtly era. There are assuredly features of the Virgin Mary in Guinivere's character (unless it is the Virgin Mary who is borrowing Guinivere's characteristics), Guinivere who incontestably represents the ancient universal mother-goddess whom people have not ceased to worship since the dawn of time.

So let us listen to what the troubadours have to say: "Whiter is she than ivory, no other idol do I wish to see. . . . All the joy of the world is ours, lady, if we both love one another" (Guillaume IX of Aquitaine). "When the cool breeze wafts from your land, it seems to me I breathe in a wind from paradise, because of the love of my comely girl who has caused me to submit to her, and to whom I have given my passion and my heart. For I have quit all women for her, she has enchanted me so" (Bernart de Ventadour). "I do not believe the beauty of another lady can equal hers, because the rose, when it blooms, is no fresher than she; her body is well made and of gracious proportions, and her eyes and her mouth are the light of the world. For never did beauty know how to do more for her; it has so well placed in her all its power that nothing is left over for others" (Raimon de Miraval). "If I am able to say or do anything of worth, it is to her my thanks are due, for she gave me the craft and the talent that have made me a merry poet. All that I do that is pleasing including even the thoughts that rise from my heart, I owe to her beautiful body, full of grace" (Peire Vidal). "I love and desire her with a heart so full, from excessive ardor I think to be stealing her from myself, if one can lose something by loving it too well. For her heart submerges mine completely with a wave that never breaks" (Arnaut Daniel).

It has often been said that all these beautiful phrases form part of a literary expression, that they are poetic clichés, but we should nevertheless recognize that they are elements of an extremely complex and strictly measured ritual. By all evidence, around the *Domina* of courtly love there is woven a network of gestures and words that appear stereotyped (and so they are), but which come from the deep dark past. It is then that we can see, in both the troubadours' poetic expression and the mythological outlines recovered by the romancers, elements of a liturgy concerning a key figure in religious history—the great goddess, sometimes called the universal Mother, even the goddess of beginnings. Is *fin'amor* not simply the resurgence (scarcely profane, and within the framework of a society in search of its soul) of a ritual aimed precisely at bringing about a coincidence between man and his soul within the breast of a somewhat mysterious, shadowy, and ambiguous goddess?

The Goddess of Beginnings

As Mircea Eliade has demonstrated very well, there is always an *in illo tempore* in the memory of humanity wherein events explaining the world and its complexity take place. In those times there was myth. And myth became flesh and became embodied in reality. History is nothing other than this embodiment of myth, but we preserve its memory only with legendary tales that establish, as well as may be expected, the boundaries of this vague and imprecise time of "beginnings," when *everything was possible* because all was contained within the *potentiality of being*.

It is in the Babylonian epic of Gilgamesh, considered one of the world's most ancient narrative texts, that we find the expression of this field of potential, which will be set in motion by the creative play of primordial impulses. It concerns the story of Enkidu and his origin and metamorphosis through the agency of woman: "And lo the goddess moistened her hands and took the very clay of the earth, which she molded in the shape of a monster she named Enkidu."[2]

Here the creation is clearly presented as feminine—which appears much more logical than the creation described in Genesis, as revised and corrected by Moses for use by a patriarchal society wherein the male tried to convince himself he alone had the power to create. But the first creation was imperfect, in the sense that it was not finished. "And he was ferocious, as was proper for a god of combat, and his entire body was hairy. His hair was long like that of a woman, and he was clad in the skins of beasts. He roamed all day with the wild animals and, like them, fed on grasses and greens and quenched his thirst with the water of the streams." In short, Enkidu leads a plantlike existence, with no real self-awareness. All the same it is remarkable how this rude and realistic depiction was transformed by the Mosaic scribes of Genesis. It would have been a deplorable thing for the image of the Jewish God if his creature was a "wild man," for that would have been to demonstrate the imperfection of this God. Mosaic tradition has thus made Adam a perfect man in a perfect place, the Garden of Eden, for it was necessary as justification for the fall and the existence of sin. This Hebraic, or rather Mosaic, notion runs absolutely counter to original Semitic tradition, just as it is in opposition to the thought of the Druids, for whom God (whatever the meaning sealed within this meaningless word) does not exist but is becoming. In other words, in primitive myth it is normal for the creature to be rough, imperfect, and savage, because the creating deity is imperfect. As becoming is the slow dialectical unfolding of the imperfect into the perfect, thus God and his creation are obliged to go through all the stages of this becoming before making any claims about opening the doors to paradise.

This said, the presence of the wild man (who brings Merlin to mind) is disturbing to the people ruled by the wise Gilgamesh in Ereck. A hunter, who sets traps for wild animals, sees Enkidu freeing animals from these traps. How is he supposed to survive under these conditions? On the advice of his father, the hunter goes before Gilgamesh to lay out the situation.

> When Gilgamesh learned of what had happened and of the existence of this wild creature who was hampering the work of his subjects, he commanded the hunter to go find a girl of the streets and bring her to the place where the herds drank; once Enkidu arrived she would undress and try to seduce him with her charms. When they saw how Enkidu behaved in this situation, the animals would realize that he was not one of them and keep their distance from him. In this way the monster would be forced to adopt human ways and obliged to abandon his savage manners.[3]

This was done.

> Once the girl caught sight of him, she undressed and revealed all her charms. The monster, sent into raptures, pulled her close to his chest and embraced her madly. For the whole of a week he amorously lingered with her, then sated with her charms he left to rejoin the herd. But the hinds and gazelles no longer accepted him as one of their race, and when he drew near, they jumped away and fled off at a gallop. Enkidu tried to catch up with them, but one day as he was running, he felt his legs growing heavier and his limbs becoming stiff. He realized all at once that he was no longer an animal and must become a man. Swooning and out of breath, he went back to the young woman. But it was now a completely different individual who sat by her feet, looking at her intensely and hanging onto every word she said. She turned toward him; Enkidu, she told him sweetly, you have become as handsome as a god. Come, allow me to bring you to Ereck, the great city where men live, let me lead you to a sparkling temple where the god and goddess are seated on their throne.[4]

One may well ask what this story has in common with *fin'amor*. Let us listen to Bernart de Ventadour: "I no longer have any power over myself since the day she allowed me to look into her eyes, into that mirror that so delights me." And Bernard Marti: "When I am the honest thief of my lady, I do not consider my pain as bad. When I am naked in her house and I embrace and caress her flanks, I know no emperor who might win any greater reward or obtain any more *fin'amor*." We have also the testimony of Arnaut Daniel: "Each day I become a better and a finer man, for I serve and revere the most fair lady in all the world, I say so straight out. I am hers from head to foot, so let the cold wind blow, the love that floods my heart keeps me warm in the coldest of winter."

Furthermore, Enkidu as the Wild Man is singularly reminiscent of the master of wild animals encountered by the knight Yvain near the Fountain of Barenton in Chrétien de Troyes's romance *Yvain, ou le*

Chevalier au lion. "I guard the animals and control them in such a way that they will not leave this spot. . . . There is not a one who dares stir when they see me coming. For when I can get hold of one, I grab it by its two horns with my solid, powerful hands so that the others shake with fear and gather around me as if to beg for mercy. But no one else could venture among them without being killed." The description of this figure, conforming with other descriptions that may be found in the old Irish epics, is revealing. "A churl resembling a Moor, uglier and more hideous than one would believe possible, there are not words to describe a creature so ugly, holding a large club in his hand." This certainly concerns a figure equivalent to Enkidu.

This whole story is but one version of a widespread tale, known the world over in numerous versions. It is, in fact, the story of *Beauty and the Beast.* Through love, or by virtue of sexual relations, a beast—that is, a human being suffering under a curse, still in a state without self-awareness—acquires human proportions and is revealed to be a handsome prince. This is what happens to Enkidu. Here again, Genesis has reversed the polarity of the original myth: chased out of paradise, Adam and Eve are in a state of complete degradation—whereas the original being (Adam and Eve within a single individual) was still living in a state of unawareness of his own existence, which is then *revealed* to him by the snake. This is a matter, to be sure, not of a devil but of an image in negative of the goddess of beginnings, the sexual and amorous initiator, who thanks to *knowledge* (in the biblical sense) provokes the emergence of human consciousness, including the notion of good and evil. From being a wild and primitive being, man has reached a stage of autonomy, he has acquired consciousness and freedom. This is the sense of the Babylonian myth, and it should be seen as the probable original version of the tales told in the Hebrew book of Genesis.

Obviously this changes everything. There is no idea of guilt in the Babylonian story. And woman appears clearly there, with all her duties, including her sexual role. She is, moreover, a "girl of the streets." Make no mistake, in Babylon as throughout the Near East, prostitution did not have the connotations it has today in our post-Christian societies.

Sacred prostitution was a reality, and the sacred Prostitute of the Temple of Ishtar became the goddess herself in her initiatory mission. It is in this direction that we must look for the explanation of the particular role played by the lady of courtly love, image of the primitive goddess and provider of spiritual and material goods. In Babylon, a religious chant declares: "Ereck, hearth of Anu and Ishtar, city of whores, trollops, and courtesans, whom men pay for serving Ishtar." The great shadow of Ishtar, also known as Inanna and Anu (a term with kinship to the Celtic Danu or Ana), soars over the Middle East, where she has been confused with Artemis, the Scythian turned Greek, she for whom the "sweet" Iphigenia becomes a priestess—Iphigenia who betrayed the priest Hippolytus and whom the goddess abandoned to the sea monsters of Poseidon. The "goddess of life" who gives Enkidu his second birth, his birth into the human condition, is not only the "goddess of desire," however; she is also the "courtesan of love" and the "sacred whore of the temple."

The Babylonian tale concerning Enkidu translates the reality of a ritual: "the prostitute" who offers herself to the Wild Man is the embodiment of the goddess, and this union presented as uniquely sexual is in fact a hierogamy, a sacred marriage. In countless Oriental temples the *hierodulas,* or sacred whores, unite with any man who asks and who gives them payment (in every religion exists the gift of money). This gesture must be understood on a cosmic plane: it is the symbol of the union of the deity (originally feminine) and the creature (masculine in this instance). Other traditions and rituals show us the priest (representing the male god) having sexual relationships with women (the feminine principle), which represents the same hierogamy, but inverted. In sum, every religion is an attempt to reestablish the contact—interrupted by the process of creation, that is to say, by existence (in the etymological sense of the word meaning "to hold oneself outside of")—between the creating deity and the created human being. And nothing can better translate this profound desire for fusion than the sexual act.

This is so true that, in the framework of the most authentic Christianity, the mystic trances of the great saints and visionaries are often expressed by sensations and words borrowed from sexuality.

Certainly the men among them have done so discreetly: God being presented as a man, any sexual allusion would be colored with homophiliac associations. So illuminated minds such as Bernard de Clairvaux, Meister Eckhart, Ruusbroec, and others preferred to speak of the union of their soul (their *anima,* that is, their feminine principle) with God. But their devotion to the Virgin Mary, although diverted toward filial love, sometimes takes on fairly strange appearances.

The female mystics did not share the same worries or the same proprieties. Saint Theresa of Avila recounts her vision of an angel: "I saw in his hands a long golden sword that seemed to bear, at the tip of the blade, a point of fire. With this point he seemed to pierce my heart on several occasions so deeply that it *penetrated into my very entrails.* When he withdrew it, I thought he tore them out with it and left me completely afire with an immense love of God. The pain was so sharp that it caused me *to utter short gasps,* and so extreme was *the sweetness caused me by this intense pain* that no one would ever want it to stop." We need no psychoanalyst to interpret this delirious description of an orgasm. We should also recall that all the Middle Ages believed in demonic incubi and succubi who came to torment saintly individuals, even uniting with them, causing inopportune births that were fortunately free of any culpability. The great Theresa of Avila is not alone: "My heart craves the kiss of your love, my soul thirsts for the most intimate embrace joining me to you," exclaims Saint Gertrude (1256–1302), while Mechtilde von Magdeburg (1241–1299) utters some very curious prayers: "Lord, love me hard, love me long and often. I call you, burning with desire. Your burning love enflames me constantly. I am but a naked soul, and you, inside it, a richly adorned guest." It is perhaps Hedewijch, a thirteenth-century visionary, who goes the farthest in this kind of mysticosexual delirium:

> My heart and my arteries, and all my limbs quivered and trembled with desire. I felt myself so violently and dreadfully tested it appeared that if I did not give satisfaction to my lover entirely, to know him, to taste him in every part of his body and if he did not

respond to my desire, I would die of rage. . . . He came, handsome and sweet, with his splendid face. I approached him submissively, like someone who belongs completely to another. And he gave himself to me as he usually does, in the form of the sacrament. Then he came in person to me and took me in his arms and locked me in his arms. All my limbs felt this contact with his with equal intensity, following my heart, as I had desired. Thus, externally, I was satisfied and *quenched*. . . . Following which, I remained merged with my lover until I had melted entirely within him in such a way that nothing was left of me.

One would think to be reading the episode from *Le Chevalier à la charrette* in which Guinivere and Lancelot, in the chamber-sanctuary in Bademagu's palace, are possessed by joy on the bed where the blood-stains will then become both witnesses of shame and profound imprints of a bliss that seizes flesh-and-blood beings so completely it reduces them to a new state, unique and eternal. It is also reminiscent of the perpetual burning suffered by Tristan and Iseult, which they never managed to extinguish because of the infinite quality of their desire.

Union with the god or goddess is perilous, however, for every human being. The deity being by essence a supernatural, superhuman power, a human being risks grave consequences in transgressing the interdiction and establishing direct contact with the divine. The divine can strike down the human because the latter finds it overpowering. In *The Quest of the Holy Grail*, when Galahad discovers what the sacred vessel contains, he is dazzled by the divine fullness and can do nothing else but die. *Is orgasm not a kind of death?*

None may return intact from the bed of a god or a goddess. Attis, Cybele's lover, is castrated; Anchis, father of Aeneus and lover of Venus, is lamed; Tiresias, the seer who knows the secret of the goddess (and has therefore had sexual relations with her), is blind. Even Lancelot and Tristan do not emerge intact from contact with Guinivere and Iseult: both suffer a terrible, incurable wound afflicting their flesh as well as their spirits. And the same, if we can believe the troubadours, holds true for all true lovers: "I do not die, nor do I live or get well, I feel my suffering not at all, yet I suffer greatly" (Cercamon). "Love has brought me more pain than was caused the lover Tristan by Iseult the Fair" (Bernart de Ventadour). "She for whom my heart burns and gnaws itself, if she does not heal my torment with a kiss, before the new year, she will kill me and condemn me to hell" (Arnaut Daniel). "The sweet ways of my lady will have caused me harm for a long time, and I think the torments of my thoughts will kill me" (Guiraud de Calanson). "It is far more piercing than a thorn, the pain that heals with the joy of love" (Jaufré Rudel).

It is tempting to view these assertions as purely conventional examples of amorous rhetoric. But that would be an error. The style is only covering here with colorful appearances a reality that could not be expressed otherwise. Furthermore, the troubadours were not dupes. They well knew they were singing an ambiguous liturgy to the great goddess, from whom they had everything to fear and little to hope. That is just the way it is, and the lover-priest is condemned always to suffer from being a mere servant in a temple where the inaccessible is concealed. In this respect, Bernart de Ventadour seems particularly lucid: "In this my Lady shows herself indeed a woman, and I reproach her for wanting what should not be wanted and for doing what is forbidden. I have fallen in evil grace and resemble the madman on the bridge! Ah, I know too well why this has happened to me, *I sought to climb a slope that was too steep.*"

Here an observation is necessary: Tristan is less fortunate than Iseult. It is he who suffers more from a situation that Iseult always manages to face up to. It is significative of a certain inferiority of the lover in connection with his mistress. The mistress is always of higher rank. It is up to the lover to make the necessary effort to catch up with her, hence a slow work of maturing translated into suffering, hence also the key position of the mistress, who can always, because she is a goddess and thus all-powerful, forbid entry into her sanctuary (the chamber of the troubadours) to he who wishes to become her lover. The priest is required to be inferior to the goddess. And when the sacramental act has been accomplished, it is the goddess who triumphs: after the orgasm, man is *dead* in some sense, because he has been devoured by the woman whose bliss, in contrast, leads to absolute fullness. The example of the praying mantis is revealing. The man (that is, the male) believes himself always the victor of the confrontation opposing him to woman. He conquers her like a soldier invading a neighboring country. He takes the woman like a city is taken. He penetrates her like a triumphant brute. But he leaves his most intimate and profound possession behind with her, his semen. After which he is good for nothing, the natural process will take place, the new being will be born from this copulation.

We can now understand why, within the context of courtly love, penetration is in theory excluded. The act of love should not result in the male's loss of identity, in his uselessness. There is no new being to be created, or rather this new being is the couple itself, without the appearance of any third party such as the child. But because, excepting penetration, all sexual play is permissible, and said play can end with the lover's ejaculation, the problem of the man's final weakness still arises anyway. It is the lady who emerges from the trial as the victor, and as she has the possibility of experiencing multiple orgasms whereas the man requires a certain amount of time to recuperate his strength, she necessarily occupies the dominant position. She is more than ever the goddess of beginnings, she whom the people of ancient civilizations have always worshiped—but of whom they had a tremendous fear, a fear so great that we could indeed ask whether the cult of the goddess was not really more a propitiatory ritual than a ritual of love.

Here the problem arises—one we have already mentioned—of what we now call masochism. Even though it did not bear this name, masochism is visible in all the great myths of humanity and in all religious rituals. The lover knows that the relations he establishes with his lady will cause him to suffer, in the same way the priest mortifies himself before the altar of the deity. All the troubadours are unanimous in declaring that their suffering is necessary, that in the end it constitutes their deepest joy. There is no joy without the suffering that precedes it. Joy without suffering is a joy of no depth. It can be observed right now how all notion of bliss emerges from the awareness of suffering. If

Lancelot was not forced to separate the bars of Guinivere's chamber, which caused him cruel pains, he would not have experienced such intense joy with the queen. Furthermore, orgasm expresses itself with painful gasps.

This is why, in the majority of ancient religious traditions, suffering is felt to be an element that allows transcendence and the attainment of the inaccessible. On a more concrete level, each time the deity is a goddess, her appearance becomes quite ambiguous. She is represented as both attractive and repulsive, both beautiful and cruel, both good and bad. The clearest example is the figure of the goddess Kali in India. But many of Kali's aspects remain in Guinivere and Iseult, in the same way they remain in every *Domina* of the troubadours, or in every *précieuse* of the sixteenth century whose beauty and *cruelty* are praised by any drawing-room poet. When Vincent Voiture writes a letter to the redhead Mademoiselle Paulet, which in all other respects is a model of gallantry, he compares her to a lion of the Atlas Mountains, but he confesses to an ardent desire to be torn apart by her claws.[5] What difference is there between this fashionable attitude on one hand and the fanaticism of the cultists of Kali, who are ready to let themselves be devoured between the dreadful jaws of the goddess who delights only in the blood of her victims? What difference is there also with the attitude of Tristan, plucking, in the words of a baroque poet, "his death from a rosebud"?

The ambiguity goes well beyond this undeniable hint of masochism. In fact, when the Catholic priest pronounces over the altar the sacramental words that, according to Roman doctrine, cause God to appear in the form of bread and wine (which is also the case, in a more symbolic form, with the Dionysian cults and the Eleusinian mysteries), who then is the victim? Let us not forget we are dealing with the holy Sacrifice of the Mass, and that the designated victim (*hostia*, therefore "host") is God, embodied and suffering because of his love for humanity. We can perceive the relationship easily enough: there is love, even *fin'amor*, between the embodied God Jesus and the whole of humanity considered as woman, even *Domina*, in this way carrying out the creation of the *Dominus-Domina* hierogamy. And in this hierogamy, God

Jesus plays the role of the lover suffering a thousand deaths for the love of she who refuses him. The serious Roman theologians, so keen when it comes to blurring all sexual references, scarcely presented things from this angle. When on the few occasions they have done so, it has been most emphatically against their will. This brings to mind Saint Bonaventure, nonetheless a serious saint, who complains bitterly about the poor priests or the poor monks who sometimes cannot prevent themselves from ejaculating when ardently praying to the Lord.

This speaks volumes about the religious substratum surviving beneath courtly love, a refined, literary, and profane aristocratic game. The image of the goddess of beginnings appears every time one scratches beneath the veneer that androcratic civilizations and then Roman Christianity spread freely over those features of hers that were definitely too sexual and too satanic. The "inventors" of courtly love were all clerics, even if they did represent a marginal current of the Roman church. As clerics they were guardians of traditional Greco-Roman culture. And this tradition was so heavily charged with the memory of the great goddess that it gave birth to the Marian cult, when no one any longer knew what to do with the obsessive image of Artemis of Ephesus, except make her into the "good" Holy Virgin, mother of God.

It was not simply Mediterranean tradition that entered the game: in the crypt at Chartres is it not claimed that the Druids revered a *Virgo Paritura?* It is difficult to claim people knew of the existence of the Virgin Mary before she even appeared in tradition. This "Virgin about to give birth" must have something to do with the Druids, the philosopher-priests of the Celtic religion. It has often been repeated that the source of courtly love was the Arab influence on the civilization of Occitania. However, rendering homage to the woman by adorning her with all possible riches while confining her within the narrow space of a harem where she has no rights but to be pretty and keep her mouth shut hardly seems compatible with the omnipotence of the troubadours' lady. If there is a source to be sought, it is somewhere else, and most certainly more to the north. It is here, in fact, that the Celtic traditions come in.

It is not only a question of the mythological outlines recovered by writers of the twelfth and thirteenth centuries. Certainly, the figures of Guinivere and Lancelot of the Lake emerged from the Breton tradition, of both the British isle and the Armorican peninsula, as did all the so-called Arthurian cycle. Certainly, the romance of Tristan and Iseult is derived from an Irish archetype, "The Pursuit of Diarmaid and Grainne," augmented with details borrowed from other stories of Gaelic origin. Certainly, Lancelot is the courtly image of the pagan Irish hero Cuchulainn (himself the image of the great god and multiple craftsman Lug), who can also be seen in the figure of Batraz, a hero from the Scythian tradition. But whoever may be the heroines of the tales or the lady whose praises are sung by a troubadour, we can clearly perceive, through the vaporous contours of the medieval chatelaine, a unique model who has been embodied in numerous tales from the great Celtic epics.

The central figure seems to be the mysterious Dana or Danu in Ireland, Dôn in Wales. The adventures of this incontestable divine mother are never told, and we know her only through the great gods who are her children. In Ireland the *Tuatha Dé Danann,* or tribes of the goddess Dana, allegedly introduced "Druidism and sorcery" among the Gaels. They came from the "isles of the north of the world," which is a symbolic formulation, of course, but one that nonetheless shows the Nordic character of this religion. Next to masculine figures such as Ogma, Dagda, Diancecht, and Mananann, we find feminine figures with diverse names, often presented in the form of triads, or goddesses who each have three faces, who are all socialized and relativized aspects of the ancient Dana. In this way we see Morrigan (the "Great Queen"); Bodbh (the "Raven"); Macha (the "Mare"); Boann (the "White Cow"), eponym of the Boyne River, who would then be found in Vivien-Ninian (the Lady of the Lake of the Arthurian romances); and especially Brigit (the "Powerful One," the "High One"), who corresponds closely with the Gallic Minerva described by Caesar, and who will later be more or less confused with Saint Brigitte of Kildare, without counting this goddess's numerous avatars, the Eithnes, Etaines, and other Medbhs.[6]

The Welsh Dôn is also the mother of the principal gods, but they are presented in a more folkloric aspect: Gwyddion (the "magician"), Amaethon (the "laborer"), Gilvaethwy (who will become Girflet in the Arthurian romances), and Arianrhod (the "silver wheel"). Dôn is a name that could come from the ancient *duna* meaning "profound," but its etymological connection to Dana is certain. Curiously enough, Welsh tradition talks of genealogies going back to a certain Anna, more or less confused with Saint Anne of Christian tradition. We must point out that there are other families of gods and goddesses in Wales who are attached to Irish tradition. Among them, we find Branwen (daughter of Llyr and sister of Bran the Blessed), whose name means "white crow" and who is a kind of goddess of love, easily discernible in Brangwain of the legend of Tristan; then again Rhiannon (the "Great Queen"), the equivalent of Macha, who can be recognized in the Gallo-Roman Epona; and Cerridwen, who initiated the bard Taliesin and whose name is connected to the same Indo-European root that has given us the Greek Korê (Persephone) and the Latin Ceres.

There are constants throughout all this, in particular the importance of the family of Dôn-Dana. It has been noted that in all the European and Near Eastern traditions the goddess of beginnings bears names referring to two principal types. "The first, defined by the Artemis = Ardvî equivalence, is common to Greece and Iran; the second, which appears to derive from an original Tanaï/Nanaï, traveled from the Semitic world to Iran and India."[7] We need to expand the field of investigation toward the extreme west, because Dôn-Dana is incontestably connected to this type. And then, "The fact that certain names designate both the great goddess and water in general, or important rivers such as the Don or the Danube, confirms what the myth of the Danaïdes suggested: the goddess personified at the same time the fertile Earth and the fertilizing Waters."[8] This observation is particularly important because it places in evidence the bisexual aspect of the goddess of beginnings, she who will be found again later in the figure of Melusine, the woman with the serpent's tail, the barely disguised image of the primordial androgyne and also the broken model of a Virgin who gives birth without the assistance of any male god.[9]

In the Celtic domain the goddess, under any name, tends to adopt certain characteristics belonging to the particular aspect of Celtic society within which woman plays a preponderant role. Even if this whole society is primarily of the Indo-European type (that is, patriarchal), some particularly important anterior elements have survived, which come to light in the image attributed by the Celts to this goddess of beginnings. She is in fact arrayed in a sovereign and *radiant* power that each human being endeavors to approach or garner. In Celtic languages the sun is feminine, which is quite revealing. The goddess of beginnings was incontestably a feminine solar deity whose last incarnation, Grainne ("sun"), can be recognized in the figure of Iseult the Fair and to a certain extent also in that of Guinivere, whose Welsh name (Gwenhwyfar) means "white phantom," in a general sense, and "beautiful appearance," in the more precise sense of the root word *gwen/finn* (which, incidentally, is the same root that has given us *Venus*).

The solar character of the goddess does not, however, eclipse her tellurian nature (she is the Earth Mother) nor her fertilizing function (she is the deity of the Waters). These three aspects meet up again in the myth of the fairy woman who lives on a lost island in the middle of the ocean. This isle is an idealized projection, not of paradise lost, a notion totally unknown to the Celts as there was no sin in their system of logic (and for the even greater reason that there is no original sin coming back to haunt humanity), but of a future world, a paradise to be realized in a becoming that has no end.

The best description of this isle can be found in the *Vita Merloni* by the Welsh cleric Geoffrey of Monmouth:

> The Isle of the Apple Trees or Apples (word for word "of *fruits*," the Latin *pomorum* [*pomme* in French]) is also called the Fortunate Isle, because all the vegetation there is natural. It is not necessary for the island's residents to cultivate it. All farming is nonexistent, save that performed by Nature herself. The harvests are rich and the forests are filled with apples and grapes. The soil grows everything as if it were grass. People there live one hundred years and more.

Nine sisters rule there by gentle law, and let this law be known to those from our regions who go there. Of these nine sisters, there is one who exceeds all the others by her beauty and power. Morgana is her name, and she teaches the uses of plants and how to cure illness. She knows the art of changing the appearance of her face, and flying through the air, like Daedalus, with the aid of feathers.

One will recognize here the Isle of Avalon from Arthurian legend, all the more because the word *Avalon* comes from *aval* or *afal*, which, in Breton and Welsh, means "apple," with all the symbolic elements this word can include. The Isle of Avalon is the marvelous orchard (which we see again in the courtly system of logic) where reigns Morgana, who has been called the half sister of King Arthur and a disciple of Merlin but who in reality is a *Morigena* ("born of the sea"), an aquatic and solar deity at the same time as she is a *Matrona* (*Modron* in Welsh, meaning "maternal"), that is to say, Mother Earth. This is obviously reminiscent of the Gallic tradition of the Isle of Sein where lived the *Gallicènes,* the priestesses who foretold the future, unleashed or calmed the tempests, knew the secrets of nature, and welcomed (even sexually) the sailors who were wrecked on their island.

This Isle of Avalon can also be found in Irish tradition. It is *Emain Ablach* (*Ablach* being a derivative of the same root as *aval):* "Feet of white bronze supported it, shining through centuries of beauty, a beautiful land through the centuries of the world, where abound many flowers. An old tree is there with its flowers, on which the birds sing out the hours. . . . Neither grief, nor death, nor illness, nor weakness, such are the signs of Emain. Rare is such a wonder." This enthusiastic description is borrowed from *The Voyage of Bran, Son of Febal,* a very ancient Irish text that recounts how the hero Bran was invited by a fairy, who brought him an apple branch from Emain, to come meet her on the Isle of Women. With several companions, Bran sets sail in quest of this island. He accomplishes a wonderful voyage, constructed on an outline analogous to that of *The Odyssey,* with stopovers on strange islands and no less surprising encounters. Finally, when he reaches the Isle of Women, the queen of the isle seems quite enamored of him. She invites him to remain with her and gives women to his companions. But they become stricken by homesickness. They oblige Bran to depart again for Ireland. The queen warns them never to set foot on the ground. Once they are off the Irish coast, however, one of Bran's companions jumps onto the shore and collapses into dust. Bran realizes that several centuries have elapsed during his sojourn on the Isle of Women.

The Voyage of Bran was adapted later in another tale, *The Voyage of Maelduin*. The initiatory expedition here is longer and more complicated, but Maelduin is also invited by the queen of the marvelous island, whom he marries. But here we are told that the sailors remain only for the three months of winter and that these three months appear as three years to them. The notion of time is reversed, and the companions of Maelduin, after obliging him to depart, get back to their native land with no difficulty.

Another adaptation of the original tale enjoyed considerable success in medieval Europe. The pagan myth was entirely Christianized around an Irish saint, the founder of the Abbey of Clonfert, and for this reason appeared in *The Voyage of Saint Brendan* as being in search of paradise. The details of the initiatory expedition are often the same, but the moral intentions are more than obvious: it is, pure and simple, a question of replacing the image of the Land of Women (decidedly too pagan and suspect of diabolism) with a reassuring, soothing image of Christian paradise.[10] The fundamental idea remains the same, however. It is an attempt by a human being to discover the true face of the Otherworld, which sits outside time and space and is a negation of real time, a sublimation of the instincts that impel one toward infinity, all at the cost of a symbolic initiation that can sometimes reveal itself dangerous to achieve.

The model of the three tales is significative. The Christian version turns it into a quest for paradise, a sort of quest for the Holy Grail. The two "pagan" versions make it into a quest of the fairy or divine woman. In the sphere of myth these are exactly the same thing. This quest can be achieved only at the cost of hard effort through many trials, some of which are dreadful. Bran and Maelduin are comparable to the knight who, having set his sights on a seemingly inaccessible lady, does everything in his power to reach her. The paradisiacal vision of Saint Brendan is no different from what happens on the Isle of Emain Ablach—the absolute fusion of the human being with the godhead, of the lover-knight with his mistress, and this in the ineffable joy that makes one lose all sense of time, causing the couple thus created to topple into a sublime moment equivalent to eternity. The experience of Bran, like that of Maelduin, leads to the *chamber*, the lady's forbidden sanctuary in a magnificent palace, on an island that is an orchard, the ideal point where earth and sky meet, in the midst of the waters.

And on this island, woman appears in her true light. She is the initiator for that man whom she has chosen as the most capable to support the secret she reveals and to assume fully the role he must now play. The sailor, like the lover-knight, has become a veritable priest, devoting himself to the service of his lady, or, in other words, the mother-goddess, the goddess of beginnings. And because time no longer exists, the goddess of beginnings is also the goddess of final ends or, rather, the eternally young, beautiful, loving goddess who dominates the world in tyrannical fashion—that is, by giving all on condition that she be given all. This is the exaltation of *fin'amor* long before the courtly poets even discussed its defining issues.

This initiatory function of the woman, a "folkloric" image of the goddess of beginnings, is in certain texts expressed quite clearly and literally. But a curious phenomenon has come to light. Even in the most "pagan" of texts there is a tendency to clothe this initiator in a marginal and disturbing, if not downright diabolical, aspect. This is how the sorceresses appear in Welsh tradition and the "warrior women" in Irish tradition.

An episode from the tale of *Peredur*, which is the Welsh *Perceval*, in fact shows the hero, in the course of the numerous adventures sown throughout his quest, forced to fight a sorceress. This woman, seeking to have her life spared, proposes that Peredur come with her "among the sorceresses" so that he may be initiated into the vocation of arms. He accepts and remains three weeks at the sorceress's court located in Kaer Lloyw (the modern Gloucester), which is no innocent spot since the name means "City of Light." In some way Peredur will find illumination among the sorceresses of Kaer Lloyw, which will permit him at the end of the story to massacre those very sorceresses. He no longer has any need of them, having gathered within himself all the secrets they were guarding and dispensing. Peredur therefore returns from Kaer Lloyw transformed, *matured*, in full possession of both warrior and sexual capabilities, the two themes being incontestably linked.

There are also women warriors in Irish tradition with the appearance of sorceresses, who recruit, raise, and educate the young Finn Mac Cumail, making him a formidable warrior and the ferocious king of the Fiana. But the most interesting stories concern the hero Cuchulainn, who, to a certain extent, appears as one of the archetypes for Lancelot of the Lake. In his youth he did, in fact, have a duty to perfect his skill at arms and was sent to some mysterious women in Scotland who taught warrior techniques to young men at the same time as they developed their sexual skills. This no doubt concerns a time preceding the Celts, when the autochthonous societies of western Europe were of a gyneco-cratic tendency and the worship of the great goddess was still prevalent. Barring this hypothesis, it is difficult to explain and justify these strange women warriors with magic powers who alone were capable of initiating future warriors.

Two texts—one quite archaic, "The Courtship of Emer," the other more recent and more detailed, "The Education of Cuchulainn"—tell of this initiation of the hero by different warrior women. The most important episode takes place with a certain Scatach (whose name means both "She who inspires fear" and "She who protects"), who has a daughter by the name of Uatach (meaning "the very terrible one"). We find Cuchulainn on his way to the home of Scatach. He meets two young men who are practicing throwing and enlists their aid as guides. They soon reach a magic bridge, the Bridge of Leaps, which certainly has a connection to the Bridge of the Sword that Lancelot has to cross to enter the kingdom of Gorre. "When one jumped upon the bridge, it shrank until it became as narrow as a hair and as hard and slippery as a fingernail. Other times it would stretch up again as high as a mast." The theme is completely shamanic and concerns those dangerous bridges that the shaman must cross before reaching the Otherworld, in that type of ecstasy that characterizes so well this tradition from the very dawn of time.

Cuchulainn tries to jump in such a way as to avoid the test. But he slips and falls on his back. So the trial appears to be indispensable. Scatach, accompanied by her daughter Uatach, watches what is happening from the top of her house. Uatach "had white fingers and black nails. . . . When the girl saw the young man, she gave him the love of her soul." Cuchulainn explodes. Furious at having failed in his jump and angered by the jibes of the young men, he exceeds himself. "He jumped in the air, rocking back and forth as if he was in the wind, in such a way that, with one furious leap, he managed to reach the middle of the bridge. And the bridge did not shrink, nor did it become hard and slippery beneath him." Thus he successfully passed his test, and after extricating himself from a quarrel with the guards he is welcomed by Scatach into her home. He is, however, very tired and injured. Like Lancelot in the palace of Bademagu, he is covered in bloody wounds. He lies down on a bed. During the night Uatach comes to find him with very specific intentions. Cuchulainn repulses her efforts, saying: "Do you not know, girl, that it is the violation of a taboo to sleep with a woman when one is wounded?"

This sheds new light on the scene that took place between Guinivere and Lancelot in Bademagu's palace. Lancelot cares little about his wounds, and within the context of the courtly society described by Chrétien de Troyes, he no longer knows the value of the prohibition on blood: hence the revelatory stains in the bed and the accusation lodged against the seneschal Kay. The bloody wounds—like a woman's menstruations—are an obstacle to the realization of the act of love and thus are under the weight of an ancestral interdiction. Cuchulainn, within the context of his Druidic society, is fully aware of this prohibition. This is why he pushes away the young Uatach.

But she comes back a little later, completely naked this time, and slides into Cuchulainn's bed. "Cuchulainn was greatly annoyed; he extended his good hand toward the girl and met her finger in such a way that, in pushing her back, he tore the skin and the flesh and he hurt and roughly bruised her." Uatach protested energetically and threatened Cuchulainn with a *geis* of destruction if he still refused to sleep with her. Cuchulainn obstinately stuck to his refusal. It was only when Uatach promised him that he would obtain from Scatach three magic tricks— and one of them the famous *gai bolga,* or "burst of lightning,"[11] that would make him the best warrior in all the world—that he finally accepted Uatach's proposition, and she then revealed to him the necessary methods for obtaining her mother's secrets.[12]

It is thus through an amorous relationship that Cuchulainn attains the rank of the world's foremost warrior. His quest for the woman leads him to fullness. There is a striking analogy here with the story of Lancelot of the Lake, who became the best knight of the world, both for Guinivere and thanks to her, because she is both the projected goal and the unconscious initiator of her lover's maturing. This demonstrates again the mythological equivalence of Cuchulainn and Lancelot, and highlights one of the incontestable sources of *fin'amor.*

Another episode from the Cuchulainn cycle reinforces this conviction, one that is recounted in a text sometimes entitled "The Great Jealousy of Emer" and sometimes "The Illness of Cuchulainn." During a Samain festival (November 1), Cuchulainn sees two birds flying by. They are linked together by a gold chain (this is the common mythic theme of women-swans, that is to say, divine or fairylike figures appearing in the form of birds), and he tries to hit them with a slingshot. He misses his shot, managing only to wound one of them. The birds vanish in the distance. Cuchulainn is overcome with languor and, leaning against a stone pillar, he falls asleep. "He saw two women approaching: one wore a green mantle, the other a mantle of purple folded five times. The one in the green mantle drew near him, smiling, and struck him with a horsewhip. The other woman came to him, smiled, and struck him in the same manner. They spent such a long time taking turns beating him there was scarcely any life left in him. Then they left."[13]

This anecdote is strange, to say the least. The two women are obviously the two birds, thus two fairy beings. They bring to mind Iseult and her lady-in-waiting Brangwain, the solar goddess and the goddess of love, respectively. We will later learn they are actually Fand, a goddess of the Otherworld and wife of the god Mananann, and her maidservant Liban. We will also learn that Fand has been in love with Cuchulainn for a long time. But while waiting, the two fairy women treat the hero very roughly, throwing themselves into an authentic flagellation session worthy of the best "house of illusions" from the beginning of the twentieth century. We can again bring up the subject of "masochism," because this has a close connection to the sufferings of Lancelot and Tristan and to the sufferings so often described by poets confronting the cruelty of their ladies— mandatory sufferings that are accepted, with full awareness, in order to attain *joy,* this ritual of love accomplished in the sanctuary-chamber of the deity. Cuchulainn wounded before Uatach, or flagellated by Fand, this is no other figure than Lancelot, covered in bloody wounds from crossing the Bridge of the Sword and from tearing out the bars defending the entrance into Guinivere's room.

However, in the Irish story, Cuchulainn remains ill for a year. On the evening of the next Samain feast, a messenger arriving from "elsewhere" explains that Cuchulainn can be cured only by a certain Liban, lady-in-waiting and companion to Fand, the wife of Mananann who rules over the marvelous isles and whose "pigs" feed the guests at a banquet of immortality. Cuchulainn is brought to the same pillar as the previous year and the woman in green appears before him. She tells him: "I have come today to speak to you on behalf of Fand, daughter of Aed Abrat. Mananann, the son of Lir, has set her free, and now she gives her love to you. Liban is my name. I also have for you a mission from my husband, Labraid, Hand-Quick-upon-the-Sword. He will give you the woman in return if you will fight for one day beside him and against Senach Siaborthe, Eochaid Iul, and Eogan Imbir."[14]

Cuchulainn asks her where Labraid lives. She answers, "In Mag Mel," on the "marvelous plain" in the Land of the Faeries. Cuchulainn prudently decides to send his chariot driver and battle companion Loeg before giving his answer. Loeg leaves with Liban and then returns with an enthusiastic report for Cuchulainn. The hero then accepts the adventure. He routs all of Labraid's enemies and receives as his reward the beautiful Fand, with whom he remains for one month.

Subsequently, following his return to Ireland where he has arranged to meet again with Fand whenever and wherever she chooses, Cuchulainn and the fairy woman are threatened by Emer, the hero's wife, accompanied by fifty women. After numerous discussions and lamentations on the part of both women, Fand decides to leave Cuchulainn forever. But he remains prostrate, and it takes all the science of the Druids to pull him out of his languishing malady, which is in fact "love sickness." They also have to make him imbibe a drink of forgetfulness, and Mananann himself has to shake his cloak between Cuchulainn and Fand, with a magic gesture, to prevent them from ever meeting again.

This adventure of Cuchulainn bears a close resemblance to courtly love. It is in fact with Mananann's agreement, thus with her husband's agreement, that Fand may give her love to the hero. But this man, in order to obtain Fand, must pass through a certain number of tests, first illness, then journey to the Land of the Faeries, finally combat against Fand's clan enemies. So this has something in common with the attitude of a Lancelot struggling against Arthur's enemies in order to win Guinivere. The lover-knight of the twelfth century, like the lover-hero of primitive Celtic society, enters into a contract with his lady, the embodiment of a community to whom he must devote himself body and soul.

In "The Illness of Cuchulainn," there is again the famous triangle—without which the contract might remain incomplete—requiring the woman, the husband, and the lover. But the contract is broken with the appearance of a fourth person, that of Emer, Cuchulainn's wife; hence Fand must return to Mananann and Cuchulainn must drink the draught of forgetfulness. Everything becomes distorted by Emer's jealousy—just as in Tristan's story the process of death is accelerated by the jealousy of Iseult of the White Hands, who precipitates Tristan into despair with her lie that the boat's sail is black, meaning that Kaherdin has failed to bring Iseult the Fair back with him. And yet Tristan had taken the precaution of not consummating his union with Iseult of the White Hands.

This triangle, seemingly indispensable to the equilibrium of *fin'amor*, can be seen in numerous tales, particularly that of "The Courtship of Etaine," one of the most beautiful love stories of ancient Ireland. In the first part of the legend, we witness the quest for the woman (in this instance the young Etaine, daughter of an Irish king), not by the one who is in love with her, the god Mider of Bri Leith, but by his adopted son, Oengus, the Mac Oc, son of Dagda. This quest seems the equivalent of Tristan's quest for Iseult in the name of his uncle Mark. But when exposed to the jealousy of Mider's first wife, Etaine is bewitched and transformed into an insect from which she is reborn in the form of a new Etaine, who then marries the high king of Ireland, Eochaid Aireainn.

Now the high king's brother, Alill Anglonnach, falls in love with the beautiful Etaine, and as this love seems an impossible thing to him, he falls into a languishing illness. One day, however, he confesses his secret to Etaine:

> Here is the reason for my injury: there is no song upon my harp, I am incapable of speaking, I am no longer master of my reason and my heart is in similar straits. A sad thing, o wife of the king, . . . my spirit and body are ill, . . . my love is a thistle, it is a desire for force and violence, it is like the four corners of the earth, it is endless like the sky; it is the breaking of a neck, it is drowning in water, it is a battle against a shadow, it is a race toward the sky, it is an adventurous trek beneath the sea, it is love for a shadow.[15]

Such romantic strains are worthy of a troubadour's song, with, in the final analysis, more violence and poetry than you would find there. But we find in this story all the same agonies and sufferings as in the songs of the courtly lover, trembling before the image of the inaccessible, cruel lady.

Etaine lets herself be swayed by the steadfastness and suffering of her brother-in-law. She ends up telling him: "Come to my room tomorrow, in the house outside the fortress, and there I will give myself to your request and desire."[16] One would think the rest of the story would then resemble that of Tristan and Iseult, but it does nothing of the sort. For three evenings Ailill, when he is about to meet with Etaine, is stricken by an incomprehensible slumber and each time it is a "shadow" that comes to the rendezvous. Etaine ends up provoking the shadow, who then reveals that he is Mider, her former husband, and it was he who put this insane passion for her in Ailill's head, so that he might feel it himself. And Mider asks her if she truly wishes to accompany him to the land of marvels, that is, to the Otherworld. Etaine replies that she accepts on condition that Eochaid Aireainn give his consent.

Mider than turns up at Eochaid's palace and engages him in a game of chess. He loses the first game and must take on an extremely difficult task. He loses the second time too, and the task is even more difficult. He pulls it off with the help of the people of the *sidh,* that is, with the fairy beings of whom he is one of the leaders. But the third time, Mider wins the game and claims Etaine from her husband, Eochaid. The high king of Ireland prevaricates and requests a delay, which is granted. At the end of the allotted time, Mider enters the royal fortress, thwarting the snares and guards the king has placed in his way. Mider reminds Eochaid of his promise and reveals that Etaine herself has promised to follow him if Eochaid agrees. Etaine acquiesces: "I told you I would not accompany you as long as Eochaid had not surrendered me. But you may take me if Eochaid gives me up." Eochaid tries to resist, but he cannot prevent Mider from embracing Etaine. Then Mider "took the woman in his right arm and carried her through the ceiling of the house. In great shame the warriors gathered about the king. They saw two swans flying away from Tara on the plain."[17]

The mythological outline is precise: the first time Mider managed to obtain Etaine, it was by contravening established custom, on one hand because the quest for Etaine had been accomplished not by him but by his adopted son, on the other hand because he already had a wife. He therefore lost Etaine, because there was not a true accord between them. But the second time it was Mider himself who undertook the quest, and he wrested willy-nilly the husband's consent out of him. The triangle thus being re-formed, Mider has the right to take Etaine with him.

There is also another reason. Etaine, in her first existence, was a fairy, a sacred being. In her second existence, she is no more than a woman, and furthermore she is the wife of a perfectly human king. So she is in a state of decline, and only the god Mider can restore her divine aspect. That is, while the man has need of the divine Woman, this divine Woman is nothing without the male, her lover-priest. Throughout the Irish tradition, it is well known that no fairy can take any action without the presence of a man. It all concerns the couple, not the individual alone. Everything suggests that Celtic mythology realized an absolute certainty in the thought of Celtic peoples: only the couple can transform the world. The main thing is to know what foundations constitute this couple. And naturally, when we look at the later era in which these old stories were gathered and copied down, we see that the couple takes on a clearly infernal hue. Let us not forget, it was the Christian monks of Ireland and Great Britain who transcribed the old pagan epics of their ancestors.

Having said as much, it can happen that the union between the mistress and her lover takes on truly platonic aspects. There is a fairly characteristic example in a tale concerning the Welsh hero Pwyll, in whom it is easy to recognize the archetype of the Fisher King Pelles from the Quest of the Holy Grail. It is an adventure told at the beginning of the first branch of the Welsh *Mabinogion*, a collection of tales going back to the darkest times of Breton tradition. Pwyll, prince of Dyved, one day becomes separated from the rest of his hunting companions. He spies another pack of hounds chasing a stag. He drives off this pack and takes the stag for himself. A man then appears before him, the owner of this other pack, who states his name is Arawn, lord of Annwyn, and he demands reparation for the outrage he has suffered.

The name *Annwyn* is revealing. It is the Welsh term for the original Abyss, in other words, the Otherworld, the "kingdom of the dead," in the same way the Irish word *sidh* designates the "peaceful" world. In short, Arawn asks Pwyll to rid him of a rival; this is the price he must pay to make up for slighting the lord and to obtain his friendship. This seems a simple reparation, as often took place in primitive Celtic society. But in reality it is, pure and simple, an initiatory test. For Pwyll not only has to take the place of Arawn in his kingdom, for the length of one year, but he must also assume Arawn's appearance and act so that no one will notice the substitution, not even Arawn's own wife. An indecent situation if ever there was one. Pwyll therefore takes Arawn's place and appearance; Arawn takes his place and appearance in the kingdom of Dyved.

Pwyll is dumbstruck at the splendor of Arawn's court: "Of all the courts he had seen in the world, it was the best provided with food and drink, as well as golden plate and royal jewels."[18] Of course this is evocative of the legendary riches of the Otherworld. Pwyll begins by taking his ease and taking maximum advantage of the wealth of his temporary kingdom. But then it comes time to go to bed. The pseudo-Arawn has complete freedom to do whatever he wants: the true king has laid no prohibition upon him, and Arawn's queen is particularly beautiful and desirable. Pwyll could have acted like Uther Pendragon, whom Merlin through his magic cloaked in the features of the count of Cornwall and who took advantage of this to have sexual relations with the countess Ygerne (thus conceiving the future King Arthur). Pwyll, however, does nothing of the sort: "As soon as they were in bed, he turned his back to her and his face to the edge and did not speak a single word until morning. On the following day there was naught but tenderness between them and fond conversation. But no matter how affectionately they treated one another during the day, he behaved the same as he had the first night for every night of the year he was there."[19] Then after Pwyll has eliminated Arawn's rival he goes in search of the other, and both of them resume their rightful places and appearances. And this is why Pwyll will always merit his title *Penn Annwyn,* "master, or lord of the Otherworld," an honorific that fits very well the archetype of the Fisher King, guardian of the Grail.

We could certainly discuss here that curious ascetic custom among the monks in Celtic countries, of sleeping with a beautiful woman without touching her at all in order to prove they could resist temptations and transcend their human state. The test imposed upon Pwyll is no doubt of this type. But it is also a kind of trial of *fin'amor*. And emerging victorious from this trial, Pwyll is considerably transformed by the contact he has with the queen of Annwyn, who is none other than one of the images of the goddess of beginnings. This is why he earns the nickname lord of Annwvyn. In fact it is the queen who gave it to him, thus helping to transform this figure completely and to give him a divine character. Is this not the real, deep purpose of *fin'amor*?

Moreover, Pwyll's asceticism in abstaining from relations with the queen of Annwyn is not gratuitous. It constitutes a kind of necessary purification before finding oneself before the true figure of the goddess, the true figure that is impossible to contemplate without initiatory preparation. Herein lies the significance of this fable. And, shortly afterward, Pwyll (now *Penn Annwyn*) will meet and marry the gentlewoman Rhiannon, the "Great Queen," who is actually the perfect incarnation of the goddess of beginnings. This is how the hierogamy is achieved, through successive stages of initiations and purifications. This is how the infernal couple is formed, by the god of the Abyss, keeper of the world's secrets, joining with the mother-goddess of beginnings, who gives life and distributes the goods of this world among all her children.

Although the lady of courtly love is never shown in her maternal aspect (which would make no sense in her relations with her lover), she is nonetheless the symbolic mother, to whom her lovers come to find nourishment, since they are also her children. We find here a metaphysical theme that Catholic theologians never can treat without fear—which is quite understandable, given their progress toward an impasse with the theme of the Virgin Mary, wife of the Holy Spirit and mother of Jesus. Now, since the Trinity is made up of three entities, all three of them God himself, we must admit this causes several problems of interpretation. In a word, who is the Virgin Mary? Is she not the mother and lover, if not the wife, of God Jesus? The question could not be any more awkward.

A Welsh legend collected somewhat later but bearing the mark of archaic features, the legend of the bard Taliesin, throws some light on the problem of the lady, who is at the same time mother and mistress. The central figure is a certain Ceridwen, who with her husband, Tegid the

Bald, lives in the middle of a lake. The image is specific and clearly echoes the theme of the Isle of Avalon. Now Ceridwen had a son, Afang-Du, who is a kind of ill-favored monster. In fact his name means "black beaver." It seems that underneath this appearance is concealed the vague recollection of a dragon or a serpent, an animal linked to the mother-goddess that is, in reality, one of her essential symbolic components. However, in order to give her son intelligence and beauty, Ceridwen boils up a magic cauldron and orders a certain Gwyon Bach (the "little scholar") to watch over it while it cooks. Now three drops of the liquid fall on Gwyon Bach's finger, whereupon he puts his finger in his mouth and imbibes the three drops: "At that very instant, he saw everything that was to come[20] and knew he would have to protect himself from Ceridwen's wiles, for she was very cunning. Prey to an irrepressible fear, he flees to his homeland."[21] However, Ceridwen, furious, pursues him relentlessly:

> He saw her and changed himself into a hare in order to get away, but she changed herself into a greyhound and caught up with him. He fled toward the river and became a fish. But Ceridwen, in the form of an otter, pursued him under the waters so relentlessly that he had to change into a bird. She then followed him in the form of a falcon and left him no respite under the sky. And just as she was on the verge of pouncing on him and he feared for his life, he spied a pile of grain that had just been threshed on the roof of a barn. He hurried there and turned himself into a grain. But Ceridwen took the form of a high-combed, black hen and . . . swallowed him. And as the story goes, she became pregnant. When her time came and she gave birth, she did not have the heart to kill the child because of his great beauty. This is why she put him in a leather sack. She threw the sack into the sea.

Of course, the sack gets fished back out of the ocean, and the person who discovers the child inside cries out *tal iesin*, meaning "shining forehead." This is why the child, who will become the most famous and the most inspired of all bards, will be called Taliesin.[22]

All the necessary ingredients are found in this story: the goddess of beginnings in the midst of the waters; the cauldron of knowledge and inspiration, which is the heart of the goddess; the enlightenment represented by the three drops, which transform a "little scholar" into another being; the hellish pursuit, a veritable dissolution in the alchemical sense; the assimilation of the grain, the symbol of sexual union between Ceridwen and Gwyon Bach; the hero's new maturity and his second birth, that of the spirit; finally, the name of light bestowed upon him. It is well and truly a process of individual metamorphosis—through the contact (sexual or otherwise) of the primitive man with the goddess, exactly as it happened to Enkidu during his relations with the "girl of the streets" that Gilgamesh had ordered for him. And in a more mythological form, more popular as well (the vocabulary is that of an oral tale), this story means much the same as the narrative of the quest of a Tristan or a Lancelot toward the lady who haunts his thoughts, then of the joy he obtains from this lady in the chamber-sanctuary, joy during the course of which not only does the lover achieve his new birth into the light but the lady also realizes her fullness by becoming her lover's mother. *Because every woman is a mother, even if she never actually gives birth to a child.*

Ceridwen is a meaningful example of the delicate alchemy that is produced in the chamber where courtly lovers lie together. She is also the figure who can make us comprehend what lies hidden beneath the reassuring aspect of the Holy Virgin, the benevolent Mary, mother of God and of all men, otherwise known as *Our Lady*.

Our Lady the Virgin

The twelfth and thirteenth centuries witnessed the covering of Christian Europe with splendid religious buildings consecrated to Our Lady, from the smallest Roman chapel lost in the remotest countryside to the most sumptuous ogival cathedral located in the very heart of a city. This indicates a considerable fervor in honor of Mary, the mother of God, and at the very time that troubadours and romance writers were glorifying woman as *Domina*, the all-powerful mistress of hearts and minds, supreme goal of the lover-knight's actions. All this obviously did not happen by chance, nor is it difficult to establish that the cult of the Virgin Mary and the exaltation of the lady of *fin'amor* were none other than two sides of the same metaphysical reality, a reality that seems to have been lived in an exceptional and quite remarkable fashion during this era.

But then, who is this Virgin Mary that people so honored in Our Lady [Notre Dame Cathedral] of Paris, Our Lady of Chartres, Our Lady of Puy, who often took on strange names such as Our Lady of the Water, Our Lady of the Arbor, Our Lady of Pain, Our Lady of Joy, even Our Lady of the Pines, Our Lady of the Watch, and Our Lady of Charity? Her names were innumerable, and new ones were constantly created. And all of them refer to the same person, so much so that this abundance of different epithets tends to conceal the original entity in a sort of blur that makes it difficult to pick out the features of the real face.

The Scriptures speak little of Mary, the mother of Jesus. The four evangelists all agree she was present at her son's crucifixion, but Mark does not mention her anywhere else. John, the only one to recount the episode, puts her on the scene—and gives her a certain authority over Jesus—at the wedding in Cana. Matthew mentions her pregnancy before her marriage and Joseph's doubts, and then very briefly the birth of Jesus. It is Luke who writes the most on the subject, enlarging on the annunciation and the birth. As for the Acts of the Apostles, apparently written by Luke, they just show her, after the ascension of Jesus, in the midst of the Apostles. The least that can be said is that she scarcely occupies the center of the evangelical stage. We can only be surprised at the fantastic disproportion between Mary's modest journey through the Scriptures and the exceptional importance of the Marian cult.

It is not a question here of discussing the problem of Mary's real and historical existence, no more than that of Jesus. It is certain that a Jeschua (Jesus), a descendant of David, did exist historically at the time of Augustus and Tiberius; that he was involved in widespread, public action in Roman-controlled Palestine; and that he was condemned—

not by the Jews (who incidentally did not have the authority to do so), for religious reasons, *but by the Romans,* for political motives, as is indicated by the inscription INRI (Jesus the Nazarene King of the Jews)—as an agitator and enemy of Roman authority. Historically this is all we can know. The rest is the business of theologians. Was he the Son of God, as he claimed—or as it is claimed that he claimed? There is nothing original about this, the expression "son of God" being common to the Jewish community. Was he the embodiment of God? This is what was claimed by those who declared themselves his apostles, and it still seems to have taken them some time to admit it, as is testified by the stories from the Gospels. But this is primarily what was claimed by Paul of Tarsus—a Jew, a Roman citizen, Greek-speaking and of Hellenic culture, who is the historical founder of Christianity, its first historian and thus its first theologian. From here on out, a religion was born and developed with well-known success, resting on the fundamental figure of a Jesus-man who is at once man and God incarnated, and who, above all, is *Christ* or *Messiah,* that is to say, "anointed," *chosen and marked* by the deity to accomplish a mission among humans. Whether Jesus Christ was a man-god, a simple prophet, even a simple political agitator matters little; he has become the perfect model of what every human being must become: a Christ surpassing the human condition and, after his victory over Evil and Death, showing each one of us the path to eternity. This is an intellectual reality, which is what counts.

Under these conditions Mary, mother of Jesus, acquires this same value of intellectual reality. But given the modest role she played in the life of Jesus, how was it that she became, essentially in Orthodox and Catholic worship, a person so important and so venerated, almost the equal of her son? After all, the Marian devotion was nonexistent in early Christianity. It was not until the fourth century that she appeared, incidentally provoking scandals that were denounced by the Church Fathers.

In fact the Gnostic sects, in their systematic search for a tradition reaching back into the depths of the past and finding its completion in the evangelical message, very soon wished to invoke a feminine deity, recalling the ancient mother-goddesses and capable of crystallizing all the impulses of the human being toward supreme understanding. For the Gnostic theoreticians, the Holy Spirit represented the Mother of the Holy Trinity. The word used to designate the Holy Spirit was neutral in Greek, but it was feminine in Aramaic and Hebrew. Gnosticism was quick to replace the neutral Greek *pneuma* (πνευμα; literally, "breath") with the feminine *sophia* (σοφια; "wisdom"), the term being used indiscriminately for masculine or feminine but clearly designating the feminine features and characteristics of the deity. This also explains the origin of the name of the basilica of Saint Sophia in Constantinople. But *Saint Sophia* is only a name. Now the Gnostics did not stop there. They considered "Sophia" the proper mother of Jesus, and they worshiped her as a goddess.

Reaction was not long in coming. Epiphanus, one of the Church Fathers (315–403), condemned unequivocally anyone who worshiped Mary in particular: "The body of Mary is holy, but it is not divine; she is a virgin and worthy of great honors, but she must not be for us an object of adoration." As for Saint Ambrose, whose influence on Saint Augustine was considerable, he stated: "Mary was the temple of God and not the God of the Temple, that is why the only one to be adored must be He whose presence animates the Temple." But Ambrose's explanation hides a malaise: if Mary is the temple of God, then she is a container. Now, as God Jesus is the contained, then we should consider the container inferior to its contents, and the contents would risk being contaminated by its stay in the container, that is to say, in Mary. This was the starting point for a considerable theological problematic concerning Mary, mother of God, that would end up in the dogma of the Immaculate Conception—a lesser evil, in the final analysis, as it prevented Mary from being considered God's equal, that is, a "goddess."

This was, however, the view put forth by the Gnostics, expressing themselves in terms of mysticisms both mythological and cosmological, creating a fairly synthetic blend between the so-called pagan elements and the Judeo-Christian elements. The pagan elements were from the great goddess with multiple faces, multiple functions, and multiple names, but always the universal Mother, creator of all energies. The

Judeo-Christian elements were first of all the celestial Jerusalem, image symbolizing future humanity; then the *assembly* itself of the participants in this celestial Jerusalem, otherwise called the *Ecclesia,* the Church (Roman Catholic, of course). Hence the qualifications that have since been widely spread in the hyperbolic language of theologians and sermon-makers, along the lines "Our very holy mother Church." Jesus himself, according to the Gospels, alludes to this celestial Jerusalem and he speaks of it in feminine terms. Saint Paul defines it as "our mother." It is the second Eve (who comes to crush the serpent's head), the true mother of the living, through whom is communicated to us the spiritual life of Christ, himself the new Adam. Finally, the Church was represented as the bride of Christ, much as the nation of Israel was the bride of Jehovah, and "through baptism, the converted became the children of the Virgin mother, and a comparison was made between the baptismal fonts and her uterus. . . . Thus the feminine principle, personified initially by the *Magna Mater,* was transmuted into *Mater Ecclesia,* both Bride and body of Christ, and became Mother of the believers."[23] Let us not forget that in the sacrifice of the mass the priest, embodiment of the assembly that is the Church and thus the feminine principle, provokes the very nuptials of this assembly with Jesus Christ, who descends upon the altar.

Saint Paul granted little importance to this problem, which to him appeared minor if not utterly irrelevant. In contrast, the priest Arius (founder of Arianism and native of Alexandria, where Near Eastern and Gnostic elements met and merged) maintained a long ideological dispute during the first third of the fourth century with Saint Athanasius (bishop of Alexandria in 328 A.D.) on what definition to give the Incarnation. Arius, who refused to believe in the divine nature of Jesus and, because of this, denied any importance to Mary, rejected any intrusion of femininity in the Christian doctrine. Saint Athanasius, in reaction, was led to increase the significance of this feminine influence. According to him, if Mary was not the mother of the Word, this Word could not have been consubstantial *(homoousios)* with humankind. Thus Mary must necessarily be the true mother of Christ, with all the consequences this entailed, if one wanted to prove the divine nature of Jesus, paralleling his human nature. And Mary emerged from this debate as the crucible wherein was realized the fusion of the human with the divine. This idea has not ceased to haunt not only theologians but also the theoreticians of *fin'amor*.

The problem is that this is all the discussion of intellectuals, speaking through abstract concepts and perfectly aware of the symbolic value of the images and myths they were manipulating to serve their own purposes. The faithful were clueless, including the rural parish priests, who were scarcely less ignorant than their flocks. It was unthinkable to present them with such theories. They were content to follow whatever was thought good to tell them, so they could keep their flocks on the straight and narrow (the path of the Church, but also that of temporal power), their flocks hoping for only one thing—to be well rewarded in the Otherworld for their goodwill in this one.

Now, what theologians have a tendency to ignore is the weight placed on institutions by the large masses. After the early days of messianic enthusiasm, where the end of the world was promised in each and every storm, the sluggish populace was overcome with weariness. The evangelical message insisted on the determining role of Jesus and his apostles. The Church was in fact an assembly of priests (*presbutoi*, that is, "elders"), invested with powers and contemptuous of women, who were considered inferior beings. In short, Christianity—after having, however, contributed to the emancipation of woman (daughter of God), notably through the reinforcement of marriage and the recognition of her maternal role—blithely extended the patriarchal misogyny of Indo-European societies (to which Semitic societies had also rallied). Women's mysteries have always alarmed the guardians of patriarchal power. What can be done to get rid of them? What can be done to ignore them? Assuredly, the Church Fathers, basing their argument on the fact that Jesus was surrounded by only male apostles (having carefully made the burdensome presence of Mary Magdalene disappear), were not far from preaching that the paradise promised by Jesus was open only to men and that, in any state of affairs, religious problems concerned men only.

This made for an abstraction of the residual pagan substratum, notably in the Middle Eastern and Celtic countries, where the image of the goddess had left traces in popular memory. Thrown off balance somewhat by the androcratic character of the new God being presented them, the newly Christianized people had only one idea in mind. This was to find for themselves a feminine figure who was not so distant or so intransigent as the biblical Jehovah, even as revised and corrected by the "good" Jesus, who was said to have come to preach charity and universal love. This was a natural reaction. In face of an omnipotent and fearsome God, they sought a mediator, or rather a mediatrix, a female being who could speak for the weak and present requests to the Master of the universe, exactly as the mother in a family speaks for her children when the father takes refuge in law and custom.

The newly Christianized peoples, with more or less enthusiasm and spontaneity, preserved the memory of an era where they worshiped and prayed to a mother-goddess. This nostalgia joined with the memory of the experiences of the Hebrew people, whose leaders never ceased to struggle in the name of Jehovah against detestable female figures and idols going by the names of Ishtar, Astarte, Tanit, Cybele, Artemis, Aphrodite, and Venus, who were always ready to invade the Holy Land and whose more or less erotic cults contradicted the strict rigor displayed in the Temple of Jerusalem. A belief is never destroyed; it is only modified and rerouted. This is what the Church Fathers did. They tried to fight against the ancient goddess of beginnings, but she survived and rematerialized with the features of the holy Church, and then of the benevolent Virgin Mary. Thus, unable to extinguish her completely, they adopted her as their own, reserving the right to sanitize her and to give her whatever appearance they wished. Here, briefly summarized, is the genesis of the Marian cult, which would find its triumph and its flowering during the twelfth and thirteenth centuries.

First there was the Council of Ephesus of 431 A.D. This council decided to recognize Mary, mother of Jesus, under the title of Theotokos (θεοτοκωσ), which is to say the parent of God. In truth this title is not new; it belonged to the ancient mother-goddess of Ephesus. It was not by accident that it was the Council of Ephesus that officially recognized Mary as the mother of God. *Ephesus was, in fact, the uncontested capital of the cult of the mother-goddess,* honored previously under the name of Artemis, the famous Scythian Diana, simultaneously kind and cruel, virgin and sensual, inaccessible and near, the barely disguised image of the feminine solar deity of the first Indo-Europeans, combined with that of the more lascivious image of the Mesopotamian goddess of sexuality, beauty, and love.

This mother-goddess of Ephesus was too powerful and too present in people's spirits to eliminate. So she was recruited to the cause. Now they miraculously discovered the places where Mary, mother of Jesus, had resided in Ephesus and made sure to exploit them. But in fact all this was supported only by vague, uncontrollable traditions with no confirmation to be found in canonical Scripture. The essential thing was to demonstrate to the world that the great goddess was no longer Artemis (or Astarte, Tanit, or Venus), but the Virgin Mary, mother of the Savior—even if she had been stripped of some of her divinity in order to make her simply the "Temple" of God.

We know that the Council of Ephesus fully succeeded in realizing the goal it had set. This official decision of the Roman Church would provide a powerful impetus to the cult of the Virgin Mary:

> Alleged portraits of the Virgin began to appear. One of them, the Hodegetria, attributed to Saint Luke, was sent, it is said, by the empress Eudoxia in 438 A.D. to her sister-in-law Pulcheria, who placed it in the church of Constantinople. This icon was the object of a very specific veneration over the centuries. It was even transported on a chariot by the army when they campaigned against the enemy, as had been previously done with the effigy of Cybele. At the beginning of the century, it was turned to for consecrating churches and, in the sixth century, Madonnas and the infant Jesus had become one of the favorite subjects of Christian iconography. They used the same symbolic colors as had served in the goddess's icons; even her outfit seems familiar: Mary wears a crown of stars

and a starry cloak, she has her feet resting on the moon, and she is strangely reminiscent of the effigies of Aphrodite. She sometimes holds an ear of corn like the Virgin of Corn Ears *(Spica Virgo),* or is accompanied by the dove that is dear to Ishtar, treading on the serpent, which, until that time, had invariably been associated with representations of the goddess. Her history abounds in legends that once were those of Ishtar or Juno.[24]

Myths have a hardy life, probably because they represent the only reality of thought that is eternal.

It is not a good idea to speak to people in a language they do not understand. If the people want certain images, it is a good idea to furnish them, even if the original meaning is modified:

> Although directed from the very interior of Christianity, this devotion combines a triple current, at once Jewish (daughter of Zion), early Christian (Our Mother the Church), and pagan (the goddess). In fact, nostalgia for the feminine deity, the adoration of maternity, is rooted so profoundly in the human heart that it is impossible to extirpate it completely. In compliance with the law of the human heart and in opposition to dogma, the cult of the Mother of God eventually asserted itself. . . . Thus the Artemis of the Ephesians becomes the "great, sublime, glorious Mother of God." The most beautiful flower in the religion of nature fills the most apparent hole in the religion of salvation. Isis returns with Horus in her arms. Mary becomes the goddess of fertility, of love and of beauty, the most noble of all that history has known.[25]

So we now have the image—and the worship—of the mother-goddess restored in honor of Mary, mother of Jesus, who has been elevated to the rank of Theotokos (Θεοτοκωσ). But here again there is nothing new. The Virgin with child may well take part in an iconography and a thought rightfully belonging to Christianity, but it certainly is not a Christian invention. There are endless examples in all traditions preceding Christianity. Since prehistoric times, the group formed by the mother-goddess and her son was worshiped in various countries, notably Crete and eastern Russia, by the Hittites, and in Phrygia. Among the Celts, just prior to the Roman conquest of Gaul, groups of *matrones* appeared, arranged in threes (the triad being a typical Celtic symbol), holding a child on their knees. In these designs, the sovereignty of the mother is in no way diminished, as it will later be in Christianity, where we witness an overturning of polarity: the son becomes the god and the mother merely the instrument of his birth. On the contrary, among the ancient peoples, the goddess retains her full power, and her son is clearly subordinated. It is probable furthermore that we are dealing with a symbolic son, the group depicting only, in concrete fashion, the concept of maternity with which they surrounded the divinity. Later (at least in the Mediterranean basin, where the great upheaval took place when the male realized himself and took control over the female), the Mother would be depicted with two children, one of each sex. This change is also transcribed in the myth of Leto (Latona), mother of Artemis (Diana) and Apollo.

It has not always been this way. The primitive mother-goddess, at first alone, has sometimes been divided into two female figures, one made into mother and the other daughter. This is the myth of Demeter and Korê, that is, the dyad formed by an older goddess and by another, younger goddess. This dyad is common to the mythologies of the Greeks, Latins, and Etruscans but can also be found in Japan, where the goddess Amaterasu is often accompanied by her double, with the obvious signification of the goddess of the setting sun (Amaterasu herself) extended by the goddess of the rising sun. But after this trend was reversed, the girl became a son. Thus were organized the myths of Ishtar and Tammuz, Astarte and Adonis, and Isis and Horus. In reality all these myths are perfectly identical. They all include "a descent into hell suggesting a death followed by resurrection, and a dyad formed by two deities of different ages. But whereas Demeter and Korê are two goddesses, Astarte and Adonis are of different sexes. Thus we pass from the female dyad to the bisexual couple. It is the application of this principle that fertility requires the union of the two sexes," whereas in previous times, fertility was considered the exclusive domain of the feminine sex.[26] And with all allowances being made, it is this new heterosexual couple that we meet again in the infernal couple of *fin'amor*. The lady is symbolically older than her lover-knight because she is the goal to be attained, and by virtue of this fact is situated on a higher plane.

Whatever the case may be, the Virgin Mary is the heir of this ancestral tradition, and she is depicted with Jesus in the same manner as the prehistoric mother-goddess. There is a certain continuity to myth. But one large problem remains: the problem of Mary's virginity.[27]

It is in fact above all doubt that Mary, as the goddess of beginnings, is a mother. Now, biologically, in order to be a mother, a woman must first have a sexual relationship with a man—unless we go no further than the primitive belief from matriarchal eras when man was still unaware of his role and the role of sexual intercourse in procreation. Thus either the Virgin Mary is not a real virgin or she is the exact image of the ancient goddess of beginnings who achieved her parturition herself without the aid of any masculine entity. The Christian context speaks of the intervention of the Holy Ghost, which seems to settle the matter but which, in reality, only postpones any solution to the question. Because how can a spirit, even a holy one, being of immaterial nature unite with a material element without passing through the customary natural process, with spirit commanding matter, and matter realizing what the spirit demands?

Let us go back to the texts. "Mary, his mother, was engaged to Joseph; now, before they started living together, she found that she had been made pregnant by the Holy Ghost" (Matthew 1:18). On its own this statement would be profoundly shocking without the reference to the Holy Ghost. But except for describing Joseph's doubts and the appearance of an angel, the text says nothing more on the matter. There is nothing about Mary's virginity or nonvirginity. There is no mention of Mary's virginity in the entire Gospel of Matthew except for one ambiguous passage: "[Joseph] took his woman into his house and did not know her until the day she gave birth to a son" (Matthew 1:24–25). This in any case might imply that Joseph knew Mary after she gave birth to Jesus, the "firstborn son" Luke speaks of—which might easily justify the "brothers" of Jesus, who are mentioned everywhere even though pains are taken to point out that they actually were his cousins.

Let us take the Gospel of Luke, apparently the best informed on Christ's childhood. We are granted a story about the Annunciation, but although the angel Gabriel declares to Mary that she will conceive and give birth to a son who will be the "Son of God" (that is to say, a Jew like all the others!), there is no mention of the young woman's virginity, and, as is noted by the commentators of the French translation of the Jerusalem Bible, "nothing in the text puts forward the idea of a vow of virginity" (Luke 1:30–35). And the tale of the birth of Jesus provides no indication either, except that Joseph had gone to be "counted in the census with Mary, his fiancée, who was pregnant" (Luke 2:5), which, in all good faith, is a shocking detail, unless it is there as a provocation.

In short, Mary's virginity does not appear in the Gospels. It was the Church Fathers who introduced this notion into the dogma, from a commonplace in the Old Testament and in all religious traditions, the image of the *Virgin who must give birth*. But what does this word *virgin* actually mean?

The French word comes from the Latin *virgo*, and it was introduced into everyday language by a religious term originally used to designate certain saints of the Christian calendar. But the Latin word means only "young girl," with no other specific details, that is, an "unmarried woman" with no connotation of chastity. The meaning of a "physically pure young girl" can be conveyed only by the expression *virgo intacta*. The Celtic root equivalent to the root that gives the Latin *virgo* is *wraki*, whose derivatives we find in the Breton *gwreg* ("wife") and the Welsh *gwraig* ("woman"). Another derivative of *wraki* was the Celtic *wrakka*, which gave the Breton *grac'h* or *groac'h* ("old woman," then "sorceress"), and we find it again in the Gallic *virago*, which was adopted into Latin before being borrowed wholesale by French. Behind all these words we can see an ancient Indo-European root word *werg*, which means "to enclose." The virgin would therefore be the "woman enclosed upon herself," which corresponds perfectly to the idea of virginity in its narrowest sense, but also the least certain sense.

Now, the root *werg* is not isolated. In Greek, it has given us *ergon* (εργον; "action") as well as its derivatives *energieia* (ενεργεια; "energy"), *orgion* (οργιον; "religious ceremony," and "orgy"), *organon* (οργανον; "instrument," and "organ"). It can be connected to the Gallic *ver* ("great," and "powerful"), which most likely provided the augmentative Welsh prefix *guor-* and the Irish *for-*, as well as the Breton preposition *war* ("over," in the sense of the Latin *super*), and the English adverb *very*. As for Latin *vis* ("force"), whose radical is *vir* ("man" or "male"; in Irish *fer*, in Breton *gour*), it is difficult not to connect it to the same root. In this way the virgin, according to etymology (and all etymology is subject to contention), would be connected to the ideas of *force, action,* and *claustration,* all of which were covered by femininity. In thinking further on the matter, this appears perfectly compatible with the mythological image of the mother-goddess, and in accord with the power and virtue attributed to the Virgin in Christian tradition.

The Hebrew Bible uses three words to designate a virgin: *naara, betula,* and *alma.* The term *naara* comes from a root word expressing movement, agitation, and precipitation and designates "a young married or unmarried girl," *virgo intacta* or not. In truth the term is thoroughly vague and resembles somewhat the medieval word for "maiden" [*pucelle,* in French], which does not mean anything precise. The term *naara* is in fact used to describe a married woman accused of having lost her innocence before marriage (Deuteronomy 12:15–16), but also for a widow who has not remarried (Ruth 2:16), as well as in Genesis where the word in one passage describes Rebecca, who is a *virgo intacta,* and in another passage (34:3) is used to designate a young girl who lost her innocence through rape.

On the other hand the term *betula* seems clearly to designate a young or an old woman who is considered a *virgo intacta,* a woman who has kept her *betulim,* a plural word meaning "hymen." But here another problem arises, and the Jewish commentators of the Bible have not shied away from discussing it, sometimes with great irony. It is medically recognized—and the Hebrews were fully aware of this—that a woman who has "known" a man may retain a portion of this mucous membrane called the hymen, as this membrane is never exactly the same in form, size, or flexibility for all women. Historical sidebars are filled with dreadful pimps who specialize in false hymens, and the Talmud (Kutubot treatise, folio 11) foresees the case in which a woman could accidentally lose this precious portion of her anatomy by falling on a protruding object, or even, according to a rabbinical expression worth its weight in gold, "by wounding herself with a piece of wood." It is true that Genesis (30:14–15) reveals a curious transaction between Leah and Rachel regarding mandrake roots.

The third term, *alma,* comes from a root word meaning "to conceal, to hide from sight." It designates a young girl whose innocence is complete, who is "hidden from the sight of men." The word is also seen in Phoenician with the meaning of *virgo intacta,*[28] but it seems a matter more of a moral than of a physical form of virginity. For the masculine *elem* designates a young unmarried man, thus a virgin in principle, if not in practice, since circumcision does not allow the least proof to be obtained of a man's virginity. The Jewish commentators, moreover, found the definition of a virgin quite troubling. One reads in the Talmud (Hhaghiga treatise, folio 14) that "a virgin who has become pregnant may become the wife of a high priest. For Schemuel (Samuel) says: I can know a woman several times without causing the loss of her virginity." We find this curious passage in Proverbs (30:18–20): "There are three things beyond my ken and four I know not: the way of the eagle in the sky, the way of a serpent on a rock, the way of a ship in the open sea. Finally *the way of a man in a virgin (alma).* Such is the way of the adulterous woman: she eats and wipes her mouth and she says: I have done no wickedness." The Talmud (Kutubot treatise, folio 6) states again: "Most men are practiced in approaching a woman without injuring the signs of her virginity." There is even an appendix to this chapter, seriously laying out the necessary methods for succeeding at this kind of endeavor.

From just these few examples, we can see that Mary's virginity, in a Latin context as well as in a biblical context, is open to lively debate, since no one agrees on the very definition of virginity, and knowing that different terms exist whose meaning changes according to circumstances. These considerations shed light on the fact that the virginity in question is in any case a moral or psychological state, not a physical state. We remember all those "maidens" who people the universe of the Welsh and Irish legends as well as in the Arthurian romances, whether they are guardians of fountains, chatelaines with downcast eyes, ladies-in-waiting to a queen, orphans with great hearts, prisoners of a wicked lord, even fairy queens. These "maidens" are incontestably virgins in the wider sense of the word; that is, they are not in a husband's power, *they are not under the authority of any man.* Looked at this way, if we trust the Gospels, Mary was not Joseph's wife and there is no indication that she married him.

The fundamental idea in the case of the Virgin Mary, as in the case of the "maidens" in the Arthurian romances, is the independence of the woman with regard to the man. Even the lady of courtly love is free, to the extent that she controls the destiny of her lover-knight and the destiny of her own husband. The Virgin is the Free Woman, always available, always new, always *possible,* the dazzling symbol of renewal, of youth, and also, consequently, of sexual freedom. Because the Virgin is also the Prostitute.[29]

It is this aspect of the prostitute, even sacred, that was abandoned in the image that the Church Fathers, and then the entire Christian community, forged of the Virgin Mary mother of God. Unable to eliminate her sexual role completely, they crystallized this role in parturition only. She is the *mother;* that is all. It does not matter how she conceived, this does not concern the ones who invoke her, and the Holy Ghost takes care of matters. Thus we arrive at the elaboration of a Virgin Mary who is completely emptied of a part of her personality, with one part of her primordial duties amputated.

Because the Virgin, whatever one may say and whatever one may do, is also the Prostitute.

In the etymological sense, of course, we are saying "she who puts herself forward," legs spread wide, ready for any coupling. Good souls will find this shocking. But there are no good souls, there are only souls that are *both good and evil.* When Jesus goes into the desert and is tempted by the Enemy, that enemy is nothing more than a projection of himself, *a part of himself,* and the so-called dialogue with Satan is in fact just an inner dialogue, in which Jesus is strongly tempted to become the master of the material world, whereas, if we believe the Gospels, his mission is to prepare the fulfillment of a "kingdom that is not of this world." The episode of the temptation in the desert is quite clear, and what is more, it is remarkably constructed. We comprehend perfectly Jesus' inner torment, prey to his own demons, that is, to his own conflicts, because even if he is God, that does not make him any less human. And if Jesus shows himself to be *double,* enclosing within himself what we call Good and Evil, which would be better called Light and Shadow, why would his mother, the Virgin Mary, not also be double, with her being of light and her being of shadow?

The Virgin is *also* the Prostitute.

The best proof is that she is free and available to every human being, who is simultaneously her child and her lover. In this domain of metaphysics, incest does not exist. And if she is available, it is that everything is *possible* with her. Are we not told that the good Holy Virgin is tuned in to the world, is tuned in to the miseries of the world, that she is *compassionate* and always intercedes in favor of the disinherited, that is, in favor of those who need her?

Furthermore, in the twelfth and thirteenth centuries, there was no lack of stories and pious narratives to recount to us some miracle of the good Virgin coming to the assistance of sinners, and particularly women sinners. "The reverend mother of a well-known abbey one day found herself in an extremely alarming predicament. She had shown her confessor, a pious ecclesiastic, a somewhat ardent affection, and the poor woman had recently realized she was pregnant. She did not know how to extricate herself from this delicate situation. But the good Virgin Mary, to whom she had prayed, came to her aid. In the greatest secrecy the Virgin Mary helped her give birth to a handsome boy who she subsequently entrusted to a hermit of the area for him to raise." The story ends there. We are not told if the handsome boy in question became a monk and carried on the passionate tendencies of his natural parents. But such as it is, this story reveals the role that the people (that is, the faithful) wanted her to play, she who is still, *in her unconscious,* the goddess of beginnings.

Another story is also exemplary. "A nun in a convent, who performed the duties of porter (hardly a glorious task in the eyes of the sisters known as the 'choir'), had one day had enough of her job and of the convent as well. She left the keys she had charge of on the altar of the chapel and went to the town where she led the more or less merry life of a prostitute. However, several months later, she began to grow weary of this eventful, uncertain kind of existence and began to regret the tranquillity of the convent. She returned, knocked on the door, and when the sister opened it and asked her name, she remembered that she had been called Sister Agatha. The porter told her she knew her name very well, as she was a saintly and blessed woman. Very surprised, the repentant sinner looked at the sister porter more closely, and then she saw she was the Holy Virgin in person, who, during her absence, had come to replace her in the convent so that no one knew she had been gone." This pretty story is meant to be edifying. What it undeniably reveals, however, is that there is a similarity between the Holy Virgin and the sinner.

The Virgin is *also* the Prostitute.

When the angel Gabriel comes to find Mary and tells her she is going to conceive a child, Mary responds immediately: "I am the Lord's servant." She has not a moment's hesitation, which is appropriate, given that she is *available* (so as not to say "a prostitute," which would be unseemly). But what no one ever asks is what would have happened if, instead of the angel Gabriel, it had been the Enemy in person—the old Sammael, otherwise known as Satan, the devil—who throws himself in the way? How would the timid Mary have responded to the infernal angel? This brings to mind the legend of Merlin. The enchanter was born from the copulation of a holy woman (a virgin, of course) with a demon incubus. The essential thing is to find a woman who is a virgin, meaning a woman who is *available.*

The Virgin is *also* the Prostitute. But she is a *sacred prostitute*. This is what is so dangerous, because this function—inscribed in the unconscious but refused by the new consciousness of androcratic Christian society (the Trinity is only masculine)—threatens to disturb a public, moral order that had been difficult to establish on the ruins of an antiquity that had lost all sense of transcendental values. And "all that Mary was not able to get back of the dark, destructive figure of the goddess (mainly her sexual worship), the Church Fathers, then the councils, theologians, and preachers have taken back up again, giving it the appearance of a living, spiritual figure in opposition to the Virgin and to God: Satan."[30] Hence the very common depiction of the virgin crushing the head of a serpent or a dragon. Hence the parable of the wise and foolish virgins. Hence, even in astrology, the opposition (but also the complicity) between the signs of Virgo and Scorpio, Virgo taking on a certain ambivalence (pure Virgin or Scorpion-Virgin), which demonstrates how difficult it is to consider her in any way other than in her totality as the goddess of beginnings.

But chasing away the goddess actually made her return with even greater strength and power. Her luminous aspect became the object of a prodigious worship under the name of Our Lady. As for her obscure aspect, this reappears as well, and with equal force, but in a very marginalized fashion. "The witchcraft trials of the Middle Ages reveal a curious group of beliefs and practices in which pagan recollections blend with Christian elements. Witches' Sabbaths took place in deserted places under the invocation of Diana and Lucifer, who plays the role of a god of Light and Sun. The dualism here is simultaneously astral and sexual; the connection is palpable between Diana, the witches, the moon, and the night. The Sabbath echoes the ancient mysteries, and the orgy ending it is related to the ancient ceremonies of the great mother cult."[31] In short, the ancient goddess of the sun was forced to seek refuge in the friendly obscurity of the night, where she became the goddess of the moon, while Lucifer the "Light Bearer," a name indicating the Morning Star originally, became the male solar god, the god of the sun, although of a *black sun*.

The patronage of the Sabbath by Diana and Lucifer is exemplary. Diana was the Artemis of the Scythians and Greeks. In Roman mythology she became Diana the Huntress, but she also became Diana the "Chaste," she who turns men down but who on the other hand binds them to her service. Diana is therefore one of the aspects of the Virgin. As for Lucifer, incapable of bringing back the old image of the Gallic Belenos, whose name means "shining one," people conferred the alarming and monstrous—because it was marginal—appearance upon him of the biblical Sammael, that is, Satan. In this way an infernal couple is formed whose Hebrew model is undoubtedly that of Lilith and Sammael. "In the Sabbath, more than anywhere else, the devil became the god of sexuality and the witches were his sacred prostitutes. Satan took with him the sexual worship of the ancient goddess. For the Sabbath is the heir to the sexual cults of yesteryear, in this instance, the worship of the great goddess. *The black mass expresses the total redemption and even the redemptive mediation of woman.* She is the priesthood, she is the altar, she is the host that provides communion to the entire group."[32] And there, quite clearly, the Virgin is *also* the Prostitute.

But it certainly seems that, originally, the infernal couple were part of a divine triad. Lilith and Sammael were not alone, for Adam too was present. According to Hebrew tradition, carefully expurgated during the Mosaic era, Lilith was Adam's first wife, and having quarreled with him she took off and formed another couple with the Enemy, the mysterious Sammael, who was subsequently identified with the snake of Genesis. In short, we find here the archetypal, famous "triangle" of courtly love: the lady between her husband and her lover-knight.

It is a good idea to stop at this archetypal notion of the "triangle" in order to get a better idea of its meaning and significance. The first image to come forward is that of Adam-Lilith-Sammael, but it has been distorted in our memory because Lilith has been concealed, cast into the shadows, in order to benefit Eve. So then a new version of the triangle takes shape: Adam-Eve-Serpent. But here, too, everything has also been distorted, because the copyists of Genesis, through their desire to conceal once and for all Lilith's sulfurous aura, gave Eve an inferior role. Eve in fact appears singularly weak and submissive in comparison to the haughty Lilith, the rebel who does not accept the male order, and who lets him know about it. Eve, in contrast, is hypocrisy incarnated, but also *weakness.* She succumbs to the serpent's wiles, she listens to him and thus provokes her own misfortune, the misfortune of Adam, and the misfortune of future humanity. Eve is thus merely the fantasy reflection of woman as seen by men, and entirely submissive—in theory—to their will, in other words to the projection of themselves onto a different nature.

The problem is that they tried to make the serpent into the symbol of Sammael, which it absolutely is not. *The serpent is a part of Eve herself,* the part that we will see later lying at the feet of the benevolent Virgin Mary. The situation is quite clear: Adam is looking at the woman, and in the fundamental dichotomy constructed within him he sees her double, that is, her two relative and complementary aspects, in the form of woman as we are accustomed to seeing her and in the form of the serpent. Adam never talks to the serpent. The serpent does not try to tempt Adam. The dialogue between Eve and the serpent is, relatively speaking, identical to that of Jesus in the desert when he is speaking with the Enemy; in other words, it is a purely inner debate. It is Eve after the debate whom Adam is looking at, and for the first time he has the realization that woman is a double being, black and white, pure and impure, divine and satanic, creative and destructive, both resigned and in revolt. *Because Eve is none other than the elaborated, intellectualized image of the ancient Lilith.*

Thus the "trio" Adam-Eve-Serpent is only an illusion inspired by humanity's crude realization that woman is a dual being, simultaneously lover and mother. Lilith is the lover. Eve is the mother. We have come back to the primordial case of our origins: the archetype is not beneath the Tree of the Knowledge of Good and Evil, but in the foliage of Eden, with Lilith the central figure of a triangle made up of herself, Adam, and Sammael. Or if you prefer, it is Iseult, surrounded by Mark and Tristan, or even the Sun, surrounded by Night and the Moon. And we do not have to go much farther to find the Christian trinity. The main thing is to determine which of the three figures is the goddess, that is, which of them holds the real power: the power of creation.[33]

This is to say that Lilith is in a position of strength. She refuses Adam his biological primacy. She knows the ineffable name of Jehovah-God. If she were to speak it she would possess God himself, something (according to Hebrew tradition) he wishes to avoid at any price, even if that price is giving his permission for Lilith to live with Sammael, the mysterious Enemy, who is not otherwise mentioned but who seems to be the black double of the male Jehovah-God, leader of the Hebrew flock. Philosophically the vision conforms to the dialectic, as God can exist only in the presence of his double; otherwise he would have no awareness of his own existence. There is in this no casuistry: Being is nothing without Non-Being, Light does not exist without Shadow, which causes its appearance in the world of relativity. Creation, insofar as we can comprehend it, is an absurdity if we forget to include a *separation,* a *cut,* thus a gap, between the two integral parts of the great, primitive All. The word *sex,* pronounced so often, should never be spoken without reference to its etymological meaning of "separation," "cut." But cuts always leave behind painful wounds, and this is what humanity suffers through pure lovers such as Tristan and Iseult.

Iseult knows it well. She is the only one who knows it. She is also the only one to *enjoy* this triangular situation. The text of the thirteenth-century prose romance and that of the Norse saga could not be any more explicit. When Brangwain leaves the bed of Mark during the famous wedding night and Iseult takes her "normal" place at the side of the groom society intended for her, the king reawakens and asks for something to drink. Brangwain serves him the rest of the philter. The king drinks it and feels himself overcome with love for Iseult. For her part, Iseult pours out the magical potion behind her. In this way she believes she will be free to love her heart's choice, Tristan. But she has forgotten to take nature into account. King Mark "stretches out his arms toward Iseult and embraces her. As morning broke the king did not perceive the woman in his arms was different from the one he had held during the early hours of the night. For her part, Iseult showed herself submissive to the king's pleasure. As she was trying to feign pleasure, she responded to his caresses; *herself lavishing such tenderness on him that the queen conceived of the joy in it.*"[34] So what is going on here? Duplicity? Hypocrisy? Betrayal? We must admit that all this is disturbing.

However, little by little, as androcratic society gradually became more established, the goddess lost her power to the benefit of her lover, who is often her own son. At the height of the courtly era, the couple formed by Vivien and Merlin is very telling: Vivien is initiated by Merlin, she is thus his inferior. But there is a sudden reversal of the situation, a veritable return to origins. Once she is fully initiated, Vivien—who will become the Lady of the Lake, incontestable image of the mother-goddess—gains the upper hand within the dyad and locks up Merlin in an invisible castle in the air. The sole difference from the original situation is that Merlin chose his fate voluntarily: thus is formed again the infernal couple who will be the couple of *fin'amor.*

This observation is important because the Merlin-Vivien couple in the end represents the reverse-angle shot of the couple formed by the Virgin with Child. In the latter couple the Virgin Mary is only "the servant of the Lord," the principal and *theological* role being assumed by Jesus, who is God. It is the masculine element that dominates in the Christian dyad. At least officially, for we can ask ourselves the question How was this couple received by the faithful? It is probable that the people gave the better role to Mary as the mother and initiator, as well as protector of the young god. As Wolfgang Lederer put it so excellently: "The Goddess remains what she has always been, the creatress of the universe, the revealing energy of the unknown god."[35]

So here we have Our Lady the Virgin definitively in place. And what a place! She can be found in all the churches, she invades the altars, she is the perfect and exemplary saint. Her litanies are sung everywhere. She is prayed to almost more than her son. Luxurious buildings are built for her. She is represented with the features of a queen. She is crowned. She is draped in cloaks adorned with gold and embroideries. She is made to travel veritable labyrinths during processions. She appears often to her devotees. She confides her secrets to them. She

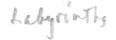

Labyrinths

cures incurable diseases. She protects the sacred springs where the faithful rush to sip of the water that confers immortality. What difference is there between the pilgrim who wends his way to Lourdes, haunted by the image of the Virgin, and Lancelot, who crosses over the Bridge of the Sword, thinking his rough journey will give him access to Guinivere's chamber?

The phenomenon is surprising. It is a long way from the timid little Galileean Mary who answers the angel with "I am the servant of the Lord" to the superb Virgin Mary who invaded, during the twelfth and thirteenth centuries, all the sanctuaries of Christian Europe. The only possible explanation is that the faithful saw in her the image of the ancient goddess of beginnings. What is more, she appears as *uniquely good;* she is stripped of the nocturnal aspects that so alarmed our ancestors and that still torment a number of people today. The Virgin Mary is Our Lady of all, but the Good Lady, the *Bona Dea* of the past. Under these conditions it is not surprising that, somewhere in a grotto in Lourdes, Bernadette Soubirous could see and hear a *white lady* speaking gentle words to her. For the white lady (a widespread theme in mythology and folklore) is the focusing of all humanity's desires for purity and happiness. She is also the fairy, and in countless folktales the Virgin gladly appears and plays the role that was at one time assumed by the fairy or the goddess. She is the goddess, at least in popular imagination.

The clergy keeps watch to ensure certain boundaries are not crossed over, however. The Trinity is always masculine. Certainly, there was an attempt to present the Holy Ghost as identical to the Virgin Mary. This is to forget that the Holy Ghost is the parent of Jesus. *If Mary should be integrated into the Trinity, it can only be in the place of God the Father.* The paternal and masculine image of the deity was imposed by the Jewish model. Of course people have need of a father and often, when there is not one, they seek him out in the form of a tyrant. But the people especially have need of a mother. And they found one in Mary. So why not a Mother-God? The importance of the Marian cult leads one to believe that this idea slyly lives on in the Christian collective unconscious. Finding it impossible to extirpate the idea, the clergy did what was necessary to neutralize a tendency that could have led to a challenge of the very theological edifice itself. On December 8, 1854, Pope Pius IX proclaimed the dogma of the Immaculate Conception.[36]

This is an important event because it recognized once and for all the dichotomy between the Virgin and the serpent. Henceforth, the Virgin was nothing more than Light, and the shadow was repressed into the monstrous forms taken by the serpent as it lurks in the deep caverns of the earth, probably in the direction of Hell. Haloed in all her light, the Virgin Mary became only the "Queen of Heaven," and as it was not possible for her to be made into a goddess, which would have been contrary to dogma, she was made into the Temple of God: Mary was thus the sole woman to escape original sin, the only one to be born in a state of absolute purity. This was obviously necessary in order to carry the Man-God in her womb. "I am the Immaculate Conception," the white lady will say to Bernadette Soubirous. And some time previously, on the rue du Bac in Paris, in a chapel today called Chapel of the Miraculous Medallion, the same white lady will appear to a humble nun, Catherine Labouré, who will say to the white lady: "Mary conceived without sin. . . ."

This obsession with purity forged the image of Our Lady the Virgin. Let us not forget, however, that the serpent is always at her feet. She owes her power to the totality of herself, and by crushing the head of the serpent she displays that power, recognizing ipso facto the reality of the serpent. It is in this regard that the Virgin Mary may be God's equal, and even more powerful than the traditional god. A nineteenth-century theologian, certainly in an ecstatic state comparable to the one Guinivere inspires in Lancelot, wrote these strange words: "Everyone obeys the orders of Mary, even God."[37] One could not express any more clearly the power of the mother-goddess, even if she remains the Holy Virgin.[38]

The Occitan troubadours and the northern trouvères, during the courtly era, echoed this almost idolatrous devotion to Our Lady. "She was in no way diminished, the deity in whom we should repose our faith, but humanity was elevated in her: he was the Father and wished to become the Son of his Daughter and always to obey her, *because he made her queen of the firmament*: this is why I serve her devotedly" (an anonymous inhabitant of the Picardy region in France). "I belong to a lady who says and does nothing but perfect things. . . . Her power is such that kings and emperors honor her and sing her praises, she who is pure of all wicked qualities. . . . My Lady wants no conceited lovers or suitors, but a sincere lover. . . . She has never had a true lover who did not receive his just reward from her. . . . My lady has a face so perfect that no improvement is possible" (Folquet de Lunel). Even a homosexual poem written by a female troubadour has been found: "Lady Mary of merit and subtle value, the joy that comes from you, your mind and your precious beauty, your manner of welcoming and giving honor, your value, your tender language and your amiable company, your kind face and your light-hearted charm, your tender glance and your loving manners, all these qualities that are yours and that none can equal incline my heart toward you with no deceit . . ." (Bieiris de Romans). And what is to be said about the numerous miracles attributed to Our Lady that the romance writers relate to us in detail before the playwrights ever put them onstage? The cleric Theophile, who had signed a pact with Satan, was he not saved from hell by the Virgin Mary? It is true that the Virgin Mary knew the serpent very well since he, originally, made up a part of her.

The most moving example of this devotion to the Virgin is without doubt the well-known medieval fabliau *Le Jongleur de Notre Dame* ("The Juggler of Our Lady"). A poor wandering poet is welcomed into a monastery, where he is told in glowing terms of the merit and beauty of the benevolent Virgin Mary. Not knowing how to honor Mary, he goes to the chapel and performs his profane dances before the statue of the Virgin, to the great scandal of the other monks, who view what is going on in there as reeking of the fires of hell. But when the poor juggler drops dead and the Holy Virgin appears and opens the gates of paradise to the dead man, they understand that it is possible to give great honor to the queen of heaven even with profane songs and dances. Because there is not a bit of difference between the profane and the sacred.

Under these conditions we can compare the worship of Our Lady the Virgin and the worship of the lady by her lover-knight. The poor juggler was also the lover—and the son—of the Virgin. And the Virgin may not abandon any of her lovers, in that she is the very holy mother of all humanity. In the courtly era, one would have been tempted to respond to the eternal question Who is God? with the answer Our Lady the Virgin. Whatever name she is given she will always be the goddess of beginnings, and she will lead us to our end. "The third returns, it is still the first," says Gérard de Nerval, who in his mystical trance confuses the Virgin of the Christians, the goddess Isis, Venus of the Romans, and Artemis of the Ephesians, not to mention Aurélia, Jenny Colon, and Sylvie.

But through her beauty and her bounty—once the danger of the serpent has been removed, which still ties her to the Earth (Chton)—is not Our Lady the Virgin, queen of heaven, like the lady of *fin'amor* a little too remote, a little too inaccessible? "Love of a faraway land," says Jaufré Rudel, "through you my entire heart suffers. No remedy can I find, if at first I do not make my way, drawn by intoxicating love, to an orchard, protected by curtains, next to the friend I long for." The orchard is paradise, not lost but yet to come. One finds there, as in Avalon or Emain Ablach, fruits that stay ripe all year round, and there is no grief, no sadness, no illness, nor death. May Our Lady the Virgin, who rules over these faraway places, lead there the poor troubadour who is dying of love beside a dried-up fountain.

The Chamber and the Orchard

The image of paradise (which is, according to the Persian etymology of the word, the orchard) has haunted human beings for as long as the world has existed; or rather, since the primordial couple, Adam and Eve, were chased by the angel with the flaming sword from the enchanted Garden of Eden; or in other words since humanity became aware that somewhere there existed in an unspecified time a "place" where perfection would be possible. This is the meaning behind the test of the Tree of Good and Evil. But since then, human beings know there is another tree in the middle of the Garden of Eden, and if they eat its fruit they will become as a god. These are things that Catholic theologians do not like at all to mention, although the text of Genesis (3:22) is perfectly clear: "Jehovah the Lord said: here man has become likened unto us for knowing good and evil! May he not stretch forth his hand, nor pick from the tree of life, nor eat of it, nor live forever!" The human being *knows*. But the entrance to Eden is forever guarded by the angel with the fiery sword. The orchard is therefore well and truly forbidden, and he who would dare adventure there would be burnt atrociously by the fiery sword.

It is here that we rediscover the wounding, that burning suffered by Tristan and Iseult and, through them, all lovers. There is a burning between the lover's desire and the realization of that desire. The forbidden orchard represents the beginning of a process to ease the burning. But inside the orchard is the Tree of Life. And in the symbolism of the troubadours, there is the chamber. The problem rests in the prohibition against entering the orchard. So this orchard, would it be dangerous?

There is a strange story in the *Book of Merlin,* which is the first part of the immense *Prose Lancelot* from the thirteenth century, of Cistercian origin but still strongly influenced by Robert de Boron and the Clunisian monks of Glastonbury. The aging enchanter Merlin has met the young Vivien in the Forest of Brocéliande, and he is trying to seduce her by revealing to her all of his secrets. One day while he is out walking with her, and passing near a beautiful lake, he tells her what once happened there. Diana, the hunter goddess, had settled in the forest and had had a manor built at the edge of this lake. She had a lover, Faunus, and she had made him swear to renounce the world for her. Then she fell in love with another knight, with the name of Felix, and started to think of getting rid of Faunus. One day when he was wounded during a hunt, she made him go down into a tomb, under the pretext of healing him by magic, and then closed the stone on top of him. This is how Faunus perished, but when Diana told Felix what she had done, he cut off her head. And since that time this lake is Diana's lake.

Certainly, coming from Merlin, this tale foretells what will happen to him when he is locked up in an invisible castle by Vivien.[39] But the story is interesting insofar as it tells of the "chaste" Diana, who, however, still has lovers she does not hesitate to get rid of when necessary. It is an assertion of the omnipotence of the goddess of beginnings, because Diana obviously recovers this primitive entity. She is simultaneously beautiful, good, and cruel. She is the very image of the lady of *fin'amor*. She is the very image of the Indian Kali, sometimes worshiped under the name of Durga, the "Inaccessible One," the "Dangerous One," or even under the name of Parvati, the Daughter of the Himalayas. This Kali is most often depicted clad entirely in red (the color of blood and violence, but also the color of love), standing at the prow of a boat sailing on an ocean of smoking blood. She stands there in the middle of the flux of life, like the eternal mother, ready to kill whoever approaches her but also ready to create new life-forms that she will nurse with her inexhaustible milk. She is the goddess of beginnings and of the end. She is the Virgin Mother, eternally available, sacred prostitute and admirable parent of the world. She is the witches' Diana, Lucifer's accomplice, the most beautiful of all the archangels, and also the Diana described by Merlin as if she were Vivien, the future Lady of the Lake. She is the lady of courtly love waiting in her chamber while her lover suffers injury in the dangerous orchard he must traverse before winning to her side. It was definitely an orchard that Lancelot sneaked through before attacking the bars that forbade entry into Guinivere's chamber. It was definitely in an orchard that Tristan poured wood shavings into the stream that ran past Iseult's chamber, to let her know he was soon arriving. It is definitely in an orchard that a troubadour, all a-shiver with cold and fear, waits for the moment when the door to his lady's chamber will open. To dazzle the young Vivien, did Merlin not create with his magic a marvelous orchard, not far from the Lake of Diana, and an enchanted palace with a secret room, the sanctuary-chamber where the delicate alchemies of love will be worked out?

But Diana has betrayed her lover and even killed him. The crime is serious, even if she did have the right, because she is a virgin, hence available and a prostitute. And Felix knows quite well that Faunus's fate will be his fate when Diana replaces him with another. He kills Diana by cutting off her head. Justice is served. But this justice is androcratic, it is men's revenge for the wicked acts committed by females. Since that time, nothing works properly anymore. There is no goddess anymore. Thus there is no couple anymore. In his wisdom, Merlin is in the process of warning Vivien that the role of the goddess is perhaps to devour her lovers, but that these must then live on in the very interior of woman. Otherwise, the symbolism is clear. The orchard is pubic hair. The chamber is the vagina. "The cultures that considered the sexual act as an act of piety in the service of the goddess were aware of its signification. The sexual act is 'the return to the mother.' It is natural that the 'gynecophobic' schools of thought found it shocking, such as early Christianity, which could conceive of only one return, that of the soul, the spirit's returning to the Father, and not the body's returning to the Mother; *the sexual cavern thus became the viscous ditch of hell.*"[40] The infernal couple no longer exists, both because of the crime of the goddess and because of the vengeance of the "youngest son." Nothing works in the world anymore, and nothing will ever be as before, if this infernal couple— formed within the "viscous cavern" or in its equivalent, the room "with the bloodstained sheets"—is not formed again by the goddess and her lover-priest, and also son.

In the courtly problematic, the orchard is guarded by figures who are all fantastic projections of the lady herself, sometimes in terrifying form that could be called phallic or castrational. The Greek myth of Circe lives on through medieval imagery. The *Roman de la Rose* (at least William of Lorris's version, which is the only one written in the courtly spirit) restores this ambiguous atmosphere. Allegorical figures such as Danger and False-Seeming, lying in wait for the lover in his labyrinthine journey toward the Rose, are none other than aspects of the lady, and they originate in the *serpent* part of the Virgin. In *Erec et Enide,* Chrétien de Troyes adopts the mythological theme with the deliberate intention of turning it into an initiatory test. This is the well-known episode of the

"Court's Joy." Erec has entered an enchanted orchard where he must fight a certain Mabonagrain (a name in which we can recognize Mabon-Maponos, son of Modron, the "Maternal One," a sort of young solar deity), who is obliged by love for his lady to forbid passage to all knights. Chrétien's description highlights Erec's prowess.

The corresponding Welsh text, *Geraint and Enid*, which originates from the same source text, remains closer to the mythical structure. The test here is known as "the enchanted games within the Hedge of Mist." The hero is moving forward through a heavy mist. "When he emerged from it he found himself in a large orchard with an open space in the center in which he spied a pavilion. . . . Its door was open. Facing the door was an apple tree, with a large hunting horn hanging from one of its branches. Geraint dismounted and entered. There was only a maiden within, seated in a golden chair, across from her was another chair, which was empty." Of course the hero sits in the empty chair, repeating the Celtic ritual enthroning of the king[41] and prefiguring also the Perilous Seat in the quest of the Holy Grail,[42] bringing down upon himself the maiden's reproaches. He is forced to fight a knight. He defeats this knight and sounds the horn; immediately the mist disappears. The spell is lifted. The mystery of the orchard is no more. The hero is thus free to go farther.

And farther along is the chamber. The passage through the orchard is mandatory in order to reach the holy of holies. These are in short "door prizes," represented by the adventures in the orchard. One is certainly free to linger there and not go any farther: courtly love offers many different ways of loving. The orchard is the next to last stage, a little like the white stage of the Philosopher's Stone in traditional alchemy. The final stage is the chamber, the *red* stage of the Philosopher's Stone, which gives perfection and joy, the universal panacea, representing the complete metamorphosis of the individual.

Let us listen to the troubadours again: "In an orchard, beneath the leaves of a hawthorn, the lady has kept her friend close to her, until the watchman cries out he has seen the dawn" (*Dawn*, anonymous). "May

God . . . give me the power to see this love faraway, truly, with my eyes, so that the chamber and the orchard appear to me like an eternal palace" (Jaufré Rudel). "I want to be a hermit in the woods, provided my lady comes with me. There the leaves will provide us cover" (Bernard Marti). "I will have my joy in either chamber or orchard . . . for as close as the finger is to the nail, I would like to be, if it pleases her, with her in her chamber" (Arnaut Daniel). Both the orchard and the chamber are enclosed spaces, removed from the ordinary world. And courtly love is not ordinary.

"The troubadour projects into a poetic sky the carnal aspirations not satisfied by marriage, the needs of the soul in quest of something beyond the passions. He clothes them in the most beautiful purple stanzas, he celebrates their worship. He is truly love's official. . . . One enters poetry, that is, into the ideal world of love, as into a cathedral, observing the ritual, here the ritual of stanzas and mandatory themes, of vulgar language made sacred by the elevated use it is put to."[43] And the marginality that might have, in a definitive way, separated courtly love from its era finally integrates it in a remarkable search for psychological and social equilibrium. It does this by means of *ritual*. But this ritual smells of fire and brimstone. "If there was no *heresy of love* existing in medieval Occitania, it is at least certain that the *trobar* had the hieratic quality of a scandalous cult. Adultery was regarded here as the primary condition for a moralization of love. A kind of adultery that had nothing to do with married love, as it in no way abolished this marriage."[44]

There is in fact a ritual, which is logical, the lover-knight being the priest of a religion that is crystallized entirely around the lady, incarnation of the goddess of beginnings. The troubadour, like Tristan and Lancelot, "has since recognized the principle that requires his truthfulness in a perfect love. Thus he does not have to formulate his desire nor question its meaning; it is less a requirement for learning than it is a practice, an exercise, at his own expense, such as the exercise of mysticism. His quest makes no demand but fulfills the gesture of a sacrificial offering. He surrenders himself like a burnt offering to his God, to the Unique, to his Lady, not as a means of identifying himself, but to experience the Other's will."[45] We would hardly be surprised to hear Lancelot speaking the words of a heretical *pater:* "Our Mother who art in Heaven, Hallowed be thy name, Thy reign come, Thy will be done on earth as it is in Heaven." But the reversal of the masculine/feminine polarity is seen as an outrage, even in the search for the absolute purity recognized in the original woman. "This phenomenon of catharsis, generator of aesthetic enthusiasms, finds itself in a double bind. First from the Church, which had to find its hour had come with the Albigensian crusades and the Inquisition, and had to absorb feminist exaltation into the cult of the Virgin. And on the other hand from the ruptures caused by inner tension: the poet is always in danger of not being able to maintain himself at the level of true love. Hence the intensifying of the formulae: ritual ensures faith when the soul is distracted."[46] But beware. This ritual, though quite often parallel to Christian liturgy, still bears the mark of sin, and the fairy atmosphere surrounding it only increases this infernal aspect. "Adultery and Fairy work hand in glove: the adventure reserves for the hero only the woman forbidden him by law."[47]

Everything is about the transgressing of a taboo, and this is the reason the courtly couple is an infernal couple. Without the taboo there could be no transcendence. Thus it is necessary for the lady to be inaccessible, dangerous, above all, *married,* which considerably increases the attraction she exercises through her beauty and moral perfection. The Virgin Mary is beautiful, perfect, good, and she contains not even a shadow of wickedness because she has been made to crush the head of the serpent, the serpent that has been forced out of her and that represents her primordial "blackness." Also, is it not surprising that the Virgin Mary is not the object of any erotic worship? But this is not the case with the lady of *fin'amor.* She retains the whole Kali aspect of the goddess of beginnings, whether she is Guinivere or Iseult, or any queen, fairy, or maiden encountered in the Arthurian romances. Here is an established erotic cult of great refinement and of a rare subtlety. The lady is a little like a spider, in a corner of her web, waiting for the lovers she will put to the test and perhaps devour like Kali or transform into animals like Circe. She is also the queen in the game of chess, who can move anywhere on the board and who plays with her knights, her rooks, and her pawns, whereas the king, indispensable but useless, remains stuck in the most exposed corner as regards his enemies. She is also the serpent itself, coiled around an imaginary axis, ready to bite the imprudent individual who passes by. Then there is the woman-serpent of the Melusinian type, both good and evil, beautiful and disturbing, cloaked in mystery. What does she do on Saturday, in her cavern, in the shadowy "slime from hell," ready to flee if her secret is discovered?

The ritual of courtly love is necessarily painful. The lover's joy is born from his suffering. But it is possible that his lady suffers equally from this situation, which she sets up, however, and in which she is an accomplice. It is a very delicate matter, to analyze all the profound motivations behind such erotic behavior, but we can be sure of one thing: love is tied to suffering and often, in its final phase, to death. This is the famous *liebestodt* of the German Romantics, singularly more "tortured" than their French counterparts. And this is what Richard Wagner felt so surely when building his "Death of Iseult" upon an overpowering series of descending chromatic scales. Pleasure nearly always passes through hell, even if it opens the gates to paradise. And this concerns the affective life as much as it does the sexual.

How does this courtly love ritual take place? The fact that the ideal lover is a knight—that is, a warrior—indicates a very close link between war and sexuality, to which we must add a third element—magic, which retrieves and sometimes provokes the mysterious feeling of love. It well and truly concerns the initiation of a neophyte, of his complete preparation to attain the state of hero, which will consecrate both the victory of this hero and that of the lady, who has been successful in capturing the one she needs in order to achieve self-realization. The murky stages of this initiation are quite simple, however. From exploit to exploit, the knight completes the various stages and elevates himself to a degree where he can claim the right to a reward. This reward may consist of a simple look or a simple word. Then, the knight is encouraged to continue his efforts. He knows now that he can reach the orchard and, from there, the chamber.

From the glance or the word, we come to the brushing of hands, then to the chaste kiss. If he has shown himself persevering in his "quest," and if he has followed his lady's advice, advice that is actually more like a command, he will win other rewards. He will then be admitted into his lady's chamber, officially, at the pleasure of the lady herself, not like a shy voyeur looking through a basement window or a keyhole. This is what the troubadours and theoreticians of *fin'amor* tried hard to depict as an initiatory ceremony, the *assais* ("attempt"), that is to say a "test." "The *assais* was a test during which the lover had to demonstrate he was capable of loving purely, that *Love existed in him,* at the very time he received the rewards of his fidelity. He could look at his naked lady and do with her all that passion required: *tener* (embrace her), *baiser* (kiss her), *manejar* (caress her); everything except the actual *deed (lo fag).* The woman in the *assais* took her revenge on her imperious, tyrannical husband, on the brutal desire that was too fast. The man that 'she had lie next to her' had to obey all her whims and succumb to the temptation only as much as she wanted to succumb herself. The more meritorious the test for the lover, the more meritorious it became for her, and perilous to her honor."[48]

So there is no possible doubt concerning this point. The satisfactions granted the lover—and shared by his lady—have nothing to do with what is generally called "platonic" relationships. It absolutely concerns sexual relations. First, the lover is allowed to see part or all of his lady's body, followed by caresses that are more and more precise and more and more intimate. But although these "games" could in most cases end with the orgasm of either the man or the woman or both, never, at least in the context of strict *fin'amor,* could they perform coitus, which was banned more for magical reasons than moral ones. It was in fact believed that the penetration of the male organ within the sex of the woman was sufficient to produce a phenomenon of impregnation, and the legitimate line (that is to say, the husband's children) would be altered because of it. Moreover, coitus was the exclusive privilege of the husband, and marriage was considered null and void without it. And let us not forget the common canonical, thus doctrinal, belief in Roman

Catholicism: original sin is transmitted exclusively be male semen. By definition, it was normal that any transmission of this original sin was removed from this pure eroticism known as *fin'amor*. This is so true that, before the Council of Trent, marriage was nothing but the recognition by the church of a sinful state, which was necessary for the reproduction of the species but a sin nonetheless.

Now *fin'amor*, particularly the *assais*, was structured around a sacramental act performed in service of God and his spouse (the community of the faithful), an obvious memory of the pagan hierogamy between the god and the goddess. But this has absolutely nothing in common with marriage, an economic and social action in which the woman is obliged to submit to conjugal duty. In the *assais* (and this is what still smacks to a certain degree of the infernal component), it is the lady who decides *whom she desires, when she will accept, and what she wants.* The difference is huge.

If we think further on the matter, the techniques of *fin'amor* are extremely scabrous but have the merit of being of such refinement as to border on preciosity. True, not all the troubadours showed the same delicacy. Some even go very far into obscenity that is not solely intended to amuse a jaded aristocracy but that translates into crude images a mythological substratum clothed in fantasies. This is the case with an anonymous parody of a *cobla* by the troubadour Folquet de Marseille: "In you I would like to place my dangling prick, and sit my balls above your ass; and I am only saying this out of desire to bang a lot, for I've set my mind on fucking. Doesn't the prick sing when it sees the cunt smile? And for fear the jealous one shows up, I will stick her with my prick and hold back my balls."[49] There is here even a clear allusion to coitus interruptus, necessitated by fear of the "jealous one," that is, the husband. Let us translate: Despite the violence of my desire, I will not go all the way, not as far as the *deed*.

In this way, even in parody, pains are taken to respect the law of *fin'amor*. Burlesque and obscenity sometimes say more than learned sermons. A story by Boccaccio—who constantly parodied and desanctified courtly love—in this way, thanks to a ferocious but healthy derision, restores the mythical structure of the infernal couple of Lilith and Sammael. The story concerns a pious hermit who takes into his hut a poor young girl who has lost her way. Obviously this cohabitation awakes in him a sexual desire of great violence, and not knowing really what to do to overcome the young girl's naiveté, he claims, with proof to back him up, that when the "devil" becomes too arrogant and angry, he must be immediately placed in "hell." The reader will understand that the devil is the hermit's own sexual organ and hell that of the young girl. But, subsequently, the girl acquires a liking for this game and does her best to keep the devil perpetually "arrogant." The unhappy hermit, who eats nothing but roots, cannot keep up with her demands and has to beg for mercy. Sammael devoured by Lilith . . . What a beautiful picture of hell Boccaccio gives us and what a profound analysis! There could be no better definition of the voracity of the lady of courtly love.

Furthermore, this voracity is explained by the fact that the lady asks *everything* of her lover in the trial by *assais.* And *everything* can also mean inaction and immobility as well as orgy, in the double sense of the term. Beneath the obscenity of a *tenson* by the troubadour Montan, we discover all the scope and significance of the *assais:* "I come to you, Sire, with my skirt up, because I have heard your name is Sire Montan. I never get enough fucking to satisfy my needs, and for two years I have been keeping a chaplain, his clerics and his retinue all busy at it. I have a large, plump, quivering ass, and the biggest cunt of any woman in this world." This is the lady's invitation. Her lover cannot abstain from replying: "And I, I come to you with my trousers down and a prick that is bigger than an ass in heat; and I will kiss you with an ardor so you'll have to wash your sheets tomorrow because they'll need to be laundered, you'll say; and we are not leaving here, neither me nor my big balls, until you've been so well fucked you are left on your back, swooning." But these are only words. The lady wants real action: "Since you have threatened me so much with your fucking, Sire, I would like to know what there is to your boasting. For I have courteously reinforced my door to withstand the hammering of your big balls; next I will start to fling myself about in such a way you will not be able to keep hold of my thatch in front and you will have to start over again from behind."[50] The details are simultaneously precise and evocative. When the lady says she has courteously reinforced her door, the situation she describes is identical to that of Guinivere in her room, separated from Lancelot by a grille that he must break in order to gain entry into her sanctuary. It is a provocation, pure and simple, a challenge, René Nelli says, that implicates both the lover's virility and his self-control. "Because, in every country of the world, women have invented ways to test their men to see whether they are truly loved, with love, or only desired for as long as it takes to fuck them."

The *assais* is therefore an essential element in the ritual of courtly love. It is the moment of truth, but it is also the moment of action, in which the infernal couple fully realizes itself. Regarding *fin'amor:* "It is a waste of time to wonder whether it was chaste or sensual, because it obviously was both at once. The *assais* is, beyond all shadow of doubt, the best-conceived test to isolate love from sexuality, for a time, and to make it then flow back into that sexuality, in the close union of bodies and souls: which truly constitutes the actual—and perhaps eternal— essence of passionate love."[51]

This kind of test, both ritualistic and initiatory, cannot help but bring to mind Eastern Tantrism. We know that this philosophical and practical system appeared in the lands bordered by India and China between the sixth and seventh centuries A.D. The goal of Tantra is to realize the union between the divine male principle (Shiva) and the divine female principle (Shakti), to rediscover the original cosmic union through a sexual union, whether real or spiritual, that is within the reach of every human being. Currently Tantrism is experienced in two ways in the Indian world. Those who follow the Tantra of "the right-hand path," within both Hinduism and Buddhism, wish to attain the liberation of being, its inner peace, by sublimating—in a negative fashion—the most potent energy in existence: sexual energy. This path is summed up in a single word: chastity. It is through an intensive asceticism, a perpetual effort over oneself and through following appropriate techniques (prayers and meditations), that one manages to transcend this sexual energy and open the path to enlightenment. Hence a mandatory continence. It goes without saying that the Western Christian knows the Tantrism of this right-handed path perfectly, even if not by name. This is the path that was chosen by Saint Paul and the Church Fathers, it is Christian asceticism. It is also the image of the Virgin Mary crushing the serpent's head. It is also the Marian cult, cleansed of all eroticism and concentrated on maternal love. It is finally the justification for the chastity expected of Christian priests.

But there is also a form of Tantra known as "the left-hand path," and this is the one closest to *fin'amor*. The goal is the same as for the ascetic Tantra, to achieve liberation and to open up the path to enlightenment, that is to say, the path to cosmic fusion. But here the technique is no longer individual; it rests entirely on the couple.

The basic postulate is that physical desires and sexual needs must find their fruition, their satisfaction, and their contentment. Liberation is not possible if one is tortured by the needs of the flesh. Hence a series of sexual techniques and activities that are (and this needs to be emphasized) extremely strict, extremely difficult, and even extremely dangerous. This asceticism (for it is one also), if it is not controlled, can very frequently lead to either madness or death. It concerns the search for total mastery of the physical impulses, the main one being sexuality, not by denying them—which is considered impossible—but by channeling them and utilizing them to achieve a state of superior spiritual development. In this way the dichotomy between what is spiritual and what is carnal is abolished.

The sexual energy utilized is obviously Shakti, without which Shiva cannot take action. In the human body Shakti is thought to be sleeping at the base of the spinal column. This primordial and *potential* sexual energy is represented in the form of a serpent (as if by chance!) called Kundalini, which is coiled at the base of the back. Tantric practice therefore consists of awakening this Kundalini, to make it spread out and ascend to Shiva, which is placed at the top of the skull, by passing through the five intermediary chakras, located at the level of the sexual organs, the navel, the heart, the throat, and between the eyebrows. "A long and difficult discipline is indispensable, nourishing desire and, at the same time, keeping it in check. During a first period, the man must serve the young woman (initiated and carefully prepared in advance) and sleep in the same room as her, at her feet. He will then sleep with her for another four months, keeping her on his left, always desiring her but having no physical contact with her. It is only after this period that coitus is allowed."[52] The connections with the initiatory stages of *fin'amor* are obvious, the major difference bearing on the ejaculation of sperm in the woman's belly, which is considered necessary in Tantrism and is forbidden in *fin'amor*. But in certain more recent forms of Tantrism, this emission of sperm must be controlled. At the end of a series of exercises that are simultaneously physical, psychological, and spiritual, the Tantric practitioner must attain sufficient mastery to be able, at the moment of orgasm, to halt ejaculation and turn it back toward himself, as much for the man as for the woman. Here the analogy with *fin'amor* is clearer. But the goals are not strictly identical. In Tantrism, the semen must be reutilized for a subtle reascension toward the top: the Kundalini unfurls, passes through the different chakras, attains Shiva, and in this way reconstitutes the original unity. In *fin'amor*, if the couple actually reaches that intimate fusion in which there is now only one being, it is because procreation (and thus marriage) should not be confused with love, and the ejaculation of sperm within the woman is excluded. But in both one case as in the other, we can say:

> And it is now that Shakti can begin to make the human being understand that he is not one, but multiple, and that he partici- pates at the same time in both sexes. This vertiginous bundle of a myriad of separate facts that make up the universe of objects offered to our view, our selves receive it through the channel of what we call soul and body, a psychosomatic mechanism in which our individual consciousness seems imprisoned and isolated. The activity of the goddess takes on a new form, which can be symbol- ized by her fertile womb. All the objects perceived by our imagina- tions in temporal experience and the entire course of our individ-

ual existences in the immense universe find their source in this dance or in this belly; that is, but we do not know it, in ourselves!"[53]

This erotic process requires a couple, of course, and a couple composed of a man and a woman. All reference to homosexuality is banned from Tantrism, as it is from courtly love as well. The man is really the male principle of Shiva and the woman the female principle of Shakti. There can be no displacement here or else the climb of the Kundalini, the female serpent, toward the male knot of Shiva no longer has any significance. Hence the considerable importance of the woman in Tantric techniques, as *she is the sole element who is truly active*. "The Tantric spirit is continually absorbed and fascinated by that radiant image (of the goddess) and all women are, in his eyes, the living replica. But, for him, it is not the woman who personifies the goddess. Rather, it is the goddess who appears in the woman. . . . It is only through cooperation with women that the Tantric male can progress. Man and woman must continually satisfy and complete each other. It is only at the end of a long experience of mutual exchanges that either can alone carry out complete Tantric rituals. Nevertheless every human act of love is, in fact, a shadow of the cosmic art, and the more completely it is performed the closer it comes to the divine primal act."[54] We understand why, in the purely Western context of *fin'amor*, the meeting of the lady and the lover can occur only at the end of a long initiatory quest. It is necessary for this union to take place under the best possible conditions. Hence an interminable series of symbolic adventures, even misadventures, sufferings, injuries, separations, *tearing apart*, before it is possible to restore the integrity of this prodigious infernal couple. It is only at the price of these sometimes intolerable sufferings—for the lady as well as for her lover—that the couple can incarnate the primal dyad.

Tantrism is not *fin'amor*. But it participates in the same quest for fullness starting from the individual's inner impulses. The specific objective of *fin'amor* as an ascetic ritual is the creation of this infernal couple, which will put an end to the perpetual conflict persisting between men and women because neither one nor the other has understood they are two faces of one single reality. The couple in courtly love restores this profound reality, for the duration of an embrace. But the duration of an embrace can last an eternity.

This is to say that courtly love, centered on the couple, and the unique couple at that, cannot tolerate dispersal. The lover can love only one lady. And whatever may be said of the sacred prostitute (always virginal, that is, always available to give herself to the first comer), the lady can only love but one single lover (the husband obviously has no standing in this precise problematic). An anonymous lay from the end of the twelfth century provides an excellent translation of this *exclusiveness,* without which it serves nothing to undertake any activity seeking fullness. I am speaking of the *Lai d'Ignauré.* The hero, named Ignauré, is truly an anti-Tristan or an anti-Lancelot, and his attitude demonstrates the false path he has taken. The consequence of his choice is death, for himself as well as for those women who made themselves his accomplices.

So Ignauré—a Breton knight completely within the norms of courtly life, brave, handsome, well taught—is attractive to women. Instead of contenting himself with one lady, he has a dozen, each of whom he praises in turn. But each of his twelve ladies has no idea she is sharing his love. Now, one day, the twelve women find themselves all together and decide to play the game of confession. This is how they learn they have a single lover, Ignauré. Furious, as it is easy to understand, they decide to kill the impostor. But he has a gift for pleading: he presents his case so well that the women allow themselves to be swayed. He must simply choose one from among them and stop there, which is done. But a *lausengier* has witnessed all of this and, claiming a large reward, he reveals what has happened to their twelve husbands. The husbands, after deliberating on the matter among themselves, seize Ignauré, castrate him, then kill him. They then invite their wives to dinner and have them eat Ignauré's heart and sexual organs, revealing to them afterward what the meal really was that they had just eaten. The twelve women declared they had never eaten anything better and that they would never eat anything else again. And they allowed themselves to starve to death.

This tragic story refers to the same theme as the well-known legend of the Chatelain of Coucy and the Lady of Fael. In reality, the theme of "the eaten heart" was widespread and knew a great success during the Middle Ages. It has a definite connection with the symbolic exchange of hearts, a strange ceremony that took place sometimes when two people—a man and a woman—after realizing that they loved each other but that their love was impossible, decided to plight their troth through a mutual oath to love each other in an entirely spiritual fashion. The "eaten heart" is the concrete, dramatized reflection of this oath, with in addition a resurgence of ancient erotic cannibalistic customs. And if the theme has been exploited in stories of marital vengeance, it is primarily because it corresponds in an entirely symbolic manner to this "exchange of hearts," one of the highest summits of amorous reasoning before the appearance of *fin'amor.*

In the case of the *Lai d'Ignauré,* however, the theme of the eaten heart is not the only one. First there are the sexual parts of their lover's body that the ladies share among them. Sexuality erupts into the original theme (which concerned just spirituality) and completely alters its scope. The inspired communion then becomes a veritable communion in the Catholic sense of the word: the twelve ladies, like the twelve apostles, share the heart and the sex of their lover as if these were the flesh and blood of Christ. It is a Last Supper that is described to us by the *Lai d'Ignauré,* but one with almost sacrilegious connotations. The Black Mass is not far away, and the eternal life promised by Christ to those who eat and drink of his body is now an eternal love in death. We find here the romantic, Wagnerian *liebestodt.* The problem is that a curse rests on all this, and this curse comes from the lover's lies and hypocrisy. If Ignauré had not lied to the twelve ladies, the secret of his love with a single lady would not have made its way into rumor, and there would not have been any regrettable consequence. The courtly couple would have been normal, and the secrecy that must necessarily surround it would have been completely preserved. Thus it is Ignauré's lies and hypocrisy that unleash the tragedy. The moral of this story is very clear: one can love only one lady, and, consequently, a lady may have only one lover. *Sharing—which does not come into play with regard to a husband— is intolerable with respect to a lover or a mistress.*

But there is something else in the *Lai d'Ignauré* that is essential for any understanding of *fin'amor*. In fact, who devours the heart and *the sex* of the lover? The ladies. Does this thereby give them something in common with the terrifying vision of the devouring, castrating Mother? If the goddess "brings man into the world and into time, she also removes him from them and accomplishes his destruction. All the causes of infirmity and death—disease, famine, violence, and war—are an inevitable aspect of her activity in the eyes of man, her victim. No one can become a true Tantric if he does not face up to this reality, and if he does not assimilate it into the image he makes of the goddess. Thus many Tantric images show her with the features of the terrible Kali, her shadowy face, her tongue lolling, her fanged mouth dripping with blood. However hideous she may be, she must nonetheless still be loved."[55]

Yes, she must nonetheless still be loved.[56]

And this is where the tragedy begins. For in every tragedy, the first sentence spoken in the first scene already contains the meaning of the final sentence, before the curtain falls. Tristan's death is inscribed in his first meeting with Iseult. Lancelot's fate is inscribed in the first glance he exchanges with Guinivere; he will never find the Holy Grail because for him the Holy Grail is Guinivere. In the first glance, the first gesture, everything has already been consummated. "In the same way that Perceval, when he yet lived, was so troubled by the sight of the Lance and the Holy Grail, and knew what purpose they served, it is for me, O Best of all Ladies, when I see your graceful person, all my senses fail when I see you" (Rigaud de Barbezieux). "I wish neither for Rome's empire nor that I be named its pope, if I could not return to her for whom my heart burns and eats at itself. For if she does not cure me of my torment with a kiss before the new year, she murders me and condemns herself to hell" (Arnaut Daniel). "For my heart cannot turn elsewhere, nor my desire draw me somewhere else, as I have no other desires" (Raimbaut de Vaqueiras). "Lady, Love is thus made that when it binds two lovers, it causes each to feel, according to his own good pleasure, either pain or joy. So I think, and

I am not joking, that it is I who bear, as my responsibility alone, the hard pain of my heart" (Raimbaut d'Orange). "Lady for whom I whistle my song, your eyes are like brambles to me" (Raimbaut d'Orange).

Courtly love, as sung of by the troubadours, is filled with references to wounds that do not even bleed they are so deep. When Tristan is lying in his bed, desperately waiting for word that Kaherdin's boat is displaying a white sail, he knows that a single glance from Iseult can save him from death. But alas, Tristan, *like Iseult,* has drunk the herbed wine, *the draught of love and death.* The last word of the tragedy is also the first. And he binds the lady as his lover, because in *fin'amor* it is completely a question of re-forming the couple formed by Lilith and Sammael, that is to say, the infernal couple.[57]

If the infernal couple really exists, this can entail only suffering, and eternal suffering. But again, let us repeat with the troubadours that suffering is also joy, and that sexual bliss can be expressed only with death rattles. There is no question but that it is indeed an infernal couple proposed to us by courtly love, through all the meanderings of the dialectic and all the perilous adventures of its heroes.

When Tristan, separated for too long from Iseult, wishes to see her again while she is living at Mark's court, he finds no better option than to disguise himself as a jester to gain access to the royal dwelling and thus look on the one without whom he cannot live. He pretends to be crazy. *But he really is crazy.* And in the magnificent text of the *Folie Tristan* ["Tristan's Madness"], one of the masterpieces of the courtly era, when he asks Mark to give him Iseult, and the king asks him what he plans to do with her, the jester replies: "King, high up in the air I have a large room where I live. It is made of glass, it is beautiful and spacious; in the very center the sun darts its rays. It is suspended in the air and hangs among the clouds; no matter how strong the wind blows, it neither wobbles nor sways. Next to the room is a richly paneled crystal chamber. When the sun rises tomorrow, it will give off a great light."[58]

It is in this crystal chamber, emerging directly out of the most ancient Celtic mythology and the eternal dream of the lovers of the goddess, that Tristan wishes to bring Iseult. For here, in this chamber flooded with sunlight, is both the orchard and the chamber, and throughout the entire year the birds sing, the fruits hanging from the trees are ripe, the flowers give off their delicate fragrance. It is obviously in this paradise that the lady should dwell, even if through her smile and through her eyes—which are the gates to the Otherworld—we can already distinguish the flames of hell.

Who among us would hesitate to build for the one he loves this miraculous, admirable, crystal chamber suspended between heaven and earth, and to lead her there like a goddess—at the risk of being devoured between her monstrous teeth—to achieve with her the delicate, ineffable liturgies of absolute love?

Π⊙TES

Introduction

1. I have analyzed and critiqued this social structure in J. Markale, *King of the Celts* (Rochester, Vt.: Inner Traditions, 1994).
2. See J. Markale, *Le Christianisme celtique et ses survivances populaires* (Paris: Imago, 1983).
3. In French, "interesting" when used to refer to a woman can also mean "pregnant"—translator's note.
4. What is most remarkable about the courtly era is the intrusion of femininity into the manners and customs of the time via the indirect route of the marvelous. In all the literary texts of the twelfth and thirteenth centuries, it is the image of the fairy that is thrust forward as the lady whose praises are sung by the troubadours. Arthurian tales abound in "maidens" endowed with mysterious powers, and the fate of the world is manipulated by figures such as Vivien, the Lady of the Lake, and Morgana, the dreadful, alluring fairy of the Isle of Avalon. These women-fairies emerge directly out of folktales that have themselves borrowed fundamental elements from Celtic mythology, appearing as "evocative examples of the fundamental ideal that the restoration (within collective consciousness) of the symbolic function, a vital source of renewal for the psychic equilibrium of the group, must pass through the mediation of the feminine: the image of the woman-object is eclipsed by

the active fairy-mistress, the guide toward higher consciousness, who opens access to the Otherworld and leads to self-realization." Jean-Claude Aubailly, *La Fée et le chevalier* (Paris: Champion, 1986), 143.

5. Between 1145 and 1153, the scholar Bernard Sylvestre, in *De Mundi universitate* [republished in volume I of the "Bibliotheca Philosophorum Mediae Aetatis" series (Innsbruck: Barach, 1876)], sang the praises of sexuality, extolling the genital organs and preaching love as the sovereign remedy against death and chaos.

6. Aubailly, *La Fée et le chevalier*, 145.

7. M. Cazenave, *La Subversion de l'âme* (Paris: Seghers, 1981), 275. The author of this impassioned book devotes a good part of it to a scientific "mythanalysis" of the story of Tristan and Iseult.

Chapter 1

1. This manuscript has been kept at the Bibliothèque Nationale de Paris (fonds Latin no. 8748). The first printed edition, from the beginning of the sixteenth century, bears the title *Tractatus amoris*, and the 1610 printing is entitled *Erotica seu Amatoria*. The work enjoyed wide renown in the baroque era, quite equal to the esteem it enjoyed at the end of the Middle Ages.

2. See J. Markale, *Lancelot et la chevalerie arthurienne* (Paris: Imago, 1985).

3. "Domine non sum dignus ut intres sub tectum meum, sed tantum dic verbum et sanabitur anima mea," whose literal translation ("Lord, I am not worthy that you come under my roof, but say a word and my soul will be cured") is a far cry from what can be heard in the contemporary reformed Catholic mass.

4. See J. Markale, *Women of the Celts* (Rochester, Vt.: Inner Traditions, 1986), 147–72, the chapter entitled "The Rebellion of the Flower-Daughter."

5. René Nelli, "Sur l'Amour provençal," *Cahiers du Sud*, no. 347.

6. C. Méla, *La Reine et le Graal* (Paris: Le Seuil, 1984), 94.

7. For the *geis,* see Markale, *Women of the Celts,* 212–24.

8. See the story "La Reine des Prouesses" in J. Markale, *La Tradition celtique en Bretagne armoricaine* (Paris: Payot, 1975), 41–46.

9. See "La Saga de Yann," ibid., 148–68.

10. For the animals, see "La Saga de Yann," as well as the episode from "La Saga de Gradlon le Grand" concerning "le Chêne de Keris" (ibid., 78–91). Countless tales on this topic can be found just about everywhere.

11. For the grateful dead, see the story "Jean de Calais" in J. Markale, *Contes occitans* (Paris: Stock, 1981).

12. Markale, *La Tradition celtique,* 169–85.

13. Méla, *La Reine et le Graal,* 52.

14. Ibid., 16.

15. Ibid., 17.

16. E. Köhler, *L'Aventure chevaleresque* (Paris: Gallimard, 1974), 176.

17. *Le Coeur mangé,* presented by C. Gaignebet and D. Régnier (Paris: Stock, 1979), 330.

18. Saint Bernard de Clairvaux, *Ecrits politiques* (Paris: 10/18, n.d.), 33.

19. This concept is magnificently (if somewhat sordidly) depicted in an Italian film from the 1970s, *Wicked Stories,* with a screenplay written by Piero Paolo Pasolini. One of these stories concerns a parish priest who mounts a footstool in order to obscenely caress a statue of the Virgin Mary. One day he is found lying on the floor crushed beneath the statue, which has fractured his skull. The best part is the following scene, in which we see the priest's successor, and there is a close-up of the statue, which is now solidly attached to the wall by means of a screw that goes straight through the statue. I think this speaks for itself.

20. Méla, *La Reine et le Graal,* 26.

21. The hero Fergus mac Roig was bathing in a lake with Queen Medbh under the eyes of Aillil and some other warriors. "Medbh drew near until she was pressed right up against Fergus's chest and had her legs wrapped around him. Fergus swam away around the lake. Jealousy took hold of Aillil. Then Medbh got out of the lake

and walked away. 'It is delightful when the stag and the doe do that in the lake, o Lugaid,' said Aillil—'Why not kill him?' said Lugaid, who never missed his mark." Indeed, Aillil ordered Lugaid to hurl his spear at Fergus, thus causing the death of the hero and satisfying the husband's vengeance. J. Markale, *The Epics of Celtic Ireland* (Rochester, Vt.: Inner Traditions, 2000), 72–73.

22. Réne Louis, postface to his adaptation of *Tristan et Yseult* (Paris: Livre de Poche, 1972), 282, 284.

23. Ibid., 284.

24. Ibid., 285.

25. Ibid., 286.

26. The Brocéliande Forest is currently located in the commune of Paimpont (Ille-et-Vilaine) but is most easily accessed from Tréhorenteuc (Morbihan) in the Forest of Paimpont, which is generally regarded as being the ancient Brocéliande.

27. French translation from the Occitan by Robert Lafont, "Pour Lire les Troubadours," *Cahiers du Sud*, no. 372, 186–89.

Chapter 2

1. See Andreas Capellanus, *De Arte amandi*, and J. Lafitte-Houssat, *Troubadours et cours d'amour* (Paris: PUF, 1979).

2. M. Raynouard, *Lexique Roman, ou dictionnaire de la langue des troubadours* (Paris: Sylvestre, 1844).

3. Pierre Bec, *Burlesque et obscénité chez les troubadours* (Paris: Stock, 1984), 182.

4. Pierre Bec, *Anthologie des troubadours* (Paris: 10/18, 1979), 350.

5. Ibid.

6. Bec, *Burlesque et obscénité*, 151–52.

7. *Le Coeur mangé*, 170–71. When we recall that sexual penetration was forbidden—or at least advised against—in *fin'amor*, we can get a better grasp of the lay's title, *Le Lécheur* ("The Licker"), which has been translated more prudishly as the *Lai du Galant* ("The Lay of the Gallant").

8. Ibid., 161–67.

9. In fact, the problem goes beyond social and psychological frameworks into the metaphysical. The name Enid means "soul" in Welsh, which is quite revealing. Enide is Erec's soul and as such intervenes invisibly in his behavior. This can easily be seen in a comparison of Chrétien de Troyes's tale with its Welsh correspondent, *Gerent and Enid*—which has wrongly been presumed to be an adaptation of the French story. It is actually a parallel version taken from the previously written prototype common to both stories. The outline is typically Celtic as I have shown in my systematic comparative analysis of the two texts. See J. Markale, *L'Epopée celtique en Bretagne* (Paris: Payot, 1984), 152–65.

10. René Nelli, "Sur l'Amour provençal," *Cahiers du Sud*, no. 347, 17–18.

11. See Markale, *L'Epopée*, 166–82. As with *Erec et Enide* there is a parallel Welsh text, *Owein, or the Lady of the Fountain*, that comes from the same prototype as Chrétien's work. A comparison between the two narratives clearly displays a fundamental myth going back to the dawn of time, but it also demonstrates exactly what it was that Chrétien wished to add.

12. In the Paimpont Forest (Ille-et-Vilaine) on the Morbihan border, and accessible through the village of Folle-Pensée ("Crazy Thinking"). It is the only place in the Brocéliande Forest where the traditional legend is truly of local origin. All the other Arthurian names are the doings of clerics and scholars.

13. J. Frappier, trans., *Le Chevalier à la charrette* (Paris: Champion, 1967), 27.

14. This is the thesis I presented with supporting documentation in Markale, *Tradition celtique*, 99, 109–32, and that I revisited in *Lancelot*. Another hypothesis inspired by certain Norman scholars, J. C. Payen among them, views the legend of Lancelot as originating in lower Normandy, in the region of Domfront and Bagnoles-de-l'Orne. In their opinion, Lancelot would be the heroically transformed appearance of a sixth-century saint, a former warrior

turned hermit, Saint Frambault or Frambourg, whose coat of arms is identical to that given Lancelot of the Lake. But the localization of Arthurian sites in the western part of the department of Orne and the northern part of Mayenne derives essentially from the fact that it was Norman writers who were the first to transcribe (under orders of the Plantagenets) the legend of Arthur and his knights.

15. Frappier, introduction to *Le Chevalier à la charrette*, 12.

16. One detail needs to be qualified in this judgment (otherwise without reproach) that Jean Frappier formulates here concerning *Le Chevalier à la charrette*. Certainly, if we are to take literally the documentation that existed before Chrétien de Troyes (such as sculptures from the Modena cathedral or ecclesiastical texts from Wales), King Arthur himself intervenes when the queen is in danger or has been kidnapped. But the distinguishing feature of the Celtic king is that he is a cuckold, and it can be seen that the figure of Lancelot merely replaces numerous of the queen's other lovers in the original versions of this legend. See Markale, *King of the Celts*, 159–64.

17. Frappier, introduction to *Le Chevalier à la charette*, 12.

18. Frappier, *Le Chevalier à la charrette*, 35.

19. Méla, *La Reine et le Graal*, 270.

20. Frappier, *Le Chevalier à la charrette*.

21. Ibid., 121.

22. See Markale, *Lancelot*. We should also emphasize the ecstasy that seizes Lancelot on two occasions in Chrétien de Troyes's tale. One occasion takes place at the moment when a maiden has given Lancelot a comb used by Guinivere, which still holds a few of her hairs. "He took pains to pull out the hairs with his fingers so gently that he broke not a single one. . . . The adoration begins: to his eyes, his mouth, his forehead, and to his entire face, he bears them one hundred and one thousand times. He locks them within his breast. . . . Gold purified one hundred times and refined in fire one hundred times would be more obscure than the night that follows the most brilliant day of this summer if one looked at the gold and

the hairs side by side." Frappier, *Le Chevalier à la charrette,* 59–60. The second ecstatic trance takes place during the battle between Meleagant and Lancelot. Worn out from the wounds inflicted on the Bridge of the Sword, Lancelot weakens. One of Guinivere's maids-in-waiting arranges to hail him and inform him that the queen is present at a window. Lancelot gazes at the queen and immediately regains his strength, as if the solar rays emanating from Guinivere infuse him with new energy. In any event, the episode is consistent with the usual metaphors of courtly poetry and with baroque poetry of the sixteenth century.

23. Méla, *La Reine et le Graal,* 286, 288.
24. Frappier, *Le Chevalier à la charrette,* 129.
25. Méla, *La Reine et le Graal,* 296.
26. Bec, *Anthologie des troubadours,* 192.
27. Frappier, *Le Chevalier à la charrette,* 130.
28. Ibid., 131.
29. Méla, *La Reine et le Graal,* 296–97.
30. Ibid., 288.
31. Alexandre Micha, trans., *Lancelot* (Paris: 10/18, 1983), 1:119.
32. Markale, *Lancelot et la chevalerie arthurienne,* 67–109 for an analysis of the "standard Lancelot" and 111–55 for the "mythology of Lancelot."
33. Méla, *La Reine et le Graal,* 365.
34. For all that concerns the origin of the legend, the Irish archetype of Diarmaid and Grainne, and the possible meanings of the legend, see the chapter titled "Iseult, or the Lady of the Orchard," in Markale, *Women of the Celts,* 201–43.
35. This is particularly true for Iseult, whose mother is a magician, and who has retained even in the more sophisticated versions some aspects of a fairy, the echo of an ancient Celtic solar goddess.
36. There is one difficulty, but we do not know if the specific detail was included in Béroul's fragments, since we know it only through its German adaptation by Eilhart von Eberg. It concerns Mark and Iseult's wedding night, during which the lady-in-waiting Brangwain

takes the place of the queen, *who is no longer a virgin*. It should be noted that if a deflowering took place in the boat with Tristan, following the incident of the philter, this occurred *before the marriage* of the king with Iseult, which mitigates considerably its symbolic scope with respect to the code of courtly love. On the other hand, if we refer back to a traditional belief that has led to the aberrant forms of the "droit de seigneur," Tristan, by virtue of this, has been encumbered with a curse he is incapable of averting and one that will fall back upon him.

37. Tristan, pure lover that he is (one aware of the exceptional nature of the infernal union he has consecrated with Iseult), cannot stand the idea that *it might be better with the other*. This stems from his own individuality as well as from Iseult's. Without thinking that Iseult might be seeking something else (a simple difference), he thinks this attitude calls into question and invalidates everything he has experienced with Iseult (that is, a totality). The fact that he is excluded from the game destroys him, hence his reaction and verbal violence. But this revolt will lead him nowhere other than to an obvious observation: it is with Iseult that he formed the perfect couple of pure lovers, and thus he will gain, through his experiment (that is to say, his marriage with Iseult of the White Hands), the revelation of a profound reality over which he has no purchase, and neither does Iseult, if we are to judge from the suffering she undergoes when she learns of her lover's marriage.

38. The same detail appears in the Irish archetype of this legend, the tale of Diarmaid and Grainne. But there, it is when wandering through a valley, pursued by the Fiana, that Grainne (with whom Diarmaid has not yet had sexual relations) receives the splash of water between her thighs. She immediately uses it as a pretext to cast a *geis* on Diarmaid in the form of a provocation: this water is bolder than you are, therefore, as you are not so bold, you must be impotent! Obligated by the *geis* that casts aspersions on his virility, Diarmaid then consummates his union with Grainne. See Markale, *Epics of Celtic Ireland*, 143–44.

39. The same is true for Lancelot of the Lake. When he must conceive the future Galahad, a sorceress gives the daughter of the Fisher King the appearance of Queen Guinivere; otherwise the hero would never have been able to "deceive" his one and only lady.

Chapter 3

1. L. Foulet, trans., *Perceval* (Paris: Stock, 1947), 191.
2. *Les Plus Anciens Textes de l'humanité,* trans. T. Gaster (Paris: Payot, 1953), 27–29.
3. Ibid.
4. Ibid.
5. Vincent Voiture, *Les Oeuvres,* Nouvelle edition corrigée (Paris: Vue F. Mauger, 1702).
6. For more concerning the "gods" of the Celtic pantheon, who are, in fact, only social, functional representations of one unique deity, see J. Markale, *The Druids* (Rochester, Vt.: Inner Traditions, 1999).
7. J. Przyluski, *La Grande Déesse* (Paris: Payot, 1950), 39.
8. Ibid.
9. Markale, *Mélusine, ou l'androgyne* (Paris: Retz, 1983).
10. We can also believe in a real voyage made by the abbot Brendan, who set off over the Atlantic and landed in America. The tale of this voyage would then be merged into the legendary tale of Bran.
11. This is an impressive magical and martial trick whose name is full of significance, by virtue of which Cuchulainn will be practically invincible. It is thanks to this *gai bolga* that he will kill his old fellow student Ferdeadh, who had not obtained this secret from Scatach.
12. Cuchulainn also casts a *geis* of death and destruction on Scatach unless she grants him "the three tricks that you have never taught anyone before me, your daughter, and also the friendship of your thighs." We can see that the transmission of secrets takes place through a sexual—if not amorous—relationship. See Markale, *Epics of Celtic Ireland,* 88–90 (taking into account the erroneous translation of *gai bolga* that is provided there).

13. Translated into French by Georges Dottin, in *L'Epopée irlandaise* (Paris: Les Presses d'aujourd'hui, 1980).
14. Ibid.
15. Egerton 1782 ms., Best and Bergin translation, "The Courtship of Etaine," *Irische Texte* III (Leipzig: E. Windisch, 1880–1909).
16. Ibid.
17. Ibid.
18. Joseph Loth, trans. *Les Mabinogion,* vol. 1 (Paris: Fontemoing, 1913).
19. Ibid.
20. Almost the same thing happens to the Irish hero Finn Mac Cumail, who burns himself while cooking the "salmon of knowledge" intended for the poet Finneces and obtains the gift of prophecy and the power to heal. See Markale, *Epics of Celtic Ireland,* 132–33.
21. Markale, *L'Epopée Celtique en Bretagne,* 94 and ff.
22. See the chapter "Taliesin and Druidism" in J. Markale, *The Celts* (Rochester, Vt.: Inner Traditions, 1993), 223–51.
23. W. Lederer, *Gynophobia, ou la peur des femmes* (Paris: Payot, 1970), 158.
24. Ibid., 159–60.
25. A. de Smet, *La Grande Déesse n'est pas morte* (Paris: published privately, 1983), 172. In this work, which is primarily a medley of quotations from various authors (precisely referenced, however), the author, a modest Catholic priest, seems perfectly straightforward and knows exactly what he is talking about.
26. Przyluski, *La Grande Déesse,* 163 (quotation).
27. A distinctive feature of Roman Catholicism (followed by Byzantine orthodoxy) is to have, over the course of centuries, presented as immutable truths symbolic elements that acquire value only when their profound meaning is discovered by means of the image. But the Church transmitted only the image, not its signification. Hence the various "heresies" and the great Protestant Reformation.
28. Saint Jerome, *Commentaires,* VII.

29. This needs qualifying, however. Etymologically, a prostitute is she "who puts herself forward," she who is offered. In principle there is nothing in any way reprehensible in this attitude. But when prostitution ceases to be a sacred act and becomes a commercial transaction, then the connotation becomes obviously different and stained with ignominy.

30. de Smet, *La Grande Déesse n'est pas morte*, 178.

31. Przyluski, *La Grande Déesse*, 167.

32. de Smet, *La Grande Déesse n'est pas morte*, 184. Let me take this occasion to remind the reader that the author of these lines is a Catholic priest.

33. I am inclined to think that the image of God the Father has completely eclipsed the earlier image of God the Mother, because in the precise context of the Trinity, the genitor—thus the father, the pro-creator—is the Holy Ghost, pure and simple, and the son is Jesus Christ. Logically the role of the mother would have devolved to God the Father, entirely diverted from its original route, whose role the Virgin Mary has tended to usurp.

34. Louis, *Tristan et Iseult*, 62. The woman is obliged to obey conjugal duty. This is why theoreticians of *fin'amor* considered the marital relationship as null. Even in the full exaltation of femininity prevailing in the courtly era, the poets and storytellers could not prevent themselves from expressing their profound mistrust toward the woman suspected of hypocrisy. In all logic, it must be admitted that the woman can always *submit* and fake a pleasure she does not feel in the sexual embrace, whereas the man is incapable, *impotent*, of carrying out the same kind of deceit.

35. Lederer, *Gynophobia*, 162.

36. Let us also note the promulgation of the dogma of the Assumption by Pius XII in 1950.

37. Alphonso de Liguori, *La Gloire de Marie*, cited in H. Zimmer, *Mythes et symboles dans l'art et la civilisation de l'Inde* (Paris: 1951), 85.

38. It is quite remarkable that the great majority of Catholic sanctuaries take the name of Our Lady, with variations ad infinitum. It is

no less remarkable that, in the twentieth century, the most important pilgrimages occurred to those sites where the Virgin has appeared to some privileged souls. Fatima, la Dalette, Pontmain, and of course Lourdes have become symbols of the Marian cult and even just of simple worship, at least for France and western Europe. Lourdes is particularly important insofar as the pilgrimages here are linked to the worship of the waters. In fact, the Virgin is always honored in those places where a spring, well, or fountain is located, as if she were the resurgence of an ancient fertility goddess, fertility being connected to the Mother water without which all life is impossible.

39. See J. Markale, *Merlin, Priest of Nature* (Rochester, Vt.: Inner Traditions, 1995).

40. Lederer, *Gynophobia,* 215.

41. This ritual in Tara, Ireland, stated that any future king who sat upon the Fal Stone provoked a cry from this magical stone.

42. There is an empty seat at the Round Table, reserved for the person who is destined to bring the Grail adventures to a successful conclusion, that is, for Galahad. Any audacious soul who sits there is swallowed up by the earth—the Earth Goddess, of course, with a satanic coloration.

43. Lafont, "Pour Lire les Troubadours," 167–68 (both quotations).

44. Ibid.

45. Méla, *La Reine et le Graal,* 258.

46. Lafont, "Pour Lire les Troubadours," 168–69.

47. Méla, *La Reine et le Graal,* 261.

48. Nelli, "Sur l'Amour provençal," 24.

49. Bec, *Burlesque et obscénité,* 171.

50. Ibid., 163.

51. Nelli, "Sur l'Amour provençal," 25.

52. Julius Evola, *The Metaphysics of Sex* (Rochester, Vt.: Inner Traditions, 1983), 240.

53. Philip Rawson, *Tantra: The Indian Cult of Ecstasy* (London: Thames and Hudson, 1973), 18–20.

54. Ibid., 17.

55. Ibid.

56. There is tragedy in the etymological sense, that is, "bloody ritual sacrifices." In fact *the lover is the victim* of this ritual intended to please the deity. But at the same time, the lover-victim transforms, sublimates, and transcends himself completely. This is what the baroque poets of the sixteenth and seventeenth centuries, the successors of the troubadours, understood so perfectly in their great lyrical outbursts celebrating a cruel lady who devours them but who deifies their very selves by this sacrifice. One cannot help but be reminded of the sonnets of Agrippa d'Aubigné collected under the title *Hécatombe à Diane*. The turbulent passion of the Huguenot for the proud Catholic Diane is expressed here in very specific mythological terminology. And coming back to the courtly era, let us note that, at the fringe of ambiguity: "The woman-snare who allows herself to be coveted by a knight-voyeur is a possible threat, but the implicit appraisal that she takes advantage of in the chosen one when he quits the feudal world for her is not a sign of immaturity, much rather a choice and a preference. In fact, the threatening and intrusive femininity embodied by seductive queens . . . is conjured up by a relay figure, a yet more powerful femininity that is seductive and imperious by the conditions she imposes, but *reassuring and comforting by the gifts she brings* and the pardon she offers. An interrogation born from childish fantasies or communal dreams, it distinguishes a dual woman, both the wicked stepmother and the beneficial mother who offers soothing answers and utopian harmony." *Le Coeur mangé*, 331–32.

57. All notion of an infernal couple assumes the existence of a conflict that can be found within as well as outside the couple in the social context, and often both together. This is the case for Tristan and Iseult: while they are in conflict with the outside world (adultery) they also suffer inner conflict (jealousy). And in the story of the legend as it has come down to us in the French, German, and

Norse versions, the only solution can be found in the lovers' death. *But this is not at all the way the story ends in the Welsh version.* In fact, following the sojourn of Tristan and Iseult in the forest, it is King Arthur who must arbitrate over the conflict between Mark and Tristan (Iseult, it appears, is left out of the discussion). Arthur therefore formally reconciles the uncle and the nephew, but one difficulty remains: neither wishes to renounce Iseult. Then "Arthur decides that one will have her while the leaves are on the trees, the other when the trees are bare." The two rivals must choose, start-ing—as androcratic society requires—with the husband. Mark chooses the time when the leaves are no longer on the trees for a reason rich in explanations itself: "because the nights are longer." Tristan has no choice but to accept, as the law of the Fathers is ineluctable. But everything is thrown back into question by Iseult. Learning of Mark's choice, she speaks out and recites a short poem: "Three trees are of a generous species: the holly, the ivy, and the yew, who keep their leaves all their life. I am Tristan's for as long as he shall live." Markale, *L'Epopée,* 222. Feminine trickery? Definitely. But it is also a victory and triumph by woman over the society of the Fathers. And it is primarily, what is more important, the legitimation of the infernal couple, the formation of a perfect and indestructible couple that no further conflict can break apart. Henceforth, Tristan and Iseult form the eternal and omnipresent dyad thanks to which the world will again become the paradise that was never lost but remains to be established. It is also, in a firmly Celtic context, the triumph of *fin'amor* in its most natural and complete expression: the infernal couple is not monstrous, it is *in communion with nature,* and the crystal chamber to which Tristan wishes to bring Iseult is the land of eternal summer.

58. Joseph Beclier, editor, *Les Deux Poèmes de la folie Tristan* (Paris: Firman-Didot, 1967).

SELECTED BIBLIOGRAPHY

Aubailly, J.-C. *La Fée et le Chevalier*. Paris: Champion, 1986.

Bec, P. *Anthologie des troubadours*. Paris: 10/18, 1979.

———. *Burlesque et obscénité chez les troubadours*. Paris: Stock, 1984.

Cahiers du Sud, nos. 347, 372. Marseille.

Cazenave, M. *La Subversion de l'âme*. Paris: Seghers, 1981.

Chapellanus, Andreas. *De Arte amandi*. Published also as *Tractatus amoris* (first edition, early sixteenth century), and as *Erotica seu Amatoria* (1610). Manuscript in Bibliothèque Nationale de Paris. Fonds Latin no. 8748.

Le Coeur mangé. Presented by C. Gaignebet and D. Régnier. Paris: Stock, 1979.

Dottin, G. *L'Epopée irlandaise*. Paris: Les Presses d'aujourd'hui, 1980.

Egan, M. *Vie des troubadours*. Paris: 10/18, 1985.

Evola, J. *The Metaphysics of Sex*. Rochester, Vt.: Inner Traditions, 1983.

Foulet, L., trans. *Perceval*. Paris: Stock, 1947.

Frappier, J., trans. *Le Chevalier à la charrette*. Paris: Champion, 1967.

Köhler, E. *L'Aventure chevaleresque*. Paris: Gallimard, 1974.

Lafitte-Houssat, J. *Troubadours et cours d'amour*. Paris: PUF, 1979.

Lafont, R. "Pour Lire les Troubadours." *Cahiers du Sud*, no. 372.

Lederer, W. *Gynophobia, ou la peur des femmes*. Paris: Payot, 1970.

Louis, R. *Tristan et Iseult*. Paris: Livre de Poche, 1974.

Markale, J. *Aliénor d'Aquitaine*. Paris: Payot, 1979.

———. *The Celts*. Rochester, Vt. : Inner Traditions, 1993.

———. *Le Christianisme celtique et ses survivances populaires*. Paris: Imago, 1983.

———. *The Druids*. Rochester, Vt.: Inner Traditions, 1999.

———. *The Epics of Celtic Ireland*. Rochester, Vt.: Inner Traditions, 2000.

———. *L'Epopée celtique en Bretagne*. New edition. Paris: Payot, 1984.

———. *King of the Celts*. Rochester, Vt.: Inner Traditions, 1994.

———. *Lancelot et la chevalerie arthurienne*. Paris: Imago, 1985.

———. *Mélusine, ou l'androgyne*. Paris: Retz, 1983.

———. *Merlin, Priest of Nature*. Rochester, Vt.: Inner Traditions, 1995.

———. *La Tradition celtique en Bretagne armoricaine*. Paris: Payot, 1975.

———. *Women of the Celts*. Rochester, Vt.: Inner Traditions, 1986.

Méla, C. *La Reine et le Graal*. Paris: Le Seuil, 1984.

Micha, A., trans. *Lancelot*. 2 vols. Paris: 10/18, 1983–1984.

Nelli, R. *L'Erotique des troubadours*. Toulouse: 1967.

———. "Sur l'Amour provençal." *Cahiers du Sud*, no. 347.

Przyluski, J. *La Grande Déesse*. Paris: Payot, 1950.

Rawson, P. *Tantra: The Indian Cult of Ecstasy*. London: Thames and Hudson, 1973.

de Rougemont, D. *L'Amour et l'Occident*. Paris: 10/18, 1984.

de Smet, A. *La Grande Déesse n'est pas morte*. Paris: published privately, 1983.

Voiture, V. *Les Oeuvres*, Nouvell edition corrigée. Paris: Vue F. Mauger, 1702.

Zimmer, H. *Mythes et symboles dans l'art et la civilisation de l'Inde*. Paris: 1951.

ÍⁿDEX

cluny 202

Holy Ghost 199